RECONSTRUCTING LAW AND JUSTICE IN A POSTCOLONY

Interdisciplinary Research Series in Ethnic, Gender and Class Relations

Series Editor: Biko Agozino, Virginia Polytechnic Institute and State University, Blacksburg, Virginia

This series brings together research from a range of disciplines including criminology, cultural studies and applied social studies, focusing on experiences of ethnic, gender and class relations. In particular, the series examines the treatment of marginalized groups within the social systems for criminal justice, education, health, employment and welfare.

Also published in this series

Policing and Crime Control in Post-apartheid South Africa
Anne-Marie Singh
ISBN 978-0-7546-4457-6

W.E.B. Du Bois on Crime and Justice
Shaun L. Gabbidon
ISBN 978-0-7546-4956-4

Democratic Policing in Transitional and Developing Countries
Edited by Nathan Pino and Michael D. Wiatrowski
ISBN 978-0-7546-4719-5

Modernization and the Crisis of Development in Africa:
The Nigerian Experience
Jeremiah I. Dibua
ISBN 978-0-7546-4228-2

Africa Beyond the Post-Colonial: Political and Socio-Cultural Identities
Edited by Ola Uduku and Alfred B. Zack-Williams
ISBN 978-0-7546-3171-2

Reconstructing Law and Justice in a Postcolony

NONSO OKAFO
Norfolk State University, USA

ASHGATE

© Nọnso Okafọ 2009

All rights reserved. No part of this publication may be reproduced, stored in a retrieval system or transmitted in any form or by any means, electronic, mechanical, photocopying, recording or otherwise without the prior permission of the publisher.

Nọnso Okafọ has asserted his right under the Copyright, Designs and Patents Act, 1988, to be identified as the author of this work.

Published by
Ashgate Publishing Limited
Wey Court East
Union Road
Farnham
Surrey, GU9 7PT
England

Ashgate Publishing Company
Suite 420
101 Cherry Street
Burlington
VT 05401-4405
USA

www.ashgate.com

British Library Cataloguing in Publication Data
Nọnso Okafọ.
　Reconstructing law and justice in a postcolony. --
(Interdisciplinary research series in ethnic, gender and class relations)
　1. Postcolonialism. 2. Law and culture. 3. Legal polycentricity. 4. Justice, Administration of--Political aspects. 5. Law reform. 6. Law reform--Nigeria.
　I. Title II. Series
　340.3-dc22

Library of Congress Cataloging-in-Publication Data
Okafọ, Nọnso.
　Reconstructing law and justice in a postcolony / by Nọnso Okafọ.
　　p. cm. -- (Interdisciplinary research series in ethnic, gender, and class relations)
　Includes index.
　ISBN 978-0-7546-4784-3 (hardback) -- ISBN 978-0-7546-8965-2 (ebook)
　1. Legal polycentricity. 2. Customary law. 3. Postcolonialism. I. Title.
　K236.O38 2009
　340.5'2--dc22
　　　　　　　　　　　　　　　　　　　　　　　　　　　　　　　　　　2009019770

ISBN 9780754647843 (hbk)
ISBN 9780754689652 (ebk)

Printed and bound in Great Britain by
MPG Books Group, UK

Contents

List of Figures	*vii*
Series Editor's Preface	*ix*
Foreword	*xiii*
Introduction	1

PART 1: CUSTOMARY LAW FOUNDATIONS OF MODERN LAW AND JUSTICE

1	Are Traditions, Customs, and Native Laws Impotent in the Face of Modernity?	7

PART 2: INDIGENOUS VERSUS FOREIGN SOCIAL CONTROLS IN TWELVE SELECTED COUNTRIES

Introduction to Part 2		33
2	Indigenous Versus Foreign Controls in Selected Countries: Afghanistan, India, Iraq, Saudi Arabia	39
3	Indigenous Versus Foreign Controls in Selected Countries: Brazil, Kenya, Nigeria, South Africa	53
4	Indigenous Versus Foreign Controls in Selected Countries: Australia, Canada, Japan, United States of America	73
Part 2 Summary and Conclusion: Lessons from the Countries Surveyed		91

PART 3: ELEMENTS IN LAW AND JUSTICE RECONSTRUCTION

Introduction to Part 3		99
5	Obstacles to Indigenizing Law and Justice: A Case Study of Post-British Nigeria	101

| 6 | Model Law and Justice: Legislation and Enforcement | 121 |
| 7 | Model Law and Justice: Adjudication and Corrections | 167 |

PART 4: FOR A FRESH PHILOSOPHY OF JUSTICE

Introduction to Part 4   215

| 8 | Sharing the Responsibility of Law and Justice Renewal | 217 |

Summary and Conclusion: Checking the Excesses of Official Criminalization in a Postcolony: Towards Increased Role for Civil Response in a Reconstructed Justice System   229

Appendix A   *237*
Index   *241*

List of Figures

7.1	Federal Court Structure	169
7.2	Northern States Court Structure	170
7.3	Southern States Court Structure	170
7.4	Recommended Federal and States Court Structure	172

Series Editor's Preface

Biko Agozino
*Virginia Polytechnic Institute and State University,
Blacksburg, Virginia*

After 12 years and more than two dozen authors published since the inception of the *Interdisciplinary Research Series in Ethnic, Gender and Class Relations*, I am pleased to welcome to the list, a book by Dr. Nọnso Okafọ, the renowned Professor of Criminal Justice at Norfolk State University, Virginia. This volume makes a valuable and original contribution to this series by examining the customary foundations of legal systems without assuming that one system is superior or inferior to another. This sense that the legal systems in Africa are the equals of European legal systems may come as a shock to those that Edward Said identified as 'Orientalists', those who believe that European systems are always superior.

Based on an initial empirical survey of legal experts in Nigeria and built on a comparative analysis of the Nigerian experience with those of 11 other postcolonial societies, the author argues that all legal systems are based on customs and that those legal systems that remain close to the culture and traditions of their society are more effective and more efficient in dispute resolution. He calls this type of legal system, 'grounded law', as opposed to customary law, given the negative connotations that the word customary has in jurisprudence where it is assumed that only the colonized have customary law while the colonizers have scientific or modern law. This formulation by Okafọ will prove challenging because of his premise that all legal systems are indeed customary in the sense of grounded law and so none is superior to others, they are only different from one another on the ground of their different customary foundations.

This thesis of systemic legal equality is original and challenging, especially to scholars in the sub-fields of law and society or socio-legal studies. First of all, followers of Max Weber would question the assumption that all legal systems are grounded in the sense that Okafọ postulates, the sense of being based on custom. On the contrary, Weber argued in *Economy and Society* that the rational ideal bureaucratic way of administering justice is superior to all other systems of justice administration because of its technical efficiency – the reliance on trained professional judges and written rules, a hierarchy of authority, bureaucratization, routinization, and the ability to reach decisions rationally rather than on the basis of the relationships between the parties.

Okafọ challenges Weber indirectly by arguing that none of these so-called technical aspects of the civil law tradition fell from the sky, they are aspects of European customs and traditions that were invented over a long period of history and so they are equivalent to the customs that form the ground for other legal systems. The difference, as Francis Snyder would argue, is that what is often called customary law is frequently a body of rules that the colonial authorities devised and imposed on the colonized to facilitate foreign domination rather than something that the colonized retained autonomously by themselves as part of their tradition and culture.

Okafọ also makes a claim that might be perplexing to socio-legal scholars when he asserted that the legal system in the US is typical of what is found in industrialized countries as opposed to countries like Nigeria and Afghanistan which remain predominantly rural. Weber himself rejected the American system of justice for being what he called 'empirical justice', similar to what Okafọ would call grounded justice. According to Weber, the English and the American systems of common law historically denied justice to the poor because they were based on customs or traditions that privileged the rich whereas the civil law tradition is supposedly based on universal rules that would apply to anyone irrespective of class or caste, contrary to the evidence from the history of slavery, racism and the Nazi holocaust as Paul Gilroy and Zygmunt Bauman argued.

Okafọ is identifying something new here – the fact that the US system of law has changed so much that its customary law origins appear lost as codification and formal bureaucratic procedures appear to make it more like the civil law traditions of continental Europe, as Phillip Reichel observed. Yet, the US legal system remains part of the common law tradition because of the privileging of precedence (Weber's empirical justice) and allowance for judge-made-law, both of which characterize common law jurisdictions and distinguish them from the civil law traditions as C.O. Okonkwo argues in his *Introduction to Nigerian Law*. The innovation here is to recognize that all legal traditions – common, civil, socialist, religious, customary – are indeed based on customs and traditions no matter what the legal gurus might want you to believe.

Okafọ suggests that legal systems would be more effective (a principle that Weber ignored while focusing on efficiency alone, while Okafọ addresses both related concepts of industrial sociology) if they reflect more of the customs and traditions of the society that the law is trying to regulate. Having already argued that all legal systems are grounded in customs and traditions, this is not a surprising argument. This view is, however, likely to elicit challenges from those who might question such an empirical definition of effectiveness given that the custom that is invoked in jurisprudence might be decadent, repugnant, evil or unreasonable as the colonial authorities insisted when local customs came into conflict with colonial decrees. In other words, what if dictators emerge and argue that theirs is a society with long traditions and customs of dictatorship and so democratization of the law would be a foreign imposition the way apartheid fascists tried to argue? The reader is reassured here that Okafọ prescribes restorative justice as opposed to repressive justice as the direction in which to transform the law in postcolonial countries, perhaps in agreement with the innovation of the Truth and Reconciliation Commission held in South Africa under the leadership of Nelson

Mandela as opposed to the witch hunt that characterizes the history of European systems of justice.

In so doing, Okafọ distances his book from the thinking of Ronald Dworkin who defined law in the image of imperialism by arguing that the law is always like an empire issuing decrees of dos and don'ts. The suggestion in this book is that it need not always be so because there are still existing examples of participatory democratic justice systems that would be more effective when the focus is on repairing injustice rather than an obsession with punitiveness. One such society is the Igbo society of Nigeria where Okafọ, Oko Elechi (cited in this context) and I myself grew up; a society without any kings or chiefs and where community affairs are still settled in public meetings with equal say for all despite attempts by the military dictators to impose 'traditional rulers' on the radically republican Igbo whose culture forms the germinal idea for this book.

In a different sense, Okafọ appears to write from the dual typology model of the functionalist perspective of theorists like Emille Durkheim, who suggested that there are two laws of penal evolution from mechanical types of solidarity (Okafọ's rural societies; Weber's irrational forms of authority; Alfred Toenies' gemeinschaft; or Thorstein Veblen's militaristic society) with repressive types of law to organic types of solidarity (Okafọ's industrial societies; Weber's rational ideal bureaucracy; Toenies' gesellshaft; or Veblen's leisure class society) with restitutory types of law. What is different here is the suggestion that rural societies might actually be more restitutory than industrial societies, so contrary to the flawed historiography of Durkheim as David Garland contended in *Punishment and Modern Society*.

In this comparative study of criminal justice systems in twelve countries that share similar experiences of having been colonized in the past but with vastly different customs and traditions, the author offers a feast of ideas that will surely ignite debates in both postcolonized countries and the countries that colonized them. The major contribution of this book is to indicate to the former colonizers that they have something to learn from the natives of their former colonized regions. A tendency to feel superior to the colonized may be depriving the former colonizers of the opportunity to bend down low and learn from those they once ruled arbitrarily and the inferiority complex that compels the postcolonials to deride and discard their own cultural heritage is contributing to the intensification of the crisis of law and order politics as I have argued in my own work. The most important message in the book is for the former colonized people to no longer continue aping their former colonizers but to dare to be different by following their own democratic customs and traditions to more effectively and efficiently resolve disputes using 'grounded law' as Frantz Fanon concluded in *The Wretched of the Earth*.

I welcome this controversial and original contribution to the series and I look forward to reading the debates that the book is bound to provoke in scholarly circles. The book is full of lessons for all those who are interested in ending social injustice and promoting social harmony. As the author writes in his conclusion:

This book challenges the postcolonial society to appreciate, question, creatively synthesize, and use the good qualities of its indigenous and foreign law and justice systems. The postcolony is urged to make room for and encourage discourses and resolutions to determine the best law, justice, and social control for the society. Citizens and leaders of the postcolony should approach this effort with a decolonized, open mind and with a willingness to challenge those institutions and processes that have been officially presumed to be good for the postcolony for so long.

Foreword

Forewords to books are becoming somewhat rare nowadays. Perhaps they have been pushed aside for more lengthy prefaces and introductions that are necessarily more substantive in regards to a book's content. The Foreword, at least according to the *Columbian Guide to Standard American English*, often introduces the author, thus being a bit more personal. I hope the reader will permit me here to bridge the gap between the personal and the more scholarly discussion of Professor Nọnso Okafọ and his new book.

I first met Nọnso Okafọ before he had received the Ph.D. when he was a beginning doctoral student in criminology at Indiana University of Pennsylvania. As it so happened, I was the doctoral coordinator at that time in the Department of Criminology. Nọnso, as we all called him, had already some distinction among his cohort of students by his being law trained as well as holding the M.A. degree. Also, many of us could not then pronounce his original Nigerian last name of Okereafọezeke. To our chagrin, soon after most of us learned how to pronounce his name, he altered it to Okafọ. I recall, as well, the difficulty we had in the mid-nineties finding a program that would place a dot under the "O" in both of his names and the other non-English vowels. He had to go through his 300-page dissertation placing dots by hand under many of the numerous Nigerian vowels used in his writing.

Nọnso's dissertation was, in fact, one of the more unique in criminology in the mid-nineties. That is, when many were satisfied to analyze a quick student survey, he was determined to gather original data and complete a rigorous thematic analysis of cases involving disputes and infractions among the Igbos of southeastern Nigeria. Early on in his career he was fascinated with the nature of disputes and crimes among the Igbos and how they were sometimes processed through a more informal rather than a more English-styled formal judicial system. How might the Igbo system of justice be described, and does it portray a viable system of judicial processing reminiscent of pre-British occupation? The dissertation later became the foundation for his other book (*Law and Justice in Post-British Nigeria: Conflicts and Interactions Between Native and Foreign Systems of Social Control in Igbo*, Greenwood Press, USA). These early concerns have guided his research and formed a stage-setting for launching much of his more recent work.

Highlighted by this Foreword, the book at hand (*Reconstructing Law and Justice in a Postcolony*) is not only a logical follow-up but also represents critically needed analyses of law and justice systems in postcolonial nations. Many nations, perhaps a majority and the citizenry can relate to the plight of being under the yoke of an occupying power. For some, the subjugation is short-lived. For others, it is long-lasting and adjustments to being subordinated are complex and difficult. For some nations, it is a single occupying authority that places its stamp over the indigenous culture. For others, there may be sequential occupiers that make matters increasingly complicated. Some societies were victims of out-right imperialism while others fell victim to more inadvertent occupation. Regardless, the following questions and others are relevant. How do nations adapt to such cultural pluralism especially regarding matters of law and justice? How do nations cope with conflicting cultures as when multiple legal systems collide or policies of dispute resolution differ? Professor Nọnso Okafọ's book on *Reconstructing Law and Justice in a Postcolony* helps to unravel some of these questions.

The new book uses illustrations from Nigeria and other postcolonies to respond to the relevant issues. However, what is particularly credible about the book is that information is collected on 12 different postcolonies spread over the globe. Consequently, the book moves in the direction of comparative law and criminology. This is a great benefit rather than a liability given the need for scholarly work that provides a comparative perspective to law, justice, and social control, particularly with a postcolonial orientation. The book should remain at arm's reach of serious researchers on issues of cross-cultural law and justice.

W. Timothy Austin, Ph.D.
Professor, Indiana University of Pennsylvania, USA

For My Mother

Madam Bessie Nwagboro Okafọ
(Number 1)
(Nwadịrị Ọra)

Introduction

In a world of *responsive law* [as distinguished from *repressive law* and *autonomous law*], ... law's power does not stem from tradition or its formal pedigree alone, but also from its persuasiveness as good public policy. In a world of responsive law, legal institutions – courts, regulatory agencies, alternative dispute resolution bodies, police departments – are periodically studied and redesigned to improve their ability to fulfill public expectations.[1]
[Robert A. Kagan in Introduction to Philippe Nonet's and Philip Selznick's *Toward Responsive Law: Law & Society in Transition* (2001), Transaction Publishers, pp. xxiv-xxv].

Reconstructing Law and Justice in a Postcolony establishes a prototype for postcolonial or post-occupational law and justice reconstruction. The central purpose of this book is to fashion a system and process for more effective and efficient social control. This is to emerge from an honest, thorough, purposeful, and progressive scrutiny of the elements of the indigenous-based and foreign-based law and justice systems applicable in a country. Nigeria is the primary case study for the research presented in this book. However, to increase comparative understanding, the book surveys the relationship between indigenous and foreign law and justice in the following 12 countries: Afghanistan, Australia, Brazil, Canada, India, Iraq, Japan, Kenya, Nigeria, Saudi Arabia, South Africa, and United States of America. The twelve countries represent a judgmental sample chosen mainly on the basis of regional representation. On the strength of the comparative insights derived from the surveyed countries, and in particular based on an in-depth analysis of the Nigerian experience, the book recommends ways to restructure the procedural and substantive components of the justice system of a postcolony.

The four-Part, eight-Chapter book establishes procedural and substantive ingredients of quality justice, social control, and law in a postcolony. Part 1, consisting of Chapter 1, was designed to demonstrate the critical importance of indigenous traditions, customs, and native laws (customary law) even in a contemporary State. The case is made in Chapter 1 that most laws of a modern State

---

1 I added italics to differentiate and emphasize law's three types based on a society's progress. The least progressive type of law is *repressive law*, followed by *autonomous law*, and finally the most progressive *responsive law* [Nonet and Selznick, *Toward Responsive Law: Law & Society in Transition* (2001); see also Nọnso Okafọ's (2006) book review in *International Criminal Justice Review*, Volume 16, Number 3, December, at pp. 202-204]. Further, see generally Peter Fitzpatrick (1992) *The Mythology of Modern Law*, London, United Kingdom: Routledge, particularly pp. 87-91.

are rooted in customary foundations. Over time, these laws have been modified, as they should be. Nonetheless, their indigenous essences are undeniable. Therefore, customary law, in its various contemporary forms, remains critically important for modern State social control. Part 2 (Chapters 2-4) synopsizes the forms of the relationships between indigenous and foreign systems of law and justice in each of the twelve countries identified in the preceding paragraph. The indigenous/foreign justice relationships identified in the twelve countries provide the comparative background for the following consideration of law and justice reconstruction.

Part 3, which consists of Chapters 5-7, focuses on the elements of justice and law reconstruction in a postcolony, based mainly on the Nigerian example. The ingredients of law making, law enforcement, adjudication, and post-conviction actions in the reconstructed justice system of a postcolony are identified, explained, and illustrated for the reader. With full appreciation of the strengths and weaknesses of Nigeria's postcolonial law and justice system, Chapters 5-7 offer specific suggestions to rebuild and strengthen the system for more effective and efficient justice. Part 4 (Chapter 8 and Summary and Conclusion) emphasizes the need for a distinctly new outlook on law and justice. The new orientation is expected to highlight and strengthen a different, presumably better, way of understanding and applying law and other forms of social control in a postcolony.

Appendix A (Questionnaire) lists the twenty-three items used to collect some of the relevant information for this book. The information was derived from thirty-one individuals who had retired from, were working or receiving training in, the Nigerian law and justice system. Appendix A is best regarded as a means of eliciting reactions from a purposive sample, which was adjudged to possess information that would help to shape the direction of the research for this book. As is apparent, the items mostly asked the respondents to draw from their respective professional knowledge, training, and experiences to help diversify the issues, opinions, and options regarding the theme of this book. Thus, the following six items highlight the issues on which Appendix A elicited information from the respondents: the relative statuses, influences, and effectiveness of customary law and English-style law in Nigeria; the ability and potentials of customary law for effective social control in a postcolonial modern State; the respondents' reactions to the idea of indigenizing law and justice in Nigeria to treat customary law as the grundnorm; the proper roles and responsibilities for developing customary law; the appropriateness of continuing with the present universal Nigeria Police Force (NPF) for policing the country *vis-à-vis* creating multi-policing organizations at the state, local, and other levels of administration; and inputs on how to restructure the court system to increase efficiency and effectiveness.

The author does not suggest that the research participants constitute a representative sample. The sample members (university law teachers, advanced law students, legal practitioners, high ranking law enforcement personnel, Customary Court judges, etc. – all Nigerians) provided diverse pieces of information in written responses to the questionnaire items. Those items and the responses helped to guide the discussions on the issues in this book. As appropriate, the author has drawn on some of the responses to illustrate and expatiate on topical issues. Throughout this book, "Survey Reaction Participant" refers to a person (one of the 31 participants) surveyed for this exercise.

Like many science-based research publications, this book has been long in coming. I conceived the idea of this book shortly after my *Law and Justice in Postcolonial Nigeria: Conflicts and Interactions Between Native and Foreign Systems of Social Control in Igbo*, Greenwood Press. At the time of forming the idea of *Reconstructing Law and Justice in a Postcolony*, I was an Associate Professor at Western Carolina University, North Carolina. I have since moved to Norfolk State University, Virginia (both institutions are in the USA), where I have gone on to become a Professor. Even as my career moved along, the idea of, and work toward, *Reconstructing Law and Justice in a Postcolony* never left me. However, I had to always *find* time to research, think, write, and re-write in the midst of other demanding aspects of my beloved job. I am quite happy to get to the present. A follow-up research project is already in the works! It is tentatively titled *Iwu Igbo* (*Igbo Law*).

Thanks to all who encouraged me in various ways through this endeavor. A special "thank you" goes to my wife, Ezii, and sons, Chinedu, Chidozie, and Nọnso, for supporting me in this undertaking. They suffered my absence in the course of my research trips to Nigeria as well as during the innumerable hours spent analyzing the data and writing this book. I love you.

I alone am responsible for the contents of this book.

Nọnso Okafọ
LL.B.(Hons.); B.L.; M.A.; Ph.D.
Professor
2009

PART 1
Customary Law Foundations of Modern Law and Justice

Chapter 1
Are Traditions, Customs, and Native Laws Impotent in the Face of Modernity?[1]

Introduction

The core object of this chapter is to gauge the utility of customary law in a modern State. Doing so requires me to judge the effectiveness and efficiency of traditions, customs, and native laws in rural and industrial societies. Without doubt, every justice system – past or present – has its limitations (constraining factors) and limits. A justice system is incapable of anticipating and addressing every conflict situation or issue because each system includes factors that compromise its capacity to satisfactorily deal with every situation or subject matter. The justice system of an industrial society, such as the United States of America (USA or US), is widely believed to de-emphasize traditions, customs, and native laws. At this juncture, it seems necessary to clarify the uses of the "traditions," "customs," "indigenous," and "native" concepts. I am aware of the simple, archaic (Hart, 1997, particularly at p. 91), and even racist (Fitzpatrick, 1992) meanings frequently ascribed to those terms in the literature, especially when documenting the relationship between Africa and the West (see Elechi, 2006, particularly Chapter 3). On the strength of immense African contributions to modern social control, those negative connotations are unwarranted and should be discarded. For convenience, those concepts are interchanged throughout this book. The terms are used merely to identify a society's homegrown system or process *vis-à-vis* a foreign system or process imposed through colonization, occupation, conquest, etc.

However, this discourse is an opportunity to suggest a way to rise above the negativity of "*traditional* law (or system) (or process)" in the professional literature, in the same way that it will allow us to escape the disparagement of "*customary* law (or system) (or process)," as well as "*native* law (or system) (or process) and "*indigenous* law (or system) (or process)." While I use the more common concepts (tradition, custom, indigenous, and native) in this book because of the reader's familiarity with them, I recommend that they be spared condemnatory meanings. Perhaps in the future, where a reader feels unable to look beyond the unjustified negative connotations imposed on the concepts, a new set of terms may be used instead. Thus, as a way out of the unneeded and wasteful intellectual bickering,

---

1 An earlier, abridged version of this chapter was presented at the American Society of Criminology Conference, Atlanta, Georgia, USA, November 13-17, 2007 (see Okafọ, 2007).

I propose the use of *grounded* instead of *traditional, customary, indigenous*, and *native*. By this recommendation, "*grounded* law (or system) (or process)" may be used instead.

The adoption and use of "*grounded* law (or system) (or process)" will expressly acknowledge that the relevant law, system, or process is based on, and grew out of, the various cultural elements of the relevant society, which elements are rooted mainly in immemorial principles, beliefs, and practices. As such, adopting and using *grounded* to describe the appropriate law, system, or process of a society will accurately capture the homegrown character of the law, system, or process, as the case may be. Also, using *grounded* to express the appropriate law, system, or process will do away with the need to assert that such homegrown law, system, or process is not inferior to another imposed by a foreign power. Further, *grounded* law, system, or process realistically captures the fact that the law, system, or process arose from principles that have been tested through centuries in innumerable grievances, conflicts, and disputes. These tests, many of which are available in the forms of decided cases, attest to the relevant law, principle, or process. Foreign law, system, or process falsely claims a foundation in the society on which it is imposed. On the other hand, *grounded* law, system, or process sensibly and unpretentiously represents the essence of the society in which it is based. Finally, hopefully, the adoption and use of *grounded* law, system, or process, as the case may be, will dispense with the war of words in the literature over "native," "indigenous," "custom," and "tradition."

However, we now return to the issue of the relative strengths of the social control arrangements of an industrial versus rural societies. Predominantly, the system of an industrial society, such as the USA, is often assumed to be more sophisticated, more effective, and more efficient, than the system of a rural society, such as the Igbo (Nigeria) native society. But that is not necessarily correct. The widely acknowledged shortcomings of, and hostility to, the US justice system, by some of its citizens, illustrate the system's limits and limitations. Numerous justice system scholars and practitioners argue for the USA to return its justice system, at least in part, to the restorative (healing) principles, which derive fundamentally from the world's indigenous or rural societies and their practices. The fact that the advocacy has grown stronger shows that traditions, customs, and native laws (customary law) remain effective and efficient in rural as well as industrial cultures; it also shows that traditions, customs, and native laws are potent mechanisms for social control in a modern society. The objective of this chapter is to demonstrate that customary law is a strong component of social control in rural as well as industrial societies.

Consistent with the foregoing, the notion that traditions, customs, and native laws (customary law) are inferior to Western law deserves further scrutiny. For instance, Cunneen (2002, pp. 45-46) observes as follows:

> The conceptualization of 'customary law' adds weight to the preeminence of western legal forms. 'Custom' becomes circumscribed within the framework of

the 'formal' legal system. Custom might be recognized, it might be considered, it might be given a place, but it is always as Other and as inferior. As Findley notes, 'the trend in post-colonial states has been to reduce custom to the realm of mitigation and sentence within the criminal jurisdiction ... this puts custom obligation outside central considerations of liability and legality' (1999: 209).

The unjustifiable dichotomy between "superior" and "inferior" legal systems need not continue. There is no rational basis or evidence to argue scientifically that Western law is superior to other societies' customary laws. Moreover, the English common law, which highlights Western law, is based on the English traditions, customs, and native laws, which constitute the same foundation for customary law. However, the claim that customary law is inferior to Western law derives from an inaccurate sense of traditions, customs, and native laws (customary law). The correct position is that customary law is a system of laws based on the indigenous cultures, religion, practices, consensus, aspirations, etc. of a society. The customary law of a postcolony or conquered territory must be distinguished from the system imposed by the colonizing or conquering power. Thus, "customary law" in this book separates a society's indigenous, home-grown law and justice system from an imposed system.

Without an extensive excursion into rural versus urban criminology, this chapter identifies key distinguishing variables of a rural society and an industrial society. Some of the limits and limitations of a justice system are inherent, while others attach from the environment. Whether they are inborn or acquired, all the variables contribute significantly to the effectiveness and efficiency of the customary law of each society. However, the basic argument here is that, whereas rural and industrial societies differ in their justice characteristics, they may be assessed on effectiveness and efficiency if the assessment is based on what reasonably works for each society (effectiveness) and the cost involved (efficiency). This chapter uses Restorative Justice principles to illustrate traditions, customs, and native laws' (customary law) contributions to social control, justice, and law in a modern State.

Judging a Justice and Social Control System on Effectiveness and Efficiency

A viable and sustainable justice and social control system must be both effective and efficient. Otherwise, it will be discarded, sooner or later. The credibility of a justice and social control system depends on whether or not its human subjects perceive the system as effective and efficient. A system based on Customary Law, the English Common Law, Constitutionalism, Religious Law, or any other philosophy, has to be effective and efficient to be sustained over a long period of time. I will now illustrate the roles of the twin considerations (effectiveness and efficiency) with a brief consideration of their applications to traditions, customs, and native laws (customary law).

Judging the effectiveness and efficiency of a customary law system can reasonably be reduced to asking and answering these two questions. Question one – effectiveness – does the customary law work reasonably well for the members or most members of its population to help them manage their civil and criminal grievances, conflicts, and disputes? If the answer is "No," such as where a customary law is generally ignored because of identifiable deficiencies or where the law works for only a few rich and influential members of society, the customary law is ineffective. If the answer is "Yes," such as where it is widely used successfully to manage grievances, conflicts, and disputes, thus strongly suggesting that it works, the customary law is effective. Question two – efficiency – if the customary law reasonably assists in the management of grievances, conflicts, and disputes, what does it cost to do so? As an example, a customary law system that is effective because a lot of resources (money, equipment, personnel, time, etc.) that would otherwise have been used in other sectors of society are poured into the customary law system is probably too expensive for such a society to maintain. Thus, the customary law is inefficient for that society. A related point should be made here therefore that, irrespective of its indigenous source, a customary or other law system may be effective and/or efficient for one society, but not for another society.

Traditions, Customs, and Native Laws in Rural and Industrial Societies

Relative to an industrial (modern, urban) society, a rural (indigenous, traditional) society is typically small (in physical space and population); it is simple (the common purpose of the society and its leadership is clear to the average member of the society); it is genuine (the common purpose of the society is consistent with most members' aspirations and the leadership's procedure for attaining the purpose is honest, reasonable, and for the common good, as opposed to dishonest, unreasonable, and motivated by selfish expectations). Also, a rural society has fewer human alterations of the natural components of the society. The small physical land space and population of a rural society carries substantial advantages. For example, its small size facilitates more and higher quality interaction among the members of the society. It is not uncommon for a member of such a society to know every other member, sometimes by name (first name, or at least last name). The importance of knowing one another well lies in the fact that familiarity with one's neighbors and other members of a society tends to promote communication, even on sensitive, contentious issues. Such familiarity helps to mollify grievances and prevent their escalation to conflicts and disputes.[2] In a dispute situation, familiarity with other members of one's society helps to smoothen the edges for more cooperative and acceptable resolution of the dispute. The characteristics of

---

2 See Todd (1978, particularly pp. 95-96) for a sample escalating process from "grievance," through "conflict," to "dispute."

simplicity, genuineness, and fewer human alterations of the natural environment also distinguish a rural from an industrial society. However, a big rural society may have some of the enumerated advantages of a rural society if it is simple, genuine, and has a few human interferences with its natural components.

Life in an industrial society differs from life in a rural society in important respects. Unlike a rural society, an industrial society thrives mostly on impersonal existence and relationships. An industrial society typically has high population density. Compared to a rural society, the scale of social change in an industrial society is massive. Moreover, these changes occur relatively quickly and rather frequently. The result is that social life in an industrial society is highly unpredictable when compared to a rural society. Members of an industrial society are detached from one another. Rarely do they know their neighbors, let alone on first name basis. It is common for next-door neighbors to live that close to each other without meeting each other for months, even years. Where they know each other, there is almost a concerted effort to keep each other at arm's length. Industrial society members tend to feel isolated and unsafe mainly because they generally live among strangers and these members perceive themselves as targets. Also, they are typically unwilling or unable (lack of opportunity) to spend the time to get to know one other better. Kinship relationships, such as family support systems and extended family networks, either do not exist or are fast disappearing.

Conventions and norms of social control constitute critical aspects of lives in rural as well as industrial societies. Every society needs a credible, effective, and efficient social control system to be stable and to thrive. Informal case management and social control techniques are in high use in a rural society. Generally, these techniques serve to promote peace, unity, harmony, sense of common purpose, and progress. As a result of their lifestyle, members of an industrial society, unlike members of a rural society, are unable to exert an informal corrective influence on their fellow members. Thus, minor disagreements that could easily be managed peacefully between friendly neighbors, colleagues, friends, acquaintances, etc. tend to get out of hand quickly leading to formal judicial action in the formal (official) justice system.

Therefore, the absence of the rural society-type close, familial, kinship, and good neighborly relationships from an industrial society leads the industrial society's members to increase the number and diversity of contentious issues they bring before the official justice system. Consequently, there is an overburdening of the official system of an industrial society. The modern State, embodying the industrial society, is thus expected to intrude more into the (private) lives of the citizens and manage their grievances, conflicts, and disputes. On the contrary, in a rural society, private persons and groups are expected to, and do, manage most of their grievances, conflicts, and disputes, generally free of interventions by the society's formal structures. One important reason that a rural society's informal justice process is able to effectively contribute to the social control of the rural environment is that, typically, most members of a rural society consent to their (traditional) informal process. Having thus consented, they are more likely to work hard to ensure that their system works well, even if there is no threat of *substantial sanctions* (active, rather than passive, penalties) for non-compliance.

On what constitutes a *substantial sanction*, it may be necessary to explain that a threat of "mere" exclusion (ostracism) from a rural society can be a substantial sanction. The substance of this sanction depends mainly on the availability of other societies, groups, or individuals with whom an ostracized person is able to associate. If an ostracized member of a society can relocate to a neighboring society or community with relative ease, such as where the ostracized person relocates and lives with maternal relatives or in-laws in a neighboring town, the burden of the ostracism should be regarded as not-substantial. On the other hand, having to move to a far off community, where the ostracized person has no blood or close relationship and thus no support base, is a substantial sanction. However, a strong case can be made to restrict *substantial sanctions* to formal denials of, and restrictions on, fundamental human rights, such as by imprisonment (restriction of the right to movement), fine or seizure and disposal of property (denial of the right to property), and death (denial of the right to life).

The law and justice system of an industrial (modern, urban) society thrives on members' fears of mainly active, formal, and substantial sanctions for non-compliance with the system's dictates. In this mode, the system alienates at least some members of the society who may disagree with aspects of the system. Notwithstanding, the official State power, influence, and resources back the system and sustain it. On the contrary, the rural (traditional) society's justice system tends to focus on carrying the members along by winning their approval, especially on key issues. One effective way in which the rural justice system does this is to emphasize peacemaking among the members. Thus, unlike the justice system of an industrial society, a rural society's justice system regards the reconciliation of disputants as an essential part of its work. Such reconciliation tends to reinforce members' faith in the system and encourage their acceptance of, and compliance with, the system.

In the case of an industrial society, numerous sanctions-backed rules and regulations monitor the actions and inactions of members. Moreover, most of the rules and regulations emanate from persons and groups far removed from most members of the industrial society, such that the generality of the members are unable to (substantially) influence the decision makers. It is acknowledged that the actions and inactions of the members of an industrial society may need to be closely monitored because of the diverse nature of such a society. Allowing a lot of discretion among already diverse members of the society would interfere with the society's smooth functioning. Closer monitoring of an industrial society's members finds expression in the rule that each member is obligated to comply with the official process, even if he/she disagrees with the process. An industrial society's officials will forcefully obtain compliance, if necessary by seizing property, freedom, or even life. Unlike the rural, informal society, consent is neither a prerequisite nor an essential part of the justice process in an industrial, formal society.

Having identified key differences between rural (traditional) and industrial (modern, urban) societies, along with some of the differing methods in which traditions, customs, and native laws (customary law) apply to the respective societies, it is necessary to state that there are several general characteristics found in customary law, whether the law applies in a rural or industrial society. Bruce Benson, quoted in Younkins (2002, p. 3), observes as follows:

> ... customary legal systems tend to share the following basic characteristics: 1) a strong concern for individual rights; 2) laws enforced by victims backed by reciprocal agreements; 3) standard adjudication procedures established to avoid violence; 4) offenses treated as torts punishable through economic restitution; 5) strong incentives for the guilty to submit to the prescribed punishments due to the threat of social ostracism; and 6) legal change by means of an evolutionary process of developing customs and norms.

Bruce Benson's observation deserves closer examination for clarification.

To shed light on Bruce Benson's (Younkins, 2002, at p. 3) six identified characteristics of customary law, several of this law's features are relevant. For example, Benson's customary law characteristic number 1 validly concludes that, contrary to the condescending summation by some of the "modern" (typically Western) law and justice systems, traditions, customs, and native laws are capable of ensuring, and do ensure, that individual rights are provided for and enforced. However, in general, customary law seems more willing than statute-based, Western-style law to subjugate the rights of an individual to those of the group or the larger society, where a community's common purpose necessitates such suppression. Thus, in customary law, group rights generally override the rights of an individual. Benson's characteristic number 2 encapsulates the stakeholders' joint interests and efforts involved in the administration of customary law. Many groups and individuals in society participate in significant ways to interpret, apply, and enforce customary law. This is unlike the situation under the Western-style modern State law, which reserves the authority and power to interpret, apply, and enforce law to exclusive personalities and groups. Thus, the customary law process is inclusive, rather than exclusive or one-sided.

On Bruce Benson's customary law characteristic number 2 (the reciprocal quality of customary law), Younkins (2002, p. 1) explains as follows: "[Customary laws] are less likely to be violated than *enacted authoritarian laws* because they require voluntary acceptance by individuals in recognition of reciprocal benefits received."[3] Put differently, individuals to whom customary law applies are less likely to violate the law because they regard it as of mutual interest to all members, rather than of one-sided interest to the privileged members of the society. It is pertinent to ask the following questions: When Younkins (2002, p. 1) mentions that *enacted authoritarian laws* are more likely to be violated than customary law,

---

3   I added italics for emphasis.

does his *enacted authoritarian laws* include laws passed by an elected legislature in a modern State, even if the State is a well known democracy such as the USA? Why would such laws not qualify as laws based on the consent of the citizens of the relevant State? Younkins apparently answers these questions as follows. Yes, the expression includes laws passed by an elected legislature. Such laws are, in reality, not based on the consent of every member of a society. The laws may not even have the consent of a majority of the members, such as where a majority of the citizens fail to vote to elect their representatives as is common in the USA, or the occupants of representative positions gained those offices illegally by subverting the constitution and electoral laws as is common in Nigeria. Or, such laws may be based simply on the discretionary, arbitrary, or other exercise of authority or power by a few members of the society who happen to constitute a majority in the legislative process. In short, relative to customary laws, enacted statutory laws (*enacted authoritarian laws*) typically do not result from the initiative or support of all or a vast majority of the citizens. Note that this part of our analysis requires the reader to distinguish between the *source* of a law and how widely accepted the law is among the citizens to whom it applies, *after* the law is created.

It is important to note that some seemingly democratically enacted laws are mainly authoritarian, even though they profess to result from democratic processes. To emphasize this authoritarian character, Younkins (2002, p. 2) opines: "… a common law system in which law arises via judicial precedent is better than a system in which courts and judges merely apply positive laws[4] enacted by a legislative body." Based on Younkins's response, the following points can be deduced. Customary law is based on consent. Enacted legislation in a modern State is less so. Enacted legislation is more authoritarian than customary law, even if the former purports to derive from the people's consent through their elected representatives. The key point is that customary law evolved over a long period of time and all members of the society, dead and alive, have contributed to the customary law. Thus, in this sense, customary law is superior to laws enacted by a legislature.

Continuing with Bruce Benson's conclusions about customary law, his customary law characteristic number 3 ensures that, in recognition of inevitable grievances, conflicts, and disputes in society, clear rules and guidelines are established so that the parties to a case and other members of the society are reasonably well informed on how each case is to be managed in the customary law system. Such recognized rules and guidelines prevent uncertainty, speculation, and self-help tactics for managing cases. Instead, members follow verifiable, peaceful methods and procedures to manage their cases. Customary law characteristic number 4 emphasizes the importance that customary law places on reparation or restoration in dealing with some transgressions. Although customary law does not always maintain a clear separation between *crimes* and *civil wrongs* the way

---

4 Positive law equals law in its pure form – just the clear statement and objective of the law – without consideration of its morality, acceptability, wisdom, fairness, etc.

that Western-style law does, in the customary law system a responsible party is often required to make an economic amend (such as by replacing lost property, repairing damaged property, or paying the monetary equivalent of such property) if such an amend will reasonably correct the transgression. Where such amend is required and made, that obviates the need for a more punitive (criminal) sanction. The concluding section of this book ("Summary and Conclusion: Checking the Excesses of Official Criminalization in a Postcolony; Towards Increased Role for Civil Response in a Reconstructed Justice System") further discusses and offers recommendations on the need and how to reduce the wide reach of criminal law in a postcolony as well as options for expanding the uses of civil responses to criminal violations.

In customary law characteristic number 5, Benson identifies the strong interest that each individual in a customary law system has in community solidarity and cohesiveness. No member wishes to live in isolation from the group or to be identified as challenging the group norm. Thus, members willingly submit to their group's judgments and directives to avoid the negative consequences of operating outside their group. Customary law characteristic number 6 points out that the principles of substantive and procedural customary law evolve over a long period of time. The growth process of customary law distinguishes this legal form from Western-style statutory enactment that is often created over a short time, such as by a legislature. Statutes are sometimes imposed summarily, for example by a dictatorship. The evolutionary character of customary law encompasses the desirable quality of developing law from the base – the grassroots – of society, rather than imposing law from the top, privileged end of society (see Snyder, 1982; Shaidi, 1992). Strewn through Bruce Benson's six characteristics, and deserving of specific highlight, is the fact or perception that all or most customary law subjects participate in their customary law process. Their sense of involvement strengthens their faith and loyalty to the system and process.

Regardless of the common features of customary law, there can be little doubt that every society and its official (governmental) and unofficial (non-governmental) leaders will manage and apply the relevant customary law rules consistently with the available rules and the needs of each issue that comes to the leaders' attention. Thus, an identified characteristic may be applied differently between societies, even if the characteristic is universally applicable in rural and industrial societies.

Inherent and Circumstantial Limits and Limitations of a Justice System – Rural Versus Industrial Societies

Every justice system (rural society-based or industrial society-based) is circumscribed by the inherent fact that the system is a human creation. Being thus a human invention, every system carries its negatives along with its positives. Its positives constitute the strengths that justify its existence and viability among the people it serves.[5] Without the positives, the people would likely have abandoned the system or replaced it with a better system. However good a justice system is or appears to be, it is imperfect. Its imperfections are the reasons that the lawmaker strives to enact improved laws, the law interpreter (judge) decides cases by reading legal provisions along with the relevant circumstances and evolving societal standards, and the law enforcer determines which laws to enforce and to what extent, considering the society's sensitivities, preferences, and available resources. The respective actions of the lawmaker, law interpreter, and law enforcer are usually forms of discretionary exercises.

Therefore, because of system imperfections, inevitably discretion grounds the decisions and conducts of role players throughout a traditional as well as a modern justice system. It is important to point out that whether a justice system is of a rural (traditional) society or an industrial (urban, modern) variety does not, *per se*, determine the system's goodness, that is effectiveness and efficiency. Ultimately, a system's goodness is to be judged based on the system's capacity to provide its subjects with *credible* and *affordable* justice. A justice system provides credible justice when it ably manages cases brought in the system, has good reputation, and reflects the general wishes of the citizens. A system attains affordable justice if the cost of invoking the system and receiving justice is reasonable.

The justice system of a rural (traditional) society, as well as that of an industrial (modern, urban) society, is limited in terms of the issues that it anticipates and what it is able and willing to do to manage the issues. A society's justice system may not provide for the complete management of all possible issues, or even for the acceptable management of all the issues that commonly arise in the population. History, religion, customs, traditions, and cultural practices greatly inform the types of issues with which a justice system is concerned. It is reasonable to expect the justice system of a rural, land tenure, agriculture-based society to provide for an array of possible grievances, conflicts, and disputes concerning land, including

---

5   Note that a justice system both serves and subjects the persons to whom it applies. To the extent that the principles of a legal system prescribe what can and cannot be done and generally regulate conduct in a society, the members of the society are subjected to those principles mainly because a member whose conduct deviates from the dictates of law risks sanction. On the other hand, law serves its society in so far as the members can amend or abrogate its provisions, expressly or impliedly (practice) through discretionary interpretation, application, or enforcement. In this case then law and its principles are servants of the citizens.

ownership, possession, lease, mortgage, sale, gift, other disposition, and reversion. Such a society's justice system may not provide (at least not extensively) for contractual relationships and breaches of contracts if the society's members typically honor their obligations for fear of incurring the wrath of the supernatural (deity, oracle, etc.) in the case of a breach. Similarly, the criminal justice responsibility of such a society's justice system may not anticipate any form of incarceration if incarceration is unknown to the society. Where the members of a transgressor's family owe the duty to the society to correct their transgressor-relative, the need for the larger society to intervene and impose punishment for the transgression may not arise.

More than the justice system of a rural society, an industrialized, heterogeneous, fast-paced, contract-based society's justice system is likely to anticipate, require, and manage grievances, conflicts, and disputes concerning formal contractual relationships. The contractual relationships pertain to such activities as goods production and manufacturing as well as service rendering and information technology. Because most contractual relationships in an industrial society involve strangers, the society's justice system relies heavily on written contracts to determine the rights of the parties to a case. This is a major difference between traditional and modern social controls. Whereas the justice system of a traditional society relies heavily on members' goodwill, oral evidence, and oral history to determine parties' rights and responsibilities, the justice system of a modern society focuses on written verifications and concrete proofs of allegations and claims. Between disputants in a modern society, the party with the more verifiable claim, usually determined by means of witness testimony and/or documentary evidence, is more likely to succeed.

In the final analysis, the goodness of a justice system is to be determined by its capacity and utility in advancing the best interests of the members of the society it serves. The dynamic nature of society means that a system that is good in one era may not be good in another era. Society's expectations may have changed such that the characteristics they previously cherished and sought in their justice system no longer satisfy the society's members. Or, it may be, as in the example of the USA, that the society's population composition has changed so much (through immigration) that the society's members now value a different set of characteristics from that which prevailed. Further, it may be, still as in the example of the USA, that leading intellectuals, academics, and professionals in the justice system, having become exposed to, and educated in, alternative, more effective and efficient justice systems and processes, value and adopt elements of the alternative systems and processes. In any case, every justice system's capacity and utility to advance the best interests of the society's members are constantly being reassessed. This goes on even if some in a society narcissistically regard the society and its system as the best, above board, or infallible.

Thus, many people in the USA, including academics, justice professionals, researchers, policy makers, and justice clients, disagree with the punitive focus of the US official criminal justice system. The critics caution that the system's concentration on punishment threatens to turn the entire country into a giant prison where virtually every person is under some supervision of the criminal justice system. Already, the US imprisons more citizens than any other country ("1 in 100 Americans Behind Bars, Report Finds," 2008). The fact that most of the offenses for which the majority of the criminal justice subjects are punished can be more effectively and efficiently handled by other less punitive or non-punitive means worries the critics. They often point out that a look at other societies and their justice systems verify that the US criminal justice system wrongly emphasizes "punitiveness" (see definition in Okereafoezeke, 2002, pp. 28, 38, 40, 200). Nader and Todd (1978), in reference to the US justice system *vis-à-vis* more traditional systems, within and outside the USA, state:

> Within one of the most professionalized systems of law in the world we have voices crying out that the legal system is overburdened, that extrajudicial systems must be developed. We have come full circle; there has been overdependence upon the law, some say. In this context it is crucial that we look at smaller societies to see how things as a whole work. In particular, it is important to see how things work in societies where the boundaries between formal and informal systems are often blurred, and can be crossed when convenient by participants who understand and use the total system for specific ends, and where law often plays a secondary role in the management of disputes (at p. 3).

Nader and Todd (1978, p. 3) make several important points about the state of the US justice system. Four of their points deserve further mention here. Point one: the US justice system is overextended and informal processes for managing grievances, conflicts, and disputes outside of the official system must be created. Point two: the US justice system depends too much on formal law with little regard for informal law and processes. This is despite the fact that informal law and processes have the capacity to regulate many of the relationships in society, sometimes more effectively and efficiently than formal law. Point three: the US justice system should look to traditional societies within and outside the US to understand how these societies use their respective total systems to achieve justice. In these societies, the differences between informal and formal systems are deemphasized. Rather, all the relevant elements and principles of both systems are utilized as necessary to ensure just results. Point four: formal law in traditional societies often plays a minor role relative to the more informal traditions, customs, and native laws. According to Nader and Todd (1978), the US justice system will do better to borrow some of the elements, principles, and philosophies of the traditional societies.

The current trend in which the US criminal justice system puts undue emphasis on punishment is unsustainable. The criminal justice system, at all layers of administration in the US (local, state, and federal), has expanded into such a behemoth that its demands on public resources drains needed funds from other vital sectors of the society. In time, the costs of supporting the punishment philosophy are bound to deplete the country's resources and lead to decays of the society's other systems, programs, responsibilities, and life. Moreover, the huge resources expended to maintain the current US justice system encourage inordinate profiteering and corruption. The criminal justice system, which is allegedly predicated on corrections and rehabilitation, is really a business enterprise in a lot of ways. Profit-making takes precedence over the welfare of the society and the criminal justice client. The US "Corrections" system, for example, is reputed to imprison too many persons. This is a result of the dominance of profiteering in the philosophy, creation, and management of prisons (Schlosser, 1998).

Schlosser (1998), borrowing from the former US President Dwight Eisenhower's warning against "the military industrial complex," explains that "the prison-industrial complex" (PIC) exists to further the financial gains of interested parties (that is, criminal justice sector investors – stakeholders). Therefore, the PIC extends beyond relevant criminal justice professionals (prison and corrections staff and personnel, police personnel, workers in the court system, social services personnel, etc.) who are hired to provide professional services for the management of prisons. Rather, the PIC includes the following groups and activities: profiteers, such as gun manufacturers, casket makers for dead prisoners, medical professionals for prisoners' upkeep, public relations workers for laundering the image of the prisons and the criminal justice system. Also, included in the PIC are building contractors and subcontractors for constructing the facilities, beds, toilets, locks, windows, and other security features. Further, food service business chains are part of the PIC because they profit from their contracts to supply large quantities of food for the prisoners. And, clothing manufacturers profit hugely from supplying uniforms for prisoners and guards, respectively (Russell, 2009). While the list of groups and activities provided here is not exhaustive, it demonstrates the pervasive nature of the PIC.

However, for avoidance of doubt, Schlosser (1998) explains that the PIC goes well beyond persons, groups, organizations, and their activities. Instead, PIC has grown to become a culture as well (p. 5):

> The prison-industrial complex is not only a set of interest groups and institutions. It is also a state of mind. The lure of big money is corrupting the nation's criminal-justice system, replacing notions of public service with a drive for higher profits. The eagerness of elected officials to pass 'tough-on-crime' legislation – combined with their unwillingness to disclose the true costs of these laws – has encouraged all sorts of financial improprieties. The inner workings of the prison-industrial complex can be observed in the state of New York, where the prison boom started, transforming the economy of an entire region; in Texas [state] and Tennessee [state], where private prison companies have thrived; and in California [state], where the correctional trends of the past two decades have converged and reached extremes.

The centrality of profit-making in the PIC means that the stakeholders and players are willing to devise and support, and have devised and supported, policies and programs that initiate and secure massive public expenses in the US criminal justice system. Schlosser (1998, p. 4), quoting Attorney Donziger, who headed the US National Criminal Justice Commission in 1996, describes the PIC philosophy as follows: "If crime is going up, then we need to build more prisons; and if crime is going down, it's because we built more prisons – and building even more prisons will therefore drive crime down even lower." Further, the policies and programs rooted in this thinking ensure the imprisonment of a large portion of the US population.

However, many of the prisoners in the US are incarcerated for relatively minor crimes that could be better managed through other less harsh sanctions and processes. The result is that for decades the US prison population has steadily risen. In the past three decades in particular (1980s-date), the country's rate of imprisonment has increased from less than five hundred thousand to more than two and half million (a 500% increase). Today, the US incarcerates more people than any other country, including more populous countries. This is startling considering that China, as well as India, has four to five times the US population. To accommodate the astronomical growth in the number of its prisoners, the US federal as well as state governments have, for decades, embarked on massive prison building. The annual spending on prisons runs into tens of billions of dollars. It is fitting to ask: How much does the US spend for crime prevention programs? How much does it spend to treat and reform its convicts? Relative to the expenses on prisons, the budgets for prevention programs, treatment, and reform pale substantially.

It is interesting that the recent (2008-) economic downturn in the US and other economies has given rise to the idea of releasing many prisoners before their terms of incarceration end. In several states of the US, especially California, there have been strong voices pushing for the governments to release non-violent (low-risk) prisoners as a way of saving scarce resources for use in meeting the governments' other more pressing responsibilities. For California alone, some analysts have suggested that as many as thirty thousand such prisoners should be released early. One is tempted to ask: If these "low-risk" prisoners did not need to be kept behind bars, why were they incarcerated in the first place? So, but for the US economic difficulties, these prisoners would have remained incarcerated even though they did not need to be behind bars? These questions reveal the unfortunate knack of the US justice system to unfairly target and punish some of the weakest and less influential members of the society.

The parasitic nature of the PIC becomes more glaring when one considers that the PIC actors prey mostly on the less well-to-do and most vulnerable of the US population. About 70% of the prisoners in the US are illiterate. Tens of thousands suffer from severe mental illness. While up to four-fifths of prisoners have a history of substance abuse, the availability of drug treatment facilities in prisons has declined considerably. The vast majority of prisoners are members of the country's minority populations, mainly African-American and Latino. In most parts of the country, African-Americans make up more than 80% of the prison population even though this minority group constitutes only about 15% of the general US population. The marked differences in the rates of imprisonment among the racial groups are stunning. For example, the 2006 US incarceration rates, by race, show that among Whites (European-Americans), 409 are imprisoned per 100,000; among Latinos, 1,038 of 100,000 are imprisoned; and among Blacks (African-Americans), 2,468 are imprisoned per 100,000. As in most world societies, the rates differ between the gender groups, with males imprisoned at a higher rate than females. However, there are far starker rate differences when all males are compared on the basis of racial categories. The result shows that 736 of 100,000 White males are imprisoned, 1,862 of 100,000 Latino males are incarcerated, while 4,789 out of 100,000 Black males are in prison. Clearly, the numbers are daunting for an African-American male; he is more than six and half times likely to be imprisoned as a White male. In particular, the likelihood of imprisonment among males aged 25-29 years shows even greater disparity.

Perhaps, a brief comparative reference should be made at this juncture. The world rightly condemned apartheid South Africa as racist. But, even apartheid South Africa (in 1993) incarcerated about 851 Black males of every 100,000, whereas the USA (in 2006) imprisoned about 4,789 Black males out of 100,000 ("Incarceration is Not an Equal Opportunity Punishment," 2009). Thus, imprisonment appears to be used as a weapon for subjugating the less favored and relatively weak segments of the US population while the stakeholders reap greater riches (Schlosser, 1998; Russell, 2009).

Thus, Nader and Todd's (1978, p. 3) statement captures the growing frustration with the US justice system. The frustration stems substantially from the criminal justice component's strong emphasis on the punishment of all sorts of offenders, including first time offenders, minor offenders or misdemeanants, and the so-called victimless offenders, such as prostitutes and drug (ab)users. The system is also notorious for its unwillingness to divest itself of some of its criminal jurisdiction. Instead, more and more otherwise private actions between private parties are defined criminally, thus widening the criminal justice net. The formal US justice system tends to regard informal processes and lessons from informal systems as inferior and incapable of noteworthy ideas. But, the US justice system is certainly not the only system with these flaws. Many justice systems across the world, especially those versions imposed by means of colonization, example Nigeria, and conquest, example Iraq, have the flaws that Nader and Todd (1978) identify, and more. These are precisely some of the flaws a reconstructed law and justice system should avoid.

Reconstructing law and justice in a postcolony should include taking steps to avoid the identified drawbacks of the US justice system, such as its over-reliance on punishment, excessive encouragement of profiteering among criminal justice investors or stakeholders, insufficient encouragement of offender healing and reform, etc. Heeding Nader and Todd's (1978) advice will demonstrate that the justice philosophies and principles of traditional societies can produce more effective and efficient justice, in the USA as well as other societies.

Enduring Contributions of Traditions, Customs, and Native Laws to Modern Justice

In no area of modern law and justice are the contributions of traditions, customs, and native laws more pervasive and enduring than in the realm of *restorative justice*. Restorative (healing, soothing) justice aims to return the victim, offender, their relatives, community, and other stakeholders to a crime to their original conditions, as much as possible. "Original conditions" refers to the respective circumstances of the identified persons and groups prior to the crime under consideration. Many theories and principles of restorative justice, which have traditional roots, are based on the immemorial lifestyles of many small and big rural, traditional societies across the world. In the last few years, it has become fashionable to adopt many of the restorative theories and principles for the major Western justice systems, such as applies in the USA. But, it must be mentioned that these theories and principles rightly belong to their traditional societies' foundations rather than the modern-day suitors (the Western justice systems).

Thus, McCold (2000) is right to describe the evolution of restorative justice as a process of discovery rather than invention. Similarly, Younkins (2002, p. 1) describes law as follows: "The law is essentially discovered, not made. Law is a systematic discovery process involving the historical experiences of successive generations. Law reflects and embodies the experiences of all [humans] who have ever lived." This is especially so for customary law and its restorative justice theories and principles. Unfortunately, many Western justice policy makers and critics seem to have only recently discovered these theories and principles even though they have existed for a very long time in traditional societies (Mackay, 2002). Thus, the recent applications of restorative justice theories and principles to the West should not be interpreted as inventions of those theories and principles. Instead, the applications are latter-day attempts by the receiving populations to know, understand, and use what traditional societies across the world invented a long time ago.

The long histories of the restorative justice theories, principles, and practices in traditional societies justify the assertion that any attempt to borrow a restorative justice idea for use in a modern State without also borrowing its foundational justification and logic would be injudicious. Mackay (2002) explains the issues as follows (at p. 263):

> Since the antecedents of restorative justice, the roots from which it is so self-consciously drawn, are inextricably bound up with religious systems involving God or gods, spirits, ghosts and witchcraft, can we in good conscience borrow mediatory practices without their spiritual framework, and simultaneously claim

that this will suffice for the requirements of a modern criminal justice system? The debate about legal acculturation cannot be avoided. When sentencing circles and conferencing are adapted either for continued use by traditional or by modern societies, what degree of recognition is given to the spiritual elements of the original processes? ... Perhaps we must finally recognize that mediation in modern societies is indeed a child of religion.

Thus, appreciating the complete history of a restorative justice theory, principle, or practice would enhance its application and use for more effective and efficient social control in a modern State.

McCold's (2000) "restorative justice is a process of discovery rather than invention" thesis relates to the contributions of traditions, customs, and native laws (customary law) to social control in a modern society. Specifically, it evokes the idea of indigenizing law and justice in a society. Thus, the "customary law" concept should be understood to include the need to analyze the implications of indigenization in the justice system of a society, especially a former colony or conquered territory. For some researchers and justice professionals, "indigenization of social control" is achieved by recruiting natives to enforce the laws of a colonial State (Havemann, 1988, pp. 71-100). See also Cunneen (2002, p. 44). But this form of indigenization is false and oppressive. Indigenization should aim higher – at reversing and correcting existing imbalances and wrongs of the past, to the extent that this can be done, for the best interest of the indigenous and larger population. Thus, merely recruiting some members of the oppressed population to further an illegitimately foisted justice system or justice principle is not a desirable form of indigenization. Instead, to indigenize a law and justice system should mean to rediscover, develop, and modernize the indigenous system and process of law and justice to better serve the needs of the relevant population.

The following is a summary of the restorative (healing, soothing) justice theories and principles along with their traditional origins. These theories and principles have practical effects on managing grievances, conflicts, and disputes in both rural (indigenous, traditional) and industrial (modern, urban) societies (see Okereafoezeke, 1996; 2002; Van Ness, 2002; Elechi, 2006). Okereafoezeke (2002) identifies the following 12 "themes" of justice and tests each theme against the Igbo (Nigeria) Traditional and English-style justice systems. The operational definitions (descriptors) of the themes include the following restorative qualities. *Theme 1, Justice Process is Neither Created Nor Managed by Official Government*: the justice process is not created by official law; that is, the process predates the official system or came into being independently of the State, and is not run by government officials. *Theme 2, Justice is Mediation-based*: justice process emphasizes reconciliation of disputants, their relatives, associates, and the general community, over the narrow interests of either party. *Theme 3, No Lawyer Involvement in Process*: case processing does not include lawyer-participation. *Theme 4, Non-Litigious, Non-Argumentative Process*: justice process is non-adversarial. Regarding Themes 3 and 4, because lawyers typically advance the best interests of their clients at the expense of the interests of the other parties, absence of lawyers from the restorative justice process will ensure that the disputants work cooperatively to resolve their differences, with reduced friction.

Theme 5, Non-Punitive Process: justice process de-emphasizes adjudging and placing blame on a party, rather the process is designed primarily to help the parties and the community to heal or recover, not to punish *the party at fault*. *Theme 6, Stigmatizing Process*: justice process includes some steps suggesting that *a responsible party* may lose the respect of other community members, such that the party may no longer be looked up to as an exemplary community member. *Theme 7, Individualized Process*: justice process is flexible enough to accommodate relevant considerations that have the potential to affect the outcome of each case. *Theme 8, No Strict Legal Code*: laws applied in the justice system are uncodified. *Theme 9, Liberal Record Management*: justice process does not depend on strict recording of cases and their processing methods; instead much of the relevant information is committed to memory and recalled as needed. *Theme 10, Simple Process*: justice process is not complicated, thus the average person can understand and follow it without the assistance of a lawyer or special training. *Theme 11, No Cost or At Least Little Cost of Invoking Process*: a person seeking justice in the system can invoke the justice process at minimal or no financial or other material cost. *Theme 12, Peacemaking Emphasis*: justice process is designed to achieve and maintain peaceful coexistence among disputants, their relatives, associates, and the general society.

Relatedly, Van Ness (2002) identifies and explains the following four components of restorative justice. One is Encounter, which includes a meeting, narrative, emotion, understanding, and agreement between the disputants. Two is Amends. Amends involves the party responsible for the challenged behavior tendering an apology, making restitution, and changing his/her behavior. Three is Reintegration, by which the complaining party and the other community members accord some respect, material assistance, and moral/spiritual direction to the responsible party. And, Four – Inclusion of persons and groups with direct and indirect stakes in an issue – requires acknowledgement of their respective interests, inviting them to participate in a healing process, and acceptance of alternative approaches to a healing settlement.

As predicted, Okereafǫezeke (2002) finds that the Igbo Traditional justice system is more restorative than the English-style justice system in Nigeria. This means that the Igbo Traditional justice system, more than the English-style justice system in Nigeria, incorporates, utilizes, and is greatly influenced by, the enumerated restorative justice principles. The data from Igbo (Okereafǫezeke, 1996; 2002), as well as Van Ness (2002), provide further support for the position that restorative justice theories and principles originated from traditional justice systems and processes, rather than from modern, Western-style justice systems. See also Weitekamp and Kerner (2002) for the other examples of societies in which the theories and principles of restorative justice are important aspects of their respective systems.

Another related issue is the ownership of a society's ideas, principles, artifacts, and practices. Where such ownership is established, what is the proper form of expressing and documenting the ownership? Consider also that the product (idea, principle, etc.) may have been forcefully and/or fraudulently arrogated by a dominant power albeit without the consent of the inventing society. For indigenous populations, this is particularly challenging in view of the extremely invasive colonization by the West, which has stolen innumerable ideas, principles, artifacts, and practices from the colonized indigenous societies. Brown (1998) regards proposals to copyright indigenous peoples' ideas with skepticism. How can the ideas of a people be clearly distinguished from the ideas of other peoples? But, the skepticism is misplaced because there is no reason that ideas and their expressions that are unique to an indigenous people or traditional group should not be protected by copyright. Copyright protection applies to Western individual and group ideas and their expressions, why not to indigenous peoples and traditional groups and their expressions of ideas? Brown's (1998) argument against copyright-protecting indigenous ideas and their expressions will have the absurd, reprehensible, and unacceptable consequence of protecting works by Western authors and other investigators of preexisting indigenous ideas and expressions, while denying the same protection to the original owners of such ideas and expressions. Thus, despite Brown's (1998) skepticism, traditional systems and societies deserve full credit for the restorative justice theories and principles emanating from them.

In view of the origins of traditions, customs, and native law (customary law) principles and practices, their contemporary uses to manage grievances, conflicts, and disputes in a modern State should be fully acknowledged. The modern-day uses should not dilute the traditional origins or time-honored essences of the principles and practices. The fact that statutes (formal, written laws) dominate the modern society does not negative the informal, traditional roots of the statutory laws. Most written and unwritten *laws of a modern society*[6] are based on the society's immemorial traditions, customs, and native laws. On many issues, modern statues have merely reduced immemorial customary law provisions to writing. Many of the substantive criminal law definitions of crimes and the procedural criminal law guides of modern States are sheer written documentations of customary law principles and rules that had been used to manage grievances, conflicts, and disputes long before the advent of modern writing. A major consequence of writing customary law has been the gradual (and sometimes, rapid) elimination of the differences among the members of a population to which a customary law system applies. The English "common law" example suffices here.

Today, the common law is a unifying system in England. The system emphasizes the common features of the English traditions, customs, and native laws. Yet, the common law had developed from numerous conflicting traditions, customs, and native laws applicable in the pre-Norman Conquest English tribes.

---

6 That is, those laws that truly and freely developed from within the society, as opposed to those forced upon the society by a foreign power, such as a colonizing agent.

Over time, the circuit judges and other officials whom the Norman Conquerors of England assigned to English villages and towns to interpret, apply, and unite the English customary laws succeeded in creating a largely unified system that applies throughout England. Writing has been a major method of documenting and preserving judicial decisions based on the existing customary laws. Through its colonization of many world populations, Britain came into contact with many cultures. Almost without exception, Britain concluded that its system of "common law" was better than the system of every culture. In time, Britain imposed its "common law" system on many other societies that it colonized throughout the world, including Nigeria and the USA.

Thus, being the precursor to modern statutory law, customary law cannot be inferior to statutory law. In many respects, customary law is richer than statutory law. As the foundation for a modern legal system and law, a strong case can be made that customary law is superior to statutory law. Moreover, Younkins (2002, at p. 4) is correct when he observes that, on many issues, "rules and laws need not be created or enforced by a central authority" because customary law satisfactorily manages those issues. He continues (at p. 4): "Customary law has many advantages and continues to govern a wide range of social interactions and to promote order in many areas of modern society. Unfortunately, today's intellectual climate largely fails to recognize the existence and potential for customary law creation."

The lack of (sufficient) recognition for the critical role of customary law in modern State social control is indefensible. This is especially so in view of the history and relationship between modern State law, on the one hand, and other legal forms, on the other hand. Simply put, modern State law's domination of the contemporary society is based on raw State power and largely forceful usurpation of the control of resources, rather than on any claim of superior justice or superior social control ability. Younkins (2002) ably summarizes the modern State law's imposed superiority over Customary Law, Natural Law, Canon Law, and other systems of law and justice, thus (p. 3):

> States amassed enough power to claim monopoly in law relatively recently and only after a long battle with competing legal systems. State law gained dominance in the competition among medieval European legal systems such as Canon law, the Law Merchant, feudal (manorial) law, etc. State law forged ahead in part to the state's success in military conquests. In addition, the state's power to tax allowed it to subsidize its legal services. Royal law absorbed the functions of the Law Merchant by adopting its precedents and enforcing them at lower prices. Royal law, and eventually state law, wielded greater coercive power than competing legal systems which depended on reciprocity and trust. The state was able to lower its costs and legitimize its claims as the monopoly source of law by establishing courts backed by the threat of violence. Citizens in a given geographical area began to view the sovereign as the sole legitimate source of law. Eventually, the state formulated and imposed its own laws in addition to claiming to be the source of existing customary laws. Early codes of

kings were mainly codifications of customary law. The influence of Christianity provided the throne with a godly character thus enabling kings to assert a divine mandate. When kings reformed royal law to absorb portions of the Church's Canon law, the state's legal system gained the strength and aura of ecclesiastical law.

As an example, the Code of Hammurabi, reputed to be the first comprehensive written law, demonstrates a convergence of custom, tradition, religion, societal changes, and individual authority, among other things. Specifically, the Code essentially documented the existing customs, traditions, and native laws of the Babylonians. The Code's main value could be found in its ability to minimize confusion about the law's expectations. Modern-day legal codes and statutes are similarly aimed at avoiding or minimizing uncertainty about the law's statements, even though the principles may be based on long establish customs, traditions, and native laws (customary law). Therefore, it is ignorant to argue that customary law is irrelevant in a modern society. Or, even that customary law is of limited importance in a modern State. Rather, customary law in all its forms is the foundation of social control in the modern State. Customary law continues to ground, inform, guide, and influence virtually every aspect of a modern State's law and justice.

However, despite some erroneous arguments that customary law is irrelevant in a modern society, it is heartening that some justice observers and researchers recognize the important role of customary law in the social control of a modern society. Nader and Todd (1978, p. 3) clearly and strongly express such recognition. This is an example of the increasing clamor for the official, Western-based justice systems to recognize and expand the roles and influences of customary law theories, principles, and practices, which originated from traditional societies, for more effective and efficient social controls in Western and non-Western societies. The clamor for the adoption of these restorative theories, principles, and practices (or at least some of them) for the US justice system, for example, supports the position that these tradition-based restorative justice ideas can improve the justice system of a rural, non-Western as well as an industrial, Western society, by making its justice system more effective and efficient.

Chapter Summary and Conclusion

In view of the constraints on all systems of law and justice, every system is handicapped in terms of its capability to anticipate and manage certain issues that may arise among its subjects. The effectiveness of a set of traditions, customs, and native laws, also called customary law, can be determined by examining the usefulness of the system to manage grievances, conflicts, and disputes and maintain effective social control among the members of the population. In this regard, an important question is: Are the members of the society reasonably confident in the ability of their traditions, customs, and native laws to regulate relations in the society? A "yes" answer would mean that the system is effective. A "no" response would represent the system's ineffectiveness. The efficiency of a customary law is to be determined by ascertaining the cost (money, time, personnel, equipment, etc.) of achieving effectiveness in the system. If there is no cost or the cost is reasonably low, then the system is efficient. Otherwise, it is an inefficient system. Based on the foregoing criteria, are traditions, customs, and native laws impotent in a modern (as opposed to a traditional or rural) society?

Research evidence shows that traditions, customs, and native laws are capable in the face of modernity. In fact, they are very powerful, viable, effective, efficient, and in wide use, even in a modern State. In many instances, however, especially in modern States, traditions, customs, and native laws and their theories and principles are not (sufficiently) credited for their contributions to social control. The theories, principles, and practices of what is today commonly called *restorative justice* constitute some of the most important bequests of traditions, customs, and native laws to modern societies. Restorative justice emphasizes the soothing, healing, and restoration of victims, offenders, their relatives and associates, as well as the affected society, as much as possible. The healing essence of restorative justice derives from the legacies of various customary laws and other traditional social control and justice systems, most of which originated in non-Western societies. Nonetheless, Nader and Todd's (1978, p. 3) strong urging for the common law-based, official US justice system to borrow elements of traditional societies' law and justice systems lends credence to the utility of traditions, customs, and native laws, even in a modern society. Thus, if enhanced and fully utilized, traditions, customs, and native laws have the potential to contribute more positively to effective and efficient social control in rural, traditional as well as industrial, modern societies.

References

"1 in 100 Americans Behind Bars, Report Finds" (2008, February 28) *Associated Press*, http://www.msnbc.msn.com/id/23392251; Internet.

Brown, M. F. (1998) "Can Culture be Copyrighted?" in *Current Anthropology*, April 1998, Volume 39, Number 2, p. 193(30).

Cunneen, C. (2002) "Restorative Justice and the Politics of Decolonization" in E. G. M. Weitekamp and H. Kerner, eds. *Restorative Justice: Theoretical Foundations*, Portland, Oregon, USA: Willan Publishing, pp. 32-49.

Elechi, O. O. (2006) *Doing Justice Without the State: The Afikpo (Ehugbo) Nigeria Model*. New York, USA: Routledge.

Findley, M. (1999) *The Globalization of Crime. Understanding Transitional Relationships in Context*. Cambridge, UK: Cambridge University Press.

Fitzpatrick, P. (1992) *The Mythology of Modern Law*. London, UK: Routledge.

Hart, H. L. A. (1997) *The Concept of Law*. Second Edition. Oxford, England: Oxford University Press.

Havemann, P. (1988) "The Indigenization of Social Control in Canada" in B. Morse and G. Woodman, eds. *Indigenous Law and the State*. Dordrecht: Foris Publications.

"Incarceration is Not an Equal Opportunity Punishment" (2009 retrieved) *Prisonsucks.com*, http://www.prisonsucks.com; Internet.

Mackay, R. E. (2002) "Punishment, Guilt, and Spirit in Restorative Justice: An Essay in Legal and Religious Anthropology" in E. G. M. Weitekamp, and H. Kerner, eds. *Restorative Justice: Theoretical Foundations* Portland, Oregon, USA: Willan Publishing, pp. 247-266.

McCold, P. (2000) "Toward a Mid-range Theory of Restorative Justice: A Reply to the Maximalist Model" in *Contemporary Justice Review*, 3(4): 357-414.

Nader, L., and H. F. Todd, Jr., eds. (1978) *The Disputing Process–Law in Ten Societies*. New York, USA: Columbia University Press.

Okafọ, N. (2007) "The Custom in Every Law: Tradition-Based Social Control as the Foundation for Modern Justice". Paper presented in the session on *Contributions of Indigenous Justice to Modern Crime Control*, at the American Society of Criminology Conference, Atlanta, Georgia, USA, November 13-17, 2007.

Okereafọezeke [a.k.a. Okafọ], N. (1996) *The Relationship Between Informal and Formal Strategies of Social Control: An Analysis of the Contemporary Methods of Dispute Processing Among the Igbos of Nigeria*. UMI Number 9638581. Ann Arbor, MI: University Microfilms, Inc.

Okereafọezeke [a.k.a. Okafọ], N. (2002) *Law and Justice in Post-British Nigeria: Conflicts and Interactions Between Native and Foreign Systems of Social Control in Igbo*. Westport, Connecticut, USA: Greenwood Press.

Russell, G. H. (2009 retrieved) PrisonIndustrialComplex.Org, http://www.prisonindustrialcomplex.org/; Internet.

Schlosser, E. (1998) "The Prison-Industrial Complex" in *The Atlantic Monthly*, December, http://www.theatlantic.com/doc/199812/prisons; Internet.

Shaidi, L. P. (1992) "Traditional, Colonial and Present-Day Administration of Criminal Justice" in *Criminology in Africa*. Publication No. 47. Rome, Italy: United Nations Interregional Crime and Justice Research Institute.

Snyder, F. G. (1982) "Colonialism and Legal Form: The Creation of Customary Law in Senegal" in C. Sumner, ed. *Crime, Justice and Underdevelopment*. London, UK: Heinemann.

Todd, H. F. (1978) "Litigious Marginals: Character and Disputing in a Bavarian Village" in L. Nader, and H. F. Todd Jr. eds. *The Disputing Process – Law in Ten Societies* New York, USA: Columbia University Press, pp. 86-121.

Van Ness, D. W. (2002) "The Shape of Things to Come: A Framework for Thinking About a Restorative Justice System" in *Restorative Justice: Theoretical Foundations* in E. G. M. Weitekamp, and H. Kerner, eds. Portland, Oregon, USA: Willan Publishing, pp. 1-20.

Weitekamp, E. G. M. and H. Kerner, eds. (2002) *Restorative Justice: Theoretical Foundations*. Portland, Oregon, USA: Willan Publishing.

Younkins, E. W. (2002) "Customary Law as an Evolved Good Shortcut", *Le Quebecois Libre*, No. 112, October 26, 2002 (Online, retrieved November 1, 2005).

PART 2
Indigenous Versus Foreign Social Controls in Twelve Selected Countries

Introduction to Part 2

Part 2 of this book (Chapters 2, 3, and 4) is intended to provide the reader with international comparative perspectives on the issues of homegrown versus alien systems and processes of law, justice, and social control. It is fitting to recognize the comparative options available to a researcher in law and justice. No two countries have the same experience on law and justice issues. Even within a country, similarities of experiences are difficult to assert due to the substantial variations that are often present. Austin (2009) identifies the following optional bases on which comparative justice analysis may be carried out: Temporality, Space, Sub-unit to Whole, Specificity, and Formality/Informality. Since law and justice typically go together – and they certainly do in the discussions in this book – Austin's (2009) typology offers useful guide for these analyses. Note that the typology options overlap, such that a category may not be clearly discernible from another category. Thus, in many instances a comparative analysis with the aid of a typology involves elements of a different typology. Also, the typology options do not exhaust the opportunities for comparative law and justice.

However, as Austin (2009) points out, geographically, comparative law and justice may be studied on a number of levels, including intra-community, inter-community, local government, state (provincial, regional) government, national, and international levels. Whatever the number of geographical levels, these constitute only one form of comparative law and justice. Austin (2009) calls this form of comparative law and justice the Spatial (geographical, cross-cultural, etc.) variety. Other than the Spatial comparative type, law and justice may be compared on the basis of Temporal (ie. historical, evolutional, etc.) considerations, or considerations of Sub-unit to the Whole (contrasting a part of a law and justice system with the wider system). Also, a law and justice system may be compared on the basis of Specificity (comparisons along a continuum from micro subject-matter or criminal justice organization, such as a court division or police department, to its macro counterpart, such as the entire country's court system or police organization). And, law and justice may be compared by considering their degrees of Formality versus Informality (Okereafoezeke, 1996; 2002a; Austin, 2009). In addition to Austin (2009), law and justice systems may be compared by considering their Indigenous versus Foreign characteristics, as this book does. In short systems of law and justice may be compared on a variety of fronts. In every instance, the author has to take into account the desired form of analysis as well as the availability of research materials in the societies under examination.

Therefore, international comparative analysis of law and justice is far-reaching and challenging. However, it is essential for scholars to investigate, document, and recommend what works in different societies and offer them as models for other societies. In the spirits of those objectives, I have examined the indigenous/foreign law and justice relationship in each of the twelve countries surveyed in this book and presented the key similarities and differences among the countries. Therefore, no suggestion is made that the countries' experiences are the same. As Benton (2002) demonstrates, there is a wide variety of the forms of colonially-induced legal interventions in different cultures and the postcolonial relationship that exists between each culture and the colonial legal system affecting it. Nor does this book offer a model system or process of a country as necessarily applicable to others. Rather, the book strongly advocates the need for each country to sensibly utilize the progressive elements of its homegrown law and justice as well as foreign law and justice to rebuild its social control, to be more effective and efficient in the postcolonial world.

For avoidance of doubt, it is quite alright to compare countries at different stages of development. A "developed" (usually economically, politically, socially) postcolony does not necessarily avoid the law and justice pitfalls and challenges of "undeveloped" postcolonies. The USA, a former colony of Britain, is commonly cited as a developed country. But it struggles mightily with many of the problems that face undeveloped ex-colonies of Britain. A growing field of law and justice critics in the USA believes that the country's law and justice system is too reactionary, exclusive, and punitive, and that it does not (sufficiently) accommodate the relevant traditional, therapeutic methods and processes within and outside the country (Nader and Todd, 1978). This is especially so on issues of drug use criminalization and the criminal justice handling of drug offenses. The critics go on to argue for increase in the roles of the informal systems and processes in the US justice system. The dilemma recounted by Nader and Todd (1978) persists. Thus, for instance, according to Nader and Todd (1978), the current official US law and justice system can learn from the various Native American systems or from other societies within "undeveloped" countries. So, even a "developed" country has something to learn from an "undeveloped" country.

In the course of developing the idea for this book, a proposal reviewer asked what I consider a germane question, thus: Can countries at different stages of development be compared simply because they have all had some experience of colonization? The answer is in the affirmative. However, the comparison must accommodate differences in reasonable, generally accepted development indices, to have room for the varied needs and aspirations of different societies. "Development" indicators created to advance the selfish interests of the dominant sections of the world at the expense of the underrepresented (or unrepresented) peoples do not suffice. Therefore, it must be asked: "What is development?" A meaningful response to this question invokes the "developed" versus "undeveloped" (or "developing") dichotomy among countries. I sense that "developed" countries do not want to be pigeonholed with "undeveloped" countries because of the inferiority inherent in the "undeveloped" status. Nonetheless, what does it mean to be "developed"? The proper meaning of the term cannot be left to Westerners to coin and give to the rest of us. For too long, they have defined the term to the undeserved advantage of the West, at the expense of Africa and the rest of the world. I have had occasions in other publications to question this concept. I restate my observation (see Okereafǫezeke, 2002b, at pp. 115-116), thus:

> Development, reasonably defined, is continuing and relative. If a society is described as "developed," the question ought to be asked "developed in what respect?" A society that is "developed" in some aspects of existence may be fundamentally lacking in others. For example, the U.S. [United States of America] may be a "developed, First World" country, but in many respects its criminal justice principles, processes, and modes of offender management are viewed abroad as backward and inconsistent with sophisticated thought and reasoning. That is why, for example, the U.S. "War on Drugs," the country's insistence on the death penalty for some convicts, and its criminal justice system are frowned upon as backward, archaic, and unenlightened by many around the world.

See also Okafǫ (2003), which questions the US "developed" status in view of its 2003 illegal and immoral invasion of, and war against, Iraq. The US waged the war regardless of the United Nations Organization.

All postcolonies are not the same. However, they often share similar characteristics on the basis of which the postcolonies can be compared. Postcolonies differ in their colonial experiences and in their postcolonial evolution. Nonetheless, their differences do not preclude a scientist from analyzing the former colonies and identifying the commonalities among them: policies, practices, etc. To illustrate: The British colonizing enterprise was based mainly on the principle of "Indirect Rule" by which the British used the colonized locals and as much of their indigenous systems as acceptable to Britain, to rule each colony. The French, on the other hand, believed in "Assimilation," which meant that the colonized were expected and encouraged to imbibe the French culture and language and abandon the indigenous equivalents. What is wrong with analyzing and comparing former British colonies to determine how, if at all, the Indirect Rule has produced similar results in their postcolonial law and justice systems? Ditto for ex-French colonies? Nothing. Further, former colonies of Britain, France, and others could be compared as well.

Chapters 2, 3, and 4 are based on a purposive sample of twelve countries, namely Afghanistan, Australia, Brazil, Canada, India, Iraq, Japan, Kenya, Nigeria, Saudi Arabia, South Africa, and United States of America. The history, nature, and relationship between the indigenous and foreign systems of law and justice in each country are surveyed. Each country's efforts to reconcile the indigenous and foreign law and justice models are examined. Each country is selected based on two main factors. One, a country is selected because it is perceived as a good illustrative case of the region of the world from which it is selected, such that the country is a good case study of its continent's experiences with colonization and/or occupation. And, two, the author is confident in the availability of data and research on indigenous versus foreign controls in the selected country. The twelve case study countries are used in this book to demonstrate the variety of the relationships among the various forms of indigenous law and justice systems, on the one hand, and the imposed foreign systems, on the other hand. The survey efforts in Chapters 2-4 do not claim that the countries whose systems are reviewed here exhaustively show the indigenous/foreign justice interface.

Further, the groupings of the twelve countries into three categories of four each are merely for convenience, to avoid discussing all twelve countries in one lengthy chapter, as initially proposed. I decided to discuss the countries in three chapters because discussing them in a chapter would result in an oddly long chapter. In categorizing the countries, I have attempted to use some similarities to put countries together. However, countries within a category do not necessarily share the same selection criteria. In short, I will explain the groupings of the twelve countries into the three categories as follows. Having made the judgmental choice to study twelve countries, I decided that four countries *per* chapter would be reasonable. Generally, I made a decision as to the chapter in which to place a country based on a combination of three factors: regional location, economic developmental classification, and population dynamics. Thus, as much as possible, I have tried to place countries located in the same world region together. Similarly, as much as possible, I have considered the economic development of countries in grouping them, with a view to considering similarly developed countries together. And, again as much as possible, I have considered each country's population characteristics (mainly, religion, since religion is at the root of every law and justice system) and tried to categorize similar countries together. Despite these categorization efforts, Brazil and India proved to be the two most difficult countries to pigeonhole. As a way out of the dilemma, I assigned India to chapter 2 because, like the other countries in the chapter, it has substantial Islamic population. Conversely, I assigned Brazil to chapter 3 because, like the other countries in the chapter, it has substantial Christian population.

Following the categories, each country has been surveyed to understand the relationship between the country's indigenous law and justice system and the colonially or occupationally introduced law and justice system. Based on the relevant literature, the conditions and challenges of the interactions between indigenous and foreign controls in each country are examined to gauge the nature and extent to which the two forms of control do and should work together for improved social control. To achieve these, and considering that every one of the selected countries has a unique set of experiences, each country is discussed separately under these two subheadings: "History, Constitutionalism, Law, and Government" and "Critique of the Colonial and Postcolonial Interactions Between Indigenous and Foreign Controls." It seems that the second subheading is self-explanatory. However, the first subheading may need to be explained briefly. In this subheading, each country is examined on its historical evolution regarding governance based on established norms, rules, and laws. A country's norms, rules, and laws may be unwritten traditions, customs, and native laws (customary law), or a written constitution, or a mixture of unwritten and written varieties of these and others. Regardless of the form, the primary consideration is whether the country has a verifiable set of regulations for governance. If so, what are its historical and contemporary forms?

References

Austin, W. T. (2009) "Teaching Perspectives for the Comparative Study of Justice." Presented in the session on *Comparative Justice: Teaching Variations*, at the Academy of Criminal Justice Sciences Conference, Boston, Massachusetts, USA, March 10-14, 2009.

Benton, L. (2002) *Law and Colonial Cultures: Legal Regimes in World History, 1400-1900*. Cambridge, UK: Cambridge University Press.

Nader, L., and H. F. Todd, Jr., eds. (1978) *The Disputing Process–Law in Ten Societies*. New York, USA: Columbia University Press.

Okafọ, N. (2003) "Developed Atavism: 21st Century Colonial U.S.A." in *NigeriaWorld* (June 18). See http://nigeriaworld.com/articles/2003/jun/121.html; Internet.

Okereafọezeke [a.k.a. Okafọ], N. (1996) *The Relationship Between Informal and Formal Strategies of Social Control: An Analysis of the Contemporary Methods of Dispute Processing Among the Igbos of Nigeria*. UMI Number 9638581. Ann Arbor, MI: University Microfilms, Inc.

Okereafọezeke [a.k.a. Okafọ], N. (2002a) *Law and Justice in Post-British Nigeria: Conflicts and Interactions Between Native and Foreign Systems of Social Control in Igbo*. Westport, Connecticut, USA: Greenwood Press.

Okereafọezeke [a.k.a. Okafọ] N. (2002b) "Yoruba Hometowns: Community, Identity, and Development in Nigeria" (Book Review) in *Africa Today*, Volume 49, Number 1, Spring, pp. 115-118.

Chapter 2
Indigenous Versus Foreign Controls in Selected Countries: Afghanistan, India, Iraq, Saudi Arabia

Consistent with the criteria outlined in the Introduction to Part 2, Chapter 2 examines the indigenous/foreign law and justice interactions in each of Afghanistan, India, Iraq, and Saudi Arabia.

Afghanistan

History, Constitutionalism, Law, and Government

With a population estimated at almost 33 million (see "Afghanistan" USA CIA Estimate, 2009), Afghanistan comprises diverse tribes and cultures. Of the many ethnic groups, the Pashtuns are reputed to be the largest cluster with about 42% of the country's population. But that means that the remaining ethnic groups, including the Tajik, Hazara, Uzbek, Turkmen, and Aimaq (Aimak) constitute the other 58%. Other estimates credit the Pashtuns with about 50% of the country's population (see Dupree, 1980; Glatzer, 1998; Wardak, 2003). However, Afghanistan is a mixture of various ethnicities, cultures, religions, and languages, among other characteristics. Long before Afghanistan's encounter with the outside world, indigenous Afghans coexisted in relative peace for centuries. Ethnically different Afghans continue to coexist in contemporary Afghanistan, even if the country has become less peaceful and the various ethnic groups have become more suspicious of one another. Much of the disharmony and suspicion among Afghans grew out of Afghanistan's encounter with the outside world, especially the West.

In four decades beginning in the 1970s, the following three sets of phenomena highlight Afghanistan's encounters with the outside world: the Soviet military intervention in Afghanistan in 1979, the Mujahedin and Taliban rules in the 1990s through 2001, and the United States military intervention and the installation of the Hamid Karzai presidency. Each experience has impacted Afghanistan in a different way. There is a strong argument that the first two sets of events, coupled with the third, have coalesced to give Afghanistan the potential to create the best justice system for the country. Wardak (2004) addresses the first two sets of events and notes the events' wealthy contributions to the reconstruction of the Afghan justice system, thus (at pp. 319-320):

These influences, by and large, reflected the values, ideologies, and politics of the various governments that Afghanistan has witnessed since its emergence as a politically organized society. ... After the military coup in 1978, the Marxist government attempted to introduce a Soviet-style judicial system, but these changes were rejected before they took root. The subsequent *mujahedin* regime of 1992-96 declared *shari'a* as the basis of the state, and this was further entrenched by the *taliban*'s regime. While most of these regimes have partly used their systems of justice as tools for achieving their political goals, they have nevertheless contributed to the richness of Afghan legal culture; there is much within these different doctrines and approaches that could be fruitfully used and integrated in a post-war justice system.

The subsequent United States military intervention in Afghanistan culminated in the forceful removal of the *taliban* rulers of Afghanistan for supporting Osama bin Laden, the apparent mastermind of the September 11, 2001 air attacks on the United States. That US intervention substantially influenced, if not altered, the existing Afghan constitutional history and future justice system.

After overthrowing the *taliban*, the United States and US-appointed president Hamid Karzai presided over the promulgation of a new Afghan constitution called the *Constitution of the Islamic Republic of Afghanistan*, which came into force on January 4, 2004 (Afghan Constitution of 2004). By the new constitution, Afghanistan is an Islamic State aimed at crafting prosperity and progress on accounts of social justice, protection of human rights, protection of human dignity, enthronement of democracy, and the promotion of unity and equality among all the Afghan tribes and ethnic groups. Afghanistan is obliged to accept the international conventions that it signed, international treaties, the United Nations Charter, and the Universal Declaration of Human Rights.

Chapter II of the Afghan Constitution of 2004, on "Fundamental Rights and Duties of Citizens," which is made up of 37 Articles (Articles 22-59), provides for the protection of a variety of individual liberties, while imposing some responsibilities on the individual. The constitutional Chapter II rights include the rights to equality, life, liberty, presumption of innocence, expression, press, and media, confidential communication, movement, private property, Bachelor of Arts education paid for by the government, individual criminal responsibility (responsibility for a crime is personal to each person and cannot extend to another person), as well as the rights against torture, compelled confession, unlawful search, and forced labor.

Most of the rights provisions of the Afghan Constitution of 2004, although written somewhat differently, appear to be modeled after those in the United States Constitutional Bill of Rights. At the same time, however, the Afghan Constitution, unlike the constitutionally declared secular US society, recognizes Islam as the *grundnorm* or principal source of the laws of Afghanistan. Article 1 states: "Afghanistan is an Islamic Republic, independent, unitary and indivisible state." Further, Article 3, titled "Law and Religion," states: "In Afghanistan, no law can be contrary to the beliefs and provisions of the sacred religion of Islam." Consider that there seem to be fundamental conflicts between the following two ideals: constitutionally guaranteed individual rights and freedoms, on the one hand, and overriding religious precepts based on the same constitution's pronouncement that Islam is the basic source of Afghan laws, on the other hand. The fact that many privileged persons and groups often unbendingly and intolerantly promote organized religions, including Islam, for narrow benefits, strongly suggests that individual rights are likely to be compromised under the Afghan Constitution of 2004. This point leads to another important question: What is the nature of the relationship between Afghanistan's indigenous law and justice systems and the Afghan Constitution of 2004?

Critique of the Colonial and Postcolonial Interactions Between Indigenous and Foreign Controls

The influences of the three sets of major foreign interferences in the Afghan society are far reaching. The Afghan Constitution of 2004 (a consequence of the United States invasion of Afghanistan and defeat of the *taliban*) affords a good illustration of these influences. Since the constitution is a direct product of the US intervention in Afghanistan, it is important to assess further the nature of the relationships and interactions between the Afghan indigenous law and justice system, on the one hand, and the US-inspired, if not directed, Afghan Constitution of 2004, on the other hand. The constitution does not specifically explain its relationship with the Afghan indigenous law, justice, or social control. However, at least three provisions of the constitution are relevant to assessing this relationship. Article 3 declares that no law can contradict Islam. Article 162 (2) further states that laws and decrees contrary to the provisions of the constitution are void. Consistently with Articles 3 and 162 (2), Article 54 (2) enjoins the Afghan state to eliminate "traditions contrary to the principles of the sacred religion of Islam." These provisions have in effect entrenched the beliefs and provisions of Islam as the standards for judging the validity of all Afghan laws.

The Articles 3, 54 (2), and 162 (2) of the Afghan Constitution of 2004 mean that Afghan traditions, customs, and indigenous laws that run counter to Islam are invalid. These provisions thus constitute the "repugnancy test"[1] for Afghan customary laws. This test, wherever it is used, results in relative advantage for the constitutionally sanctioned laws. The Articles also give the constitutionally authorized courts and tribunals superior jurisdictions over their customary law-based counterparts, even if the customary law courts pre-existed the constitution-created courts. However, the Afghan Constitution of 2004 recognizes the importance of the country's indigenous institutions and their expressions. Thus, the constitution requires the State to provide "the opportunity to teach native

---

1 The "repugnancy test" is discussed more extensively in the section on Nigeria in Chapter 3.

languages in the areas where they are spoken" [Article 43 (3)]. Although this would encourage and promote teaching and research on indigenous systems and institutions (including the customary law systems), there is no evidence that the indigenous systems would have access to the same resources as the other, foreign systems. In the final analysis, the Afghan Constitution of 2004 appears to give comparative advantage to Afghanistan's foreign-based justice systems over the country's indigenous systems.

India

History, Constitutionalism, Law, and Government

India's present-day diverse society is traceable to ancient times. Historical accounts show that the Indus River and the surrounding farming communities provided the foundation for the founding of modern India. In time, many different world cultures, including those of Africa, China, and Europe interacted with, and migrated to, the lands closer to the Indus River. Vasco da Gama's 1498 journey from Europe to India highlighted the beginning of the European epoch in India. Shortly thereafter, the French, the Dutch, the English, as well as the Italians, went to India to advance different agendas, including missionary and economic expansions. The economic attraction led France, Denmark, the Netherlands, and England to establish corporations in India. England soon imposed its will on the competition and, for about 200 years, went on to dominate the Indian society. Britain, having forcefully incorporated India into the then British empire, exploited India through the English monarchy. Indians' anti-colonial struggles, highlighted by the leadership of Mohandas Gandhi (1869-1948), culminated in political independence for India in 1947 and a republican status in 1950. Shortly before independence, however, Pakistan broke away from India. Later (1971), another former portion of India seceded to form Bangladesh.

Modern India is a federal republic, with a population of more than one billion and one hundred and 48 million citizens (see "India" USA CIA Estimate, 2009). It consists of 28 states and seven union territories. On ethnicity, the Indo-Aryan (72%) dominates the country. The Dravidian and Mongoloid groups, along with other ethnic groups, make up the remainder. On religion, Hinduism (80.5%), Islam (13.4%), Christianity (2.3%), and Sikhism (1.9%) are some of the commonly identified faiths. India has fifteen official languages plus the English language (all sixteen languages are officially recognized for use in conducting official government businesses). Of course, as it did to all its other colonized peoples, colonial Britain had imposed the English language on India. And so, this language remains a prominent official language in India [see Article 120 of the *Constitution of India, 1950* (Indian Constitution of 1950)]. The imposition happened despite the fact that most Indians neither speak nor write the English language. Like the roots of the English language in India, the country's government, which is based on parliamentary democracy, is a British colonial legacy.

India is popularly regarded as "the world's largest democracy." This characterization stems from the country's immense population (second only to China) and the fact that since independence in 1947 India has sustained and practiced its version of the British parliamentary democracy, even with India's great diversity of peoples. The Indian Constitution of 1950 is the basic source of postcolonial Indian government and law. Having declared itself a republic, a president (head of State) and prime minister (government leader) lead the Indian parliamentary democracy. Also, the constitution formally recognizes a justice system anchored in the English common law with the Supreme Court as the highest judicial organ in India. However, separate personal law codes applicable to Hindus, Muslims, and Christians exist in the country. These codes address personal, rather than public, matters.

Critique of the Colonial and Postcolonial Interactions Between Indigenous and Foreign Controls

Separate personal law codes (*customary laws*) for India's Hindus, Muslims, and Christians, as well as other groups in the country, are recognized and maintained so long as such laws do not violate the Indian constitution. Article 13 (1) states: "All laws in force in the territory of India immediately before the commencement of this Constitution, in so far as they are inconsistent with the provisions of this Part, shall, to the extent of such inconsistency, be void." *This Part* refers to Part III of the Indian constitution on Fundamental Rights. And Article 13 (3) provides: "In this article, unless the context otherwise required, – (a) 'law' includes any Ordinance, order, bye-law, rule, regulation, notification, custom or usage having in the territory of India the force of law." Thus, Indian customary law remains in force, unless the law or any principle or application thereof violates any of the constitutionally guaranteed fundamental rights. A reading of the Indian constitution lead to the following question: Are India's indigenous systems of justice, social control, and law equal to the country's foreign, European-based system?

The import of Article 13 of the Indian constitution, and other similar provisions, is that the country's customary laws are subjected to the later Indian constitution, which is based on the English-inspired parliamentary democracy. Thus, customary law principles based on long standing practices are void if they conflict with the Indian constitution. In fact, the constitution specifically prohibits discrimination on grounds of religion, race, caste, sex or place of birth (Article 15) and untouchability (Article 17), both of which practices are rooted in immemorial Indian culture and way of life. Article 17, to further underline the constitution's opposition to the offensive Indian customary practice, has gone on to criminalize "any form" of the practice of untouchability. These provisions constitute serious limitations on the jurisdiction of the indigenous Indian justice system. The Indian constitution's strong objection to the customary practices outlined in Articles 15 and 17 notwithstanding, many (perhaps, most) Indians subscribe to the practices as important expressions of their history and heritage.

Indians probably view the European-style Indian constitution's meddling in the Indian indigenous life as contemptible. However, for promoters of the Indian customary law and practice, it is encouraging that Article 29 guarantees the protection of the language, script, and culture interests of minorities. There is no reason that "culture" cannot be read to include indigenous law and justice. Law and justice are expressions and instances of a people's culture. To be sure, the aforementioned limitations imposed by the Indian constitution limit the Article 29 guarantees. Thus, it seems that while taking necessary steps to discourage inhumane customary practices (including perhaps untouchability), India's postcolonial government should take equally strong steps to promote and encourage customary practices that reflect the citizens' contemporary preferences, many of which may differ from Western standards. In doing so, it will become clear that many aspects of the indigenous and foreign law and justice systems can be synthesized to create a system that caters to the needs of the majority of Indians.

Iraq

History, Constitutionalism, Law, and Government

With a population of over 28 million citizens (see "Iraq" USA CIA Estimate, 2009), contemporary Iraq is rooted in diverse historical influences. Several former and current world powers have contributed to Iraq's rich history. Specifically, the following societies and countries have, at various times, wielded power and influence over the Iraqi society: Ancient Mesopotamia (the period covering about 10,000 BC), the Sumerians (3000-2350 BC), the Akkadians (2350-2112 BC), the Empire of Ur III (2112-2004 BC), the Old Babylonian Empire (2004-1600 BC), the Assyrian Empire (1600-609 BC), the Neo-Babylonian Empire (626-539 BC), Mesopotamia under the Persians and Greeks 539 BC-637 AD), Mesopotamia under the Arabs (637-1258 AD, "Mesopotamia" was renamed "Iraq" in this period), Iraq under the Mongols (1258-1432 AD), Iraq under the Turkmen Tribes (1375-1508), Iraq under the Safavids of Iran (1508-1534), Iraq under the Ottoman Empire (1534-1918), Iraq under the British (1918-1932), the Modern State of Iraq (1932-present) (see "Iraq's History Page," 2009). The identified societies and countries have often exerted colonial authority with the result that today's Iraq has important institutions of State representing many of the interveners that have historically shaped the Iraqi nation.

Britain exemplifies countries that have intervened in Iraq multiple times. Indeed, Britain has done so in many countries of the world, refusing to grant true independence to its former colonies once and for all. In line with the colonialist view of superiority over the colonized, Britain has found it difficult to stay away from Iraq's affairs. However, in the late 20th Century and beyond, Britain has not been nearly as powerful a country as it was in the 17th through 19th Centuries. Thus, Britain has had to depend on other means and agents, such as the USA, to interfere in, and control, its former colonies around the world.

Contemporary British colonial influences are aided by the USA, whose actions, highlighted by President George W. Bush's irrational and unprovoked war against Iraq (with Prime Minister Tony Blair's Britain), justify labeling the US the late 20th and early 21st Centuries' colonizer (see Okafọ, 2003). Nowhere is the colonialist intent and mentality of Britain and the USA more displayed than in contemporary Iraq. A colonizer, such as the USA has shown in Iraq, expects the colonized to surrender to the colonizer and not resist in any meaningful way. This colonial expectation is rooted in the colonizer's narcissistic belief in the inherent superiority of the colonizer over the colonized. In the post-2003 US invasion of Iraq, Iraqis have resisted the illegal US occupation. This demonstrates that the colonizer does not always get to impose itself on a docile colonized population, especially in the 21st Century. However, the extreme destruction and damage that Blair and Bush have done to Iraq will live on even if the US formally ends its occupation of Iraq.

A little historical examination is necessary here to provide the background to the post-Hussein, US-supervised Iraqi constitution. Shortly after invading Iraq, the USA's "coalition of the willing" (including Britain) degenerated to fighting a sectarian war mainly between Islamic Shiites and Sunnis. Under President Saddam Hussein, Iraq was an oppressed but stable country in which the average citizen went about his/her business with reasonable security for life and property. After the September 11, 2001 attacks on the USA's "World Trade Center," "Pentagon," and the Pennsylvania state field, and perhaps before the attacks, President Bush and his supporters decided to violently remove President Hussein from office. President Bush, with the assistance of Prime Minister Tony Blair and some other leaders went to war against Iraq and aggressively overthrew President Hussein despite the United Nation's opposition to such a grossly irresponsible display of gangster diplomacy. In the USA's post-Hussein Iraq, the Hobbesian "nasty, poor, brutish, and short" accurately describes life.

None of President Bush's reasons for invading Iraq convinced a reasonable observer of politics and world events, including this writer. Long before the unprovoked invasion became widely unpopular, I described the US war against Iraq, tagged "operation enduring freedom," as a manifestation of 21st Century colonization (see Okafọ, 2003). Since 2003, many, if not most, of the war's previous supporters, including some of its chief architects, have opposed it or significantly diluted their initial support. Okafọ (2003) counseled that the war was immoral and illegal and was an unnecessary and unjustified destabilization, degradation, destruction, and supplanting of Iraq's systems (including its indigenous and long-practiced systems of justice and law). The subsequent Iraqi insurgency against the USA in the post-Hussein Iraq is, at least in part, a resistance against the US's attempt to colonize and dominate 21st Century Iraq.

The US supervisory role in the fashioning of the post-Hussein Iraqi constitution highlights the ongoing colonial relationship between the USA and Iraq. In 2005, a

US-inspired and backed constitution was enacted for Iraq. A fundamental question for the purposes of this book is: To what extent, if at all, does the USA-inspired *Constitution of Iraq, 2005*, protect and/or promote Iraq's traditions, customs, and native laws, and the indigenous system/s for their administration *vis-à-vis* the Western systems?

Critique of the Colonial and Postcolonial Interactions Between Indigenous and Foreign Controls

For a long time, Iraqi law and justice have been based on Islamic, civil, and other principles. The 2005 Constitution retains this foundation. Article 2 states:

> 1st – Islam is the official religion of the state and is *a basic source*[2] of legislation:
> (a) No law can be passed that contradicts the undisputed rules of Islam.
> (b) No law can be passed that contradicts the principles of democracy.
> (c) No law can be passed that contradicts the rights and basic freedoms outlined in this constitution.
> 2nd – This constitution guarantees the Islamic identity of the majority of the Iraqi people and full religious rights for all individuals and freedom of creed and religious practices.

The italicized phrase in the Article 2 means that the foundational importance of Islam notwithstanding, it is only one of the sources of Iraq's laws under the 2005 Constitution. The other sources under Article 2 are democratic principles and the constitutionally guaranteed rights and freedoms. However, Islamic beliefs operate as a major check on Iraq's laws, including those designed to advance democracy, rights and freedoms, and the freedom of creed and religious practices of non-Muslims. Similarly, traditions, customs, and native laws function subject to Islam.

Besides "legislation" (Article 2), the 2005 Constitution recognizes the country's customary law as a source of social control. However, while providing for customary law, the constitution effectively subjects this form of law to the Islamic and foreign-styled systems. Article 43 provides, *inter alia*: "2nd – The state is keen to advance Iraqi tribes and clans and it cares about their affairs in accordance with religion, law and honorable human values and in a way that contributes to developing society and it forbids tribal customs that run contrary to human rights." Thus, the constitution expressly recognizes Iraq's indigenous religions, laws, and human values and their contributions to the development of the Iraqi society (see also Article 4 of the constitution establishing Arabic and Kurdish as the two official languages for Iraq plus the right of Iraqis to educate children in their mother tongues). An important limitation on the indigenous contributions to

---

2 Italics added by this author for emphasis.

law, justice, and social control is that the traditions must not offend human rights. Considering that strong citizen loyalties to indigenous institutions and systems, Islam, as well as the new constitution are likely, it is an open question as to how contradictions among an Iraqi customary law principle, Islamic law principle, and a constitutional provision would be resolved in the country.

Chapter Two of the 2005 Constitution on "Rights and Freedoms" details the human rights of Iraqis. The rights are civil and political, economic, social and cultural rights, together with identified freedoms. The Chapter defines Iraqi citizenship and guarantees citizenship rights pursuant to the status. Other constitutional rights and freedoms for Iraqis concern trial and punishment, personal liberty, ownership, health care, education, observance of family, religion, assembly, and movement. An Iraqi customary law principle or system that contravenes any of the constitutionally guaranteed rights would be unenforceable. Therefore, the 2005 Constitution, which is Iraq's supreme law, restricts the jurisdiction of the country's indigenous systems minus the Islam-based systems. An indigenous principle that contradicts the constitution or Islam will be adjudged repugnant and unenforceable. For the Islam-based systems, the constitution both expands and contracts their scope.

Various provisions of Article 2 (quoted above) appear to contradict one another. In particular, it appears that Article 2 (a), which forbids the passage of a law that conflicts with the undisputed rules of Islam, and Article 2 (b) and (c), which respectively forbid the passage of a law that contradicts the principles of democracy, and the rights and freedoms outlined in the constitution, will produce contradiction. In view of Article 2's broad statement that "Islam is the official religion of the State and is a basic source of legislation," what will happen when, for an example, an Iraqi citizen's "freedom of thought and conscience" (Article 41) challenges Islam's apparent disapproval of conversion from the religion or criticism of the religion and/or its leaders?

In the final analysis, the 2005 Constitution of Iraq limits the role of the country's indigenous justice and law systems, but the constitution allows Islam-based systems a dominant role in the country.

Saudi Arabia

History, Constitutionalism, Law, and Government

The population of Saudi Arabia is estimated at over twenty-eight million residents, including the more than five and a half million non-nationals residing in the country (see "Saudi Arabia" USA CIA Estimate, 2009). Contemporary Saudi Arabia effectively began in 1902, when ABD AL-AZIZ bin Abd al-Rahman Al Saud captured Riyadh and launched a military campaign leading to the 1932 unification of the Kingdom of Saudi Arabia. Al Saud's military exploits established his bloodline as the ruler of Saudi Arabia to date. The head of the Saudi State and government, as well as virtually every key official of the country, is a descendant of Al Saud, specifically male descendants. The country's immense crude oil wealth has greatly helped the ruling family to maintain a privileged lifestyle without a need to overburden the citizens with the taxes that would otherwise be required to pay for the lifestyle. It is noteworthy that the Saudi oil wealth has brought it closer to the USA and other Western countries that need its oil. The close economic relationships and cooperation among Saudi Arabia and the Western countries have not permeated the social and cultural realms. Thus, Saudi Arabia remains a monarchical dictatorship with very limited freedoms for its citizens. Nonetheless, the USA, Britain, and other Western powers continue to support the pervasive Saudi political and legal systems and the Saudi rulers because of the Saudi control of important oil resources.

Saudi Arabia is a male-dominated monarchy made up of thirteen provinces. The king is the head of State and head of government. Islam dominates its government, law and justice, and other public as well as private affairs. *Shari'ah* governs the kingdom. In addition, in 1993 a law was introduced to enunciate the government's rights and responsibilities. Also, several other secular codes operate in the country and special committees manage commercial disputes. However, the courts will not apply a secular code that contradicts an Islamic principle. "The courts will apply the rules of the Islamic *Shari'ah* in the cases that are brought before them, in accordance with what is indicated in the Book and the Sunnah, *and statutes decreed by the Ruler which do not contradict the Book or the Sunnah*"[3] (Article 48 of the *Saudi Arabia Constitution of 1992*). *Shari'ah* dominates every law source in Saudi Arabia. And, with its pre-eminence as home to Mecca and Medina – two of the most important places in Islam – Saudi Arabia is widely regarded as the home, or at least chief host, of all Muslims. The Saudi *shari'ah* system of criminal law is one of the strictest in the world because it allows minimal, if any, deviation from the positive statements of the *shari'ah* code. Thus, the Saudi *shari'ah* in a sense is the standard for aspiring extremist *shari'ah* societies in the world, such as Nigeria's Zamfara state and about eleven other northern states of Nigeria.

Critique of the Colonial and Postcolonial Interactions Between Indigenous and Foreign Controls

With 83 short Articles, the *Saudi Arabia Constitution of 1992* is a rather brief statement of the rights and responsibilities of the Saudi government and the citizens. The reason that the constitution is so short is because it is actually a statement of acknowledgement of other constituents of the country's constitution. Article 1 of the 1992 Constitution states: "The Kingdom of Saudi Arabia is a sovereign Arab Islamic state with Islam as its religion; God's Book and the Sunnah of His Prophet, God's prayers and peace be upon him, *are its constitution*,[4] Arabic

---

3   Italics added by this author for emphasis.
4   Italics added by this author for emphasis.

is its language and Riyadh is its capital." Thus, more accurately, the *Saudi Arabia Constitution of 1992* directs the reader to where to find the Saudi constitution. The key principles of Islam, as expressed in the important books of the religion, *are* the Saudi constitution. It is clear then that Saudi Arabia is a religious State. The *shari'ah* dominates the society. The citizens' rights and duties are subject to the *shari'ah*. "The state protects human rights in accordance with the Islamic Shari'ah" (Article 26 of the *Saudi Arabia Constitution of 1992*). Thus, human rights under the Saudi constitution are subject to the principles of Islam. What is the implication of this religious atmosphere for law and justice and, especially, for indigenous justice systems in the country?

The *Saudi Arabia Constitution of 1992* makes only a brief reference to traditions, customs, and native laws (customary law) in Article 41, thus: "Residents of the Kingdom of Saudi Arabia shall abide by its laws and shall observe the values of Saudi society and respect its traditions and feelings." Although this Article mentions "traditions," which should include indigenous traditions, those traditions can only apply to the extent that they do not contradict Islamic principles (see Article 38). Similar to the situation in Afghanistan and Iraq, the Saudi constitution effectively cements Islamic beliefs and principles as the standards for judging the validity of all other Saudi laws, including customary law. Customary laws that contradict Islam are repugnant and thus invalid. As in Iraq, the Saudi constitution accords great advantage to Saudi Arabia's Islam-based justice system over the country's indigenous systems.

Chapter Summary

Considering the different historical and contemporary experiences of Afghanistan, India, Iraq, and Saudi Arabia, surveys of the countries were expected to show that each country addressed the issues concerning the relationship between its indigenous and colonially imposed law and justice systems differently. Afghanistan, Iraq, and Saudi Arabia have constitutional provisions stating that each country is an Islamic state. Similarly, each country declares that no law in the country can contravene an Islamic principle. For each of the three countries, then, Islam is the *grundnorm* (fundamental law), by which all other laws are judged. "All other laws" includes the customary law of each country. Thus, a customary law provision or a mode of its administration in Afghanistan, Iraq, or Saudi Arabia that offends Islam is void and unenforceable.

For Afghanistan and Iraq, in particular, the constitutional declaration of Islam as the *grundnorm* appears to betray Western expectation and standard considering the key role that the USA has played in fashioning the Afghan and Iraqi respective constitutions, after the USA violently overthrew the *Taliban* (Afghanistan) and Saddam Hussein (Iraq). The forceful changes of the regimes facilitated the creations of the countries' constitutions. However, unlike the Indian, Iraqi, and Saudi constitutions, the Afghan constitution expressly recognizes the importance of the country's indigenous institutions and thus requires the state to provide "the opportunity to teach native languages in the areas where they are spoken" [Article 43 (3)]. The importance of indigenous language to customary law use and administration cannot be overstated. A native language is probably the best medium for expressing and administering indigenous justice and law.

For India, its otherwise secular constitution voids all Indian laws that contravene the constitution. Consequently, the country's customary laws that violate the later Indian constitution establishing the English-inspired parliamentary democracy have no effect, at least officially. To illustrate this official subjection of the Indian customary law to the Western-style system, the Indian constitution specifically prohibits discrimination on grounds of religion, race, caste, untouchability, sex or place of birth. This provision affronts a long standing and widely practiced Indian custom – the caste system. The point of referencing this constitutional prohibition is not that the customary Indian caste system, for example, should be continued. Rather, the constitutional prohibition is referenced to draw attention to the fact that India's postcolonial British-style constitution has been elevated to a superior position above India's immemorial traditions, customs, and native laws.

In sum, whereas the constitutions of Afghanistan, Iraq, and Saudi Arabia accord primary importance to Islamic principles and laws over their indigenous counterparts, the constitution of India ascribes dominance to India's British-style parliamentary system and law over India's indigenous law and justice.

References

"Afghanistan" (2009) *The World Factbook*, Central Intelligence Agency, USA (Online). See https://www.cia.gov/library/publications/the-world-factbook/geos/af.html; Internet; accessed March 2009.

Austin, W. T. (2009) "Teaching Perspectives for the Comparative Study of Justice." Presented in the session on *Comparative Justice: Teaching Variations*, at the Academy of Criminal Justice Sciences Conference, Boston, Massachusetts, USA, March 10-14, 2009.

Benton, L. (2002) *Law and Colonial Cultures: Legal Regimes in World History, 1400-1900*. Cambridge, UK: Cambridge University Press.

Constitution of India, 1950 (adopted on January 26, 1950).

Constitution of the Islamic Republic of Afghanistan, 2004 (in force since January 4, 2004).

Dupree, L. (1980) *Afghanistan*. Princeton, New Jersey, USA: Princeton University Press.

Glatzer, B. (1998) "Is Afghanistan on the Brink of Ethnic and Tribal Disintegration?" in W. Maley, ed. *Fundamentalism Reborn? Afghanistan and the Taliban*. New York, USA: St. Martins.

"India" (2009) *The World Factbook*, Central Intelligence Agency, USA (Online). See https://www.cia.gov/library/publications/the-world-factbook/geos/in.html; Internet; accessed March 2009.

"Iraq" (2008) *The World Factbook*, Central Intelligence Agency, USA (Online). See https://www.cia.gov/library/publications/the-world-factbook/geos/iz.html; Internet; accessed April 2008.

Iraqi Constitution of 2005 (Online; Retrieved on September 9, 2006).

"Iraq's History Page" (Online, Retrieved March 3, 2009). See http://www.angelfire.com/nt/Gilgamesh/history.html; Internet.

Okafọ, N. (2003) "Developed Atavism: 21st Century Colonial U.S.A." in *NigeriaWorld* (June 18). See http://nigeriaworld.com/articles/2003/jun/121.html; Internet.

Okereafọezeke [a.k.a. Okafọ], N. (1996) *The Relationship Between Informal and Formal Strategies of Social Control: An Analysis of the Contemporary Methods of Dispute Processing Among the Igbos of Nigeria* (1996). UMI Number 9638581. Ann Arbor, MI: University Microfilms, Inc.

Okereafọezeke [a.k.a. Okafọ] N. (2002) "Yoruba Hometowns: Community, Identity, and Development in Nigeria" (Book Review) in *Africa Today*, Volume 49, Number 1, Spring, pp. 115-118.

"Saudi Arabia" (2009) *The World Factbook*, Central Intelligence Agency, USA; see https://www.cia.gov/library/publications/the-world-factbook/geos/sa.html; Internet; accessed March 2009.

Saudi Arabia Constitution of 1992 (Online; Retrieved on December 12, 2006).

Wardak, A. (2003) "The Tribal and Ethnic Composition of Afghan Society", in E. Girardet and J. Walter, eds. *Afghanistan: Essential Field Guides to Humanitarian and Conflict Zones*, Second Edition. Geneva: Crosslines.

Wardak, A. (2004) "Building a Post-War Justice System in Afghanistan" in *Crime, Law & Social Change*, 41: 319-341. See also http://www.usip.org/ruleoflaw/projects/wardak_article.pdf; Internet.

Chapter 3

Indigenous Versus Foreign Controls in Selected Countries: Brazil, Kenya, Nigeria, South Africa

Chapter 3 continues Part 2's analysis of the forms of relationships between indigenous law and justice and colonially or occupationally introduced law and justice in selected countries. This Chapter examines the situations in Brazil, Kenya, Nigeria, and South Africa. As in all three chapters of Part 2 (Chapters 2, 3, and 4), each country is discussed separately under these two subheadings: "History, Constitutionalism, Law, and Government" and "Critique of the Colonial and Postcolonial Interactions Between Indigenous and Foreign Controls."

Brazil

History, Constitutionalism, Law, and Government

Contemporary Brazil is a Portuguese postcolony. Brazil became independent of Portugal in 1822 and became a republic in 1889. Before Brazil could take meaningful steps to adjust to, and recover from, the consequences of Portuguese hegemony, postcolonial Brazilian armed forces took over the country's leadership and held it with force for more than a half century. Eventually, in 1985, the armed forces handed over the country's leadership to civilians. This facilitated the development of the *Constitution of Brazil, 1988* (Brazilian Constitution). Under the constitution, Brazil is a federal republic made up of twenty-six states and a federal district. The president heads the Brazilian State as well as its government. Portuguese is the country's official language, but the over one hundred and ninety-six million citizens speak such other languages as Spanish, English, French, and the indigenous languages. The primacy of the Portuguese language shows that, like other ex-colonizers, Brazil's erstwhile colonizer (Portugal) maintains enormous influence over its former colonial territory.

Overall, Brazil has made significant economic gains. However, the country is faced with the problem of limited access to economic advantages for its citizens. Economic prosperity and income distribution are unequal in Brazil, even in the face of the country's general economic progress. Race remains a major determinant of the availability of, and access to, success opportunities and achievement of wealth. By the official racial figures, "Whites" in Brazil have the numerical advantage. The

2000 census reported the makeup as 53.7% White, 38.5% Mulatto (mixed Black and White), 6.2% Black, 0.9% Other (including Ameridian, Arab, and Japanese), and 0.7% Unspecified (see "Brazil" USA CIA Estimate, 2009). The numerical advantage of "Whites" seems to have favored them economically at the expense of the country's other constituent groups.

But, beyond economics, what is Brazil's official position on the systems of indigenous law, justice, and social control in relationship with the colonially imposed law and justice system? The *Constitution of Brazil, 1988* is instructive for responding to these issues.

Critique of the Colonial and Postcolonial Interactions Between Indigenous and Foreign Controls

Unlike the spiritual constitution of Saudi Arabia, for instance, the secular Brazilian Constitution forbids the State and all parts thereof from establishing, maintaining, or favoring any religion as a State religion, or otherwise interfering with any religion (Article 19). Further, the constitution acknowledges the Brazilian people as the source of all State powers expressed in the document (Article 1). Thus, the provisions of the constitution are superior to all other laws. On the specific question of the relationship between Brazilian customary law and the country's Western-style law, the constitution expressly recognizes the indigenous law and system. Article 231 on "Native Populations and Lands" provides:

> (0) Indians shall have their social organization, customs, languages, creeds, and traditions recognized, as well as their native rights to the lands they traditionally occupy, it being incumbent on the Republic to demarcate them and protect and ensure respect for all their property.

Thus, Article 231 of the *Constitution of Brazil 1988* affirms the traditions, customs, languages, and other expressions of the cultures of the indigenous populations. The Article also recognizes and protects the tradition-based rights of indigenous Brazilians to property. The indigenous traditions and customs of Brazilians should include their native law and justice systems and processes, among other things. Thus, Article 231 of the Brazilian Constitution acknowledges that the Native Brazilians' customary laws and systems have the force of law.

Furthermore, the Article 231 of the constitution preserves the rights of Brazil's Native population to pursue their creeds and to use their indigenous languages in teaching and learning. However, despite constitutional preservation of the Native rights to manage their social organization, customs, traditions, religions, and languages (Article 231), the modality for the distribution of State resources between the indigenous system and the Western-style, postcolonial Brazilian system is another issue. A resources distribution formula favoring the Western-style system over the indigenous system will demonstrate an inferior position and role for the indigenous system. Article 97 of the constitution provides evidence of inequality between Brazil's indigenous justice system, on the one hand, and the Western-style system, on the other hand. By Article 97, a customary law provision that contravenes an aspect of the *Constitution of Brazil, 1988* is null and void. Article 97 empowers the Brazilian courts to "declare the unconstitutionality of a law or of a normative act of the Government."

Ultimately, as expressed in the Brazilian Constitution, Brazil's indigenous law and justice as well as the systems for their administration are subject to the imposed European systems and standards.

Kenya

History, Constitutionalism, Law, and Government

The population of Kenya is about thirty-eight million (see "Kenya" USA CIA Estimate, 2009). A multi-ethnic people colonized by Britain, Kenyans fought vigorously for their independence. Jomo Kenyatta stood out in his countrymen's independence struggles. From independence on December 12, 1963, Jomo Kenyatta led Kenya until his death in 1978, at which time Daniel arap Moi succeeded Kenyatta. It needs to be pointed out here that in spite of his significant leadership in Kenyans' independence war against Britain, Kenyatta probably stayed in office for too long (fifteen years) as the country's leader, after helping Kenya win independence from Britain. I have little doubt that Kenyatta's rather long occupation of the country's leadership post set a wrong precedent and encouraged Moi, Kenyatta's successor, to lengthen his stay in office as he did (Moi eventually occupied the country's leadership post for twenty-four years). From 1969 to 1982, the ruling Kenya African National Union (KANU) party, led by Kenyatta and later Moi, ruled the country as a *de facto* one-party State.

Kenya's ethnic groups include Kikuyu, Luhya, Luo, Kalenjin, Kamba, Kisii, and Me, as well as such other non-Africans as Arabs, Asians, and Europeans. Despite the country's multi-ethnic characteristics, varying political leanings, and other differences, the ruling KANU party in 1982 declared itself the only lawful political party in Kenya. Nonetheless, opposition groups that were forced to operate underground continued their actions against the Moi regime. Eventually, in 1991, pressures from within and outside Kenya caused the regime to liberalize the country's politics allowing lawful opposition parties. Moi's KANU party remained in charge of the country until 2002 when a coalition of multi-ethnic parties (the National Rainbow Coalition) led by Mwai Kibaki defeated the KANU party in that year's election. President Kibaki, who had campaigned on an anti-corruption platform, sought to create a new constitution for Kenya. A draft constitution was offered to the electorate in a 2005 referendum. The draft was defeated. Thus, the earlier constitution, which has been amended at various times, remains the basic law for Kenya.

Kenya, like most contemporary African countries, has had substantial colonial experiences. A British colony until December 1963, Kenya continues to struggle with the enormous disequilibrium that the British culture and life have wrought on the Kenyan society and ways of living. Kenya strives to build a credible State based on the dual elements of indigenous Kenyan systems and foreign European systems, among others. Contemporary Kenyan law and justice system is based on Kenyan statutes, English common law as adopted and applied to Kenya, Kenyan traditions, customs, and native law, and Islamic law. Of all the sources of law and justice in Kenya, the *Constitution of the Republic of Kenya*, with all the amendments to it, is the supreme law of the country.

Critique of the Colonial and Postcolonial Interactions Between Indigenous and Foreign Controls

By its Article 3, the *Constitution of the Republic of Kenya* (Kenyan Constitution) is the supreme law of the country. Any inconsistent law, including customary law, is, to the extent of the inconsistency, void. At least on the issue of real property rights, the Kenyan Constitution expressly recognizes the important role of the country's indigenous law in the lives of Kenyans. The constitution acknowledges that individual and group rights, interests, and other benefits existed before the advent of the constitution in 1963. Thus, the constitution in Article 115 vests the rights, interests, and other benefits over each piece of community land in the county council with jurisdiction over the land. The council is to give effect to the rights, interests, etc. if they are consistent with written law. Article 115 (2) provides:

> Each county council shall hold the Trust land vested in it for the benefit of the persons ordinarily resident on that land and shall give effect to such rights, interests or other benefits in respect of the land as may, under the African customary law for the time being in force and applicable thereto, be vested in any tribe, group, family or individual: Provided that no right, interest or other benefit under African customary law shall have effect for the purposes of this subsection so far as it is repugnant to any written law.

Therefore, even on the specific issue of land rights, the constitution restricts the Kenyan customary law by imposing the repugnancy test[1] for the application and enforcement of customary law (see also Article 117).

Unlike Kenya's customary civil law, it is not clear that the Kenyan Constitution recognizes customary criminal law. The constitution establishes some Western-style courts, such as the High Court and the Court of Appeal. The constitution does not establish a Customary Court. However, it authorizes the country's legislature to create such other courts as it finds necessary. In any case, any Kenyan court

---

1 The "repugnancy test" features prominently in Nigeria and is discussed in greater detail in the section of this Chapter on Nigeria.

applying customary law (civil or criminal) to a case before it has to comply with the constitutionally mandated Chapter V on "Protection of Fundamental Rights and Freedoms of the Individual," which, among other guarantees, provides for the protection of the right to life (Article 71), protection of the right to personal liberty (Article 72), protection from slavery and forced labor (Article 73), protection from inhuman treatment (Article 74), and protection from discrimination on grounds of race, etc. (Article 82). Thus, a customary law principle or practice that violates any of the guaranteed constitutional rights will be voided.

In view of the prominence afforded Western-type law and justice by the Kenyan Constitution, there is little doubt that the country's resources for justice administration are concentrated in the effort to promote the Western-style courts as created by the constitution and other laws. This means that Kenya's indigenous law and justice are relegated to the background relative to the Western-based law and justice. However, on the issue of official language for the country, it is encouraging that Kiswahili (one of Kenya's indigenous languages) is an official language of the country. The Kenyan Constitution's accord of "official" status to the country's indigenous language, even if it shares the status with the foreign English language, is a welcome deviation from the negative trend in postcolonial African States. In the Nigerian example, although most Nigerians neither speak nor write English well, it is Nigeria's "official" language in line with the British colonial legacy in Nigeria. In Kenya, Kiswahili's official status will likely encourage Kenyans to communicate in that and their other native languages. Communications in the indigenous languages will likely help Kenyans to advance other aspects of their indigenous lives and development, including their traditions, customs, and native laws.

Nigeria

History, Constitutionalism, Law, and Government

Nigeria's evolution on the issues of constitutionalism, law, and government is long, odious, and continuing. For a clearer appreciation of this evolutionary process, three main phases of Nigeria are identifiable, as follows: the pre-colonial, colonial, and postcolonial Nigeria. "Pre-colonial Nigeria" refers to the cultural, economic, political, religious, and other life contexts of the peoples, nations, ethnic groups, and other groups that inhabited the land area now called Nigeria prior to British occupation. In the mid-19th through the mid-20th Centuries, Britain colonized Nigeria. Prior to the British colonization of Nigeria, the Nigerian peoples, through their various kindred, ethnic, and national arrangements, formed and maintained informal and formal leaderships by means of governments, constitutions, traditions, customs, and other laws.

Pre-colonial Nigerians established and nurtured leaderships, in various forms, at the family, extended family, village, community (town), and regional (group of towns) levels. Typically, the leaderships of the family, extended family, village, community, and region in pre-colonial Nigeria rested mainly with male members. Because patriarchy has historically dominated among the Nigerian peoples, the leader of a family, extended family, village, community, or region has typically been male or a group of males. Note, however, that female leaders are found at all levels of pre-colonial, colonial, and postcolonial Nigeria. Nonetheless, whether the leader of a group is male or female, individual and subgroup members of the group have clearly identified and assigned roles in the overall social control scheme. Thus, as examples, respective categories of elderly, middle aged, young, and female members of an Igbo group may be assigned specific functions in their community. Similarly, based on an age grade system, young males, elderly males, and titleholders, respectively, would be assigned explicit duties to perform for the society. The leader of each of the family, extended family, village, community, and region is chosen and retains his or her office based mainly on integrity of character and positive results achieved in office. This means that pre-colonial Nigerians tended to hold their leaders accountable to the leaders' constituencies.

Constitutionalism in a pre-colonial Nigerian nation (ethnic group) means adherence to the fundamental traditions, customs, and laws of the nation. These traditions, customs, and laws are important to the existence and sustenance of each nation. They bind the nation's members together. Most members of each nation view the fundamental traditions, customs, and laws as instrumental to the continuation of their nation. In most pre-colonial, as well as postcolonial, Nigerian nations, the fundamental norms are unwritten. Rather, they form parts of generally understood and accepted customary laws. Examples of these fundamental traditions, customs, and laws are the customary laws regulating the qualifications for, and assumption and relinquishing of, traditional leadership positions. Other examples are the customary laws on religious ceremonies and the duties of religious leaders. Also, some crimes are regarded as fundamentally relevant to a traditional nation because the crimes can compromise the nation's future. The Igbos call such crimes *aru* or *alu* (crimes that are so serious that they pollute the entire society and threaten the existence and progress of the society). *Aru* crimes include *ochu* (homicide), incest, and desecration of religious institutions or symbols. Considering their importance to the Igbo society, these morality-based crimes (Okereafoezeke, 2002; 2003) should be regarded as parts of the constitutional foundation of the Igbo nation (see Elechi, 2006).

Pre-colonial Nigerian nations and societies also recognized and articulated ordinary, non-fundamental crimes, civil violations, and other issues. Note that in traditional society, the word "civil," for instance, does not necessarily carry the same meaning as it does in English law. Also, a traditional society may not clearly separate a "civil" from a "criminal" matter. However, in recognition of the ordinary, non-fundamental crimes, etc., the various nations and societies established and have maintained, in various forms over time, the processes for managing the crimes and issues. "Ordinary, non-fundamental crimes, civil violations, and other issues" are common, routinely encountered, and managed disputes in each society. Generally, they are administered by means of unwritten criminal and civil laws designed to address less serious violations (they are not *arų* or *alų* crimes). Typically, these unwritten laws have been passed down from previous generations.

However, in a variety of modern traditional Nigerian societies, some of these laws are enacted and they change from time to time in society (see as example, Okereafọezeke, 2002). The laws on ordinary crimes and other violations and issues deal with everyday concerns and disputes, including those that the English common law defines as "civil" and most "criminal" matters. Civil law matters include breach of contract, tort, and civil trespass. Non-fundamental criminal laws include the laws against stealing, destruction of property, fraud, and assault. In a Nigerian nation, such as the Igbo, although the concerns and disputes may be important to the parties involved, it is unlikely that the majority of the citizens generally will regard the issues as directly affecting the society's future. And because such a concern or dispute is perceived as having limited impact on the general society, ordinary crimes and other laws of a Nigerian society are distinguishable from the society's fundamental laws.

Against the long-established Nigerian traditional society background, the British colonization of Nigeria injected the British law and justice system into the Nigerian societies. After decades of the British colonization and usurpation of many aspects of the Nigerian personality, Nigeria gained political independence on October 1, 1960. Since then, Nigerians have run the country. However, decades after political independence, there remain numerous key manifestations of the British-imposed colonial systems of control in Nigeria (Saleh-Hanna, 2008). More broadly, one of the enduring features of the British colonization of Nigeria, even long after the British colonial rule ended, is the creation of the modern State and its supplanting of the pre-colonial Nigerian nations. The *Constitution of the Federal Republic of Nigeria, 1999* (Nigerian Constitution 1999), for example, proclaims that the country is a federation of thirty-six states and a federal capital territory. Because of the powers arrogated to it by Nigeria's colonizers and sustained by the successive post-independence Nigerian military as well as civilian governments, the modern State institutions of the country have enormous powers and influences, above the powers and influences of the pre-colonial Nigerian nations. The result is that in postcolonial Nigeria, the modern State structure and its units are highly visible in every aspect of justice, social control, and law, in civil as well as criminal grievances, conflicts, and disputes.

The following subsection will analyze in some detail the relative positions of the Nigerian customary laws and their English counterparts in the postcolonial State structure.

Critique of the Colonial and Postcolonial Interactions Between Indigenous and Foreign Controls

An important question examined in this subsection is as follows. Considering the official, modern State structure, constitution, and laws of Nigeria, what are the relative positions of the country's indigenous law and justice systems *vis-à-vis* the foreign English law and justice system? Asked another way, how, if at all, do Nigeria's postcolonial constitution and laws provide for or support the country's customary laws in view of the English system imported into Nigeria by colonial Britain? In view of Nigeria's post-independence constitutionalism, legal development, and history, the differences between the laws of a civilian government and those of a military administration ought to be noted. The several military regimes, which usurped State powers in the country in violation of existing laws, significantly stalled post-independence Nigerian constitutional and legal development. Each military regime took steps to preserve and legitimize itself by enacting Decrees and Edicts mainly with the aim of removing or dampening official and unofficial oppositions. Considering the inherent nature of military regimes and the character of law making in those governments, the military's law making idiosyncrasies should not surprise anyone.

In the military-dominated circumstances, the role and influence of customary law received little or no positive consideration. Attention to the development of customary law was scant. A conflict between customary law and a Decree or Edict provision was certain to be resolved in favor of the Decree or Edict. This did a lot of damage to the ownership psyche of the average Nigerian who was thus denied participation in formulating, applying, or enforcing the laws that governed the country. On law making, for instance, Onagoruwa (2009) points out that the process in a military government is essentially self-serving. He states (at pp. 1, 2, 3):

> Principally, law making under the military was designed to subjugate the populace ... Thus, whilst in a civilian regime the people are mostly the beneficiaries of laws enacted, the military is the primary beneficiary of decrees ... The procedure under the military is quite ignoble, bearing in mind that the fine-tuning and quality processing which involves public opinion, vigorous debate, and cross fertilization that constitute a democratic law making process are non-existent in the military regime. Principally, their laws are designed to subjugate.

Although Onagoruwa's (2009) characterization is mainly accurate, it would be wrong to say that all laws made by military regimes are convenient for the regime or useless for the general citizenry, just as it would be inaccurate to claim that civilian government laws are all altruistic or utilitarian (greatest good for the greatest number of citizens). Many military-enacted laws are desirable and serve useful purposes, while a lot of civilian-enacted laws violate the best interests of the majority of the citizens, particularly where an illegitimate or undemocratic civilian regime takes over power. Beyond the process for its enactment, the quality of a law depends mainly on the character of the law maker. An honest, patriotic, intelligent, selfless, and forward-looking law maker, civilian or military, is likely to enact a good law. On the other hand, a law maker that lacks the identified character components will probably enact a bad law.

However, to explain Nigeria's post-military government position on the relationship between customary law and English law in Nigeria, the Nigerian Constitution 1999 should be examined. The 1999 constitution specifies the officially assigned role of Nigeria's customary laws in the country's social control. The constitution expressly recognizes the existence of customary law in two main ways.

One, the constitution creates or provides the basis for the creations of customary law-based trial and appellate courts. These courts are typically parts of the respective official judicial systems of Nigeria's 36 states and the federal capital territory. The customary law-based courts are established to hear and decide disputes over Nigeria's traditions, customs, and native laws applicable within the jurisdiction of each court. The customary court jurisdiction is largely civil (as opposed to criminal), except for few instances of criminal violations of local Ordinances and where particular conducts cause the court to invoke its inherent power to punish for contempt. Every state in the country has a Customary Court Law (or its equivalent) that establishes the state's trial court for matters involving disputes over an aspect of the state's customary law. Also, section 280 (1) of the Nigerian Constitution 1999 provides for the setting up of a Customary Court of Appeal in each state, thus: "There shall be for any State that requires it a Customary Court of Appeal for that State." The constitution gives the court "appellate and supervisory jurisdiction in civil proceedings involving questions of Customary law" [section 282 (1)]. As to be expected, the constitution goes on to declare that a person shall not be qualified to be appointed as a judge of a Customary Court of Appeal of a state unless, among other requirements [section 281 (3)],

> (a) he is a legal practitioner in Nigeria and he has been so qualified for a period of not less than ten years and in the opinion of the National Judicial Council he has considerable knowledge and experience in the practice of Customary law; or
>
> (b) in the opinion of the National Judicial Council he has considerable knowledge of and experience in the practice of Customary law.

Two, the second way in which the Nigerian Constitution 1999 expressly recognizes the existence of customary law is that the constitution assigns judicial roles to persons educated in customary law. Some of these customary law educated judges sit on appellate state and federal courts. Thus, where appropriate, the constitution requires the participation of customary law trained judges in hearing and determining customary law-based cases before an otherwise English-style court, such as the Court of Appeal. For an example, section 237 (2) (b) of the Nigerian Constitution 1999 creates the Court of Appeal and declares that the members of this court are a Court of Appeal President and no less than forty-nine justices of whom at least three "shall be learned in Customary law." Ostensibly, the customary law trained justices are intended to provide the court with opportunity to understand more thoroughly the customary issues to be decided in each case.

However, in light of section 237 (2) (b), it must be asked "Do the opinions of the customary law justices sitting on the Court of Appeal weigh heavier than those of the other justices when the court decides a customary law-based case?" The constitution does not address this. Although the following position is speculative, it seems reasonable: Non-customary law justices would defer to the customary law justices because of the latter's more in-depth understanding of the issues in such a case. After all, they have a form of expert knowledge of customary laws and issues. Ignoring their uncommon and critical knowledge could easily lead to miscarriage of justice. Also, ignoring the knowledge would make it difficult to justify the presence of customary law justices on the court.

So, how is a prospective customary law judge deemed to be learned or educated enough to judge cases involving the interpretation of Nigeria's customary law? The constitution answers this question in section 288 (2), thus:

> (2) For the purposes of subsection (1) of this section -
>
> (b) a person shall be deemed to be learned in Customary law if he is a legal practitioner in Nigeria and has been so qualified for a period of not less than fifteen years in the case of a Justice of the Supreme Court or not less than twelve years in the case of a Justice of the Court of Appeal and has in either case and in the opinion of the National Judicial Council considerable knowledge of and experience in the practice of Customary law.

Although this constitutional provision is made for the expressed purposes of subsection (1) of section 288, it should be alright to use it as a guide for determining who is "learned" or "educated" in the context of the other relevant provisions of the constitution.

However, despite its explicit recognition of Nigeria's customary law, the Nigerian Constitution 1999, as demonstrated in section 282 (1), limits the customary courts' subject matter jurisdiction to civil cases. Thus, the constitution reserves the country's criminal jurisdiction for the various state and federal English-style courts. This is a major curtailment of the customary courts' powers.

Nigeria's constitutionally created customary courts are official attempts to codify the powers of the country's pre-colonial tribunals for adjudicating grievances, conflicts, and disputes, for modern Nigeria. In their original (pre-colonial) forms, the pre-colonial courts, at different levels of societal organization, heard and determined virtually all civil and criminal issues. The pre-colonial tribunals also heard and decided a variety of issues that the English law and justice system may regard as non-justiceable.[2] Case processing in the contemporary traditional system

---

2 A non-justiceable issue is a matter on which legal remedy does not exist and which thus should not be litigated.

commonly involves maters unknown to English law and justice. Indeed, even the postcolonial official Customary Court hears and decides civil disputes that the official English-style courts are not prepared to manage (Okereafoezeke, 1996; 2002). However, the constitutional and other postcolonial legal limitations of the customary court jurisdiction to civil matters takes away a substantial portion of the jurisdiction previously held by the pre-colonial customary tribunal in Nigeria.

In addition to the postcolonial limitation of Nigeria's customary courts' jurisdiction to civil cases, there is an overarching officially-imposed test for the applicability of a customary law principle. This test is commonly expressed as the "repugnancy test" (Okereafoezeke, 1996; 2000; 2002). By means of *Proclamation No. 6 of 1900*, the British colonial regime in Nigeria instituted the repugnancy test to facilitate the dominance of the British traditions, customs, and native laws over their Nigerian counterparts. Regrettably, the various postcolonial Nigerian governments have continued the policy in various forms, even long after Nigeria's independence from Britain. The provisions of the *Proclamation No. 6 of 1900* deserve closer scrutiny.

By the *Proclamation No. 6*, for a customary law or tradition to be enforceable, it cannot be "repugnant to natural justice, equity, or good conscience, nor contrary to any official law." This test, in its various forms, subdues Nigeria's traditions, customs, and native laws to the official, English-style laws. Within this Proclamation (and its equivalents), a customary law principle will be denied application and enforcement if the principle is contrary to any official local, state, or federal law. Alternatively, a customary law principle, which does not contravene an official law, may nevertheless be denied application and enforcement if an official court determines that the customary law opposes natural justice, equity, or good conscience. The concepts of "natural justice," "equity," and "good conscience," being as fluid as they are, their interpretations are left to each official court to make. Each court is expected to interpret the concepts reasonably. However, because of their English heritage and biases, Nigeria's English-style courts and judges are also expected to, and often do, interpret "natural justice, equity, or good conscience" in line with the English, rather than Nigerian, standards. It seems clear that although Nigeria's colonial experiences are relevant to the interpretation of its statutes, the country's contemporary circumstances and aspirations are the more important considerations for reading and interpreting the concepts of natural justice, equity, and good conscience. Unfortunately, the antecedents of many Nigerian judges so far preclude them from adopting the proper judicial attitude to this offensive instrument of colonization.

Thus, as interpreted and applied, the repugnancy test empowers an official English-style court to deny enforcement to a customary law principle if the court concludes that the relevant principle offends natural justice, equity, or good conscience, even if the members of the relevant population have accepted and commonly followed the customary law principle. In fact, in *Okonkwo v. Okagbue and 2 Others* (1994), the Supreme Court of Nigeria (SCN) decided that the issue of repugnancy is a legal matter and that a court is entitled to raise the issue *suo motu* (on its own), and decide the issue, even if the parties do not raise it. According to the SCN,

> The question whether a custom is repugnant being a point of law can be raised by counsel in his address to court as was done by the plaintiff's counsel in the High Court. The court itself may raise the point *suo motu* since it is enjoined to take the law into consideration and apply it in determining whether a particular custom is applicable (at p. 101 of the Case Report).[3]

However, where the court raises the issue *suo motu*, it is expected to refer the issue to the parties for arguments before deciding on it (*Ezeanya and Others v. Okeke and Others*, 1995).

Ideally, the laws of a society should reflect the society's antecedents, experiences, ideals, and aspirations. The society's customs and traditions embody their antecedents, experiences, et al. Of course, the society's ideals and aspirations are expected to change with time and circumstances. Therefore, the laws of a society should reflect the society's antecedents, experiences, ideals, and aspirations, and the changes thereto. Changes to a society's laws should, above every other consideration, be based on the society's needs as the generality of the members interpret them. Such changes should occur only as and when the people, directly or through their true representatives, determine that changes are necessary. Then, the people would also determine the form of each change the society needs. Ideally, therefore, a people's laws should emanate from a broad spectrum of the people, rather than from a few. This is the distinction between customary law imposed from the top and customary law that develops from grassroots consultation and popular practices (see Snyder, 1982; Shaidi, 1992). Laws, which are imposed by a few, cannot become an acceptable means of social control; *a priori* where the imposition is by a foreign power, such as the British imposition of English law and system on Nigeria, which the repugnancy test and successive postcolonial Nigerian governments have reinforced.

Despite its negative effects on Nigeria's customary law, a potentially positive aspect of the repugnancy test is that it can allow for the monitoring of the operations of Nigeria's native laws and customs. Such monitoring should allow community members and other stakeholders to do away with those customary laws that have become out-of-step with societal evolution. Where appropriate, customary laws should be reformed and modified for contemporary use. These are noble ideals of a properly fashioned and implemented repugnancy test. However, the customary law monitoring allowed under the prevailing repugnancy test is available only to the official governments and their judicial personnel. Because of their origins as British citizens in the colonial era, or legal training in the English system in the postcolonial era, these officials tend to be biased in favor of the English-style law and justice system. Therefore, the present customary law monitoring system

---

3 Italics added by this author.

arms the official governments to police the indigenous law and justice systems and bring them under the official system, even where a given customary law or change to it is in accord with the aspirations of the citizens. This situation discourages and stultifies the evolution of Nigeria's indigenous justice systems without outside interference.

Curative policy and program steps to redress the repugnancy test anomaly should include Nigerian governments' official recognition of the country's customary law and indigenous institutions of justice and social control. Official encouragement and material assistance are important for the continuous revision and development of the customary law to change outdated principles and provisions of the law. Also, official legislative steps are necessary to enact appropriate laws at the Local, State, and Federal government levels to change the repugnancy test travesty, while providing for the positive monitoring of the operations of the country's traditions, customs, and native laws, as recommended in this book.

South Africa

History, Constitutionalism, Law, and Government

The history of modern South Africa can be traced to the British seizure of the Cape of Good Hope area in 1806. In response to this, many of the Dutch settlers (Boers) journeyed north of South Africa to establish their own republics. With the discoveries of diamonds and gold in the mid to late 19th Century, the immigrant Europeans stepped up their subjugation of the indigenous Africans. The Boars successfully defied British intruders until the Boar War of 1899-1902 when Britain defeated the Boars. The "Union of South Africa" resulted from these efforts. On May 31, 1910, the country received political independence from Britain. In 1961, South Africa replaced its "Union" with "Republic" following a 1960 referendum.

The Union of South Africa and later Republic of South Africa designed and operated a State apartheid system in which the State laws, programs, and officials were expressly required to implement the country's policy of the separate development of the South African races. An apartheid system, such as South Africa's until the 1990s, is designed not just to keep the races independent of one another but to subject all other races to a chosen race. An essential ingredient of apartheid is the belief that the chosen race is superior to all others and thus should be promoted and preferred over the inferior races. This belief was the driving philosophy behind the South African apartheid policy. In the apartheid era, the official policy championed the European systems and ways of life at the expense of all others, especially the African systems and ways of life. The apartheid system allowed the government to allocate the country's resources in such a way as to further its preferred European systems at the expense of their indigenous African counterparts. This apartheid thrived in South Africa until the early 1990s when multiparty representative democracy replaced the repressive apartheid regime.

The *Constitution of the Republic of South Africa, 1996*, which went into effect on February 3, 1997, governs contemporary South Africa. The country's official law and justice are based on some combination of the country's indigenous law and justice, Roman-Dutch law, and English common law.

Critique of the Colonial and Postcolonial Interactions Between Indigenous and Foreign Controls

Like most constitutions, the *Constitution of the Republic of South Africa, 1996* (CRSA) is supreme to all other laws. Where a law is inconsistent with the CRSA, the conflicting law is invalid and the constitution shall be fulfilled (sections 1 and 2 of the CRSA). It may be necessary to restate here the fact that the CRSA recognizes, protects, and promotes the country's indigenous (customary) law. Although section 166 of the constitution does not specifically create a customary court, that provision expressly empowers Parliament to establish "any court" by an Act of Parliament. The Parliament may therefore set up a customary court with a status equal to the constitutionally created High Court or Magistrates Court. Thus, based on its section 166, the CRSA anticipates and supports the role of the South African indigenous law and justice and the system for their administration.

Moreover, considering South Africa's apartheid history, the CRSA's Chapter 2 on Bill of Rights, with its wide array of rights guarantees and protections, is arguably the most important component of the constitution. Consistent with this view, the constitution in section 39 (2) requires every court, when interpreting legislation or developing the common law or customary law, to promote the spirit, purport, and objects of the Bill of Rights. This is an acknowledgement that the South African customary law is an important component of the country's justice system. In fact, section 39 (3) further evidences the expansive role and somewhat high regard with which the CRSA holds the country's customary law. Section 39 (3) provides: "The Bill of Rights does not deny the existence of any other rights or freedoms that are recognised or conferred by common law, *customary law*[4] or legislation, to the extent that they are consistent with the Bill." This should mean that even the South African official courts are expected to apply and enforce the country's customary law principles and provisions except where they are inconsistent with the Bill of Rights of the CRSA.

Section 6 (1-5) of the CRSA, on Languages, contains other key provisions demonstrating the importance of the South African traditions and customs in the country's affairs. In particular, section 6 (1) declares that the country's official languages are: Sepedi, Setswana, siSwati, Tshivenda, Xitsonga, Afrikaans, English, isiNdebele, isiXhosa, and isiZulu. Most of the enumerated official languages are indigenous African languages, which feature prominently in the conducts of South African affairs. Section 6 (2) goes on to enjoin the South African government to promote the indigenous languages, thus: "Recognising the historically diminished

---

4 Italics added by this author for emphasis.

use and status of the indigenous languages of our people, the state *must*[5] take practical and positive measures to elevate the status and advance the use of these languages." Therefore, the constitution requires the government to use, and allow for uses of, the indigenous languages in the conduct of government business. Also, the government must allocate necessary resources to strengthen and grow the indigenous languages.

South African indigenous law and justice system features prominently in the country's social control. Understandably, the indigenous languages are more likely to be used in the traditional justice process (Haffajee, 2005) because many, probably most, South Africans cannot or do not speak European languages either at all or fluently. Uses of the indigenous languages in the official justice system can and should be increased to eliminate or minimize the postcolonial tendency to operate an alien, largely irrelevant official system due to language differences. As the CRSA expressly recognizes, the indigenous languages are very important in the country's scheme of things. And so, increased allocation of resources to strengthen and grow the indigenous languages will likely lead to a stronger customary law system.

Despite the cited CRSA provisions in support of the country's customary law, to the extent that the constitution prefers a Bill of Rights provision over a customary law provision, the constitution promotes a form of the "repugnancy test," by which the customary law system is subjected to the European-style systems.

All the 12 countries surveyed in this book experienced colonization and/or occupation. Each country struggles with reconciling its indigenous law and justice system with the applicable foreign system. However, in the case of South Africa the official domination of the country's indigenous population through apartheid, which is a form of colonization, ended in the early 1990s. Consequently, I intend here to examine further some of the features of contemporary South African customary law *vis-à-vis* the imposed European and apartheid laws. Even though South Africa received political independence on May 31, 1910, the relatively few European immigrants in the country continued to dominate and subjugate the numerically overwhelming indigenous South Africans, through the apartheid policy, until the early 1990s when the European population was forced to abandon its obnoxious policy.

Under apartheid, South African customary law endured challenges comparable to those of other African countries under colonization. On independence from colonial Britain, the succeeding South African Afrikaner regimes received dual common law and customary law systems from Britain. Afrikaners enacted the *Native Administration Act* (later in 1986 this became the *Black Administration Act*) to keep indigenous Africans separate from the European settlers. By the Act, South African customary law was put up with to the extent that it was not repugnant to the European common law. Repugnant customary law was invalidated.

---

5   Italics added by this author for emphasis.

Since the official end of apartheid, South African officials and private individuals and groups have sought to re-establish and promote their traditions, customs, and native laws, which apartheid worked hard to obliterate. For instance,

> "under apartheid, traditional or customary law marriages were not legally recognized and only regarded as 'unions'. If a couple couldn't afford a common law marriage, the woman was considered a 'minor' who wasn't even allowed to open a credit account with a local grocer. Most rural women raise[d] their children alone as their husbands [were] migrant workers in mines and industrial centres." "The women couldn't buy anything. They had to wait for their husbands to return from the city in order to sell property," says Likhapa Mbatha of the Centre for Applied Legal Studies … Thus, the *Recognition of Customary Marriages Act* was passed [in 2004].

In addition to new State legislation, customary law in post-apartheid South Africa has taken on a new prominence due to the commendable examples of some of the country's greatest citizens.

As an example, when former President Nelson Mandela married Graca Machel in 2004, the couple kept their Western-style ceremony secret and simple. On the other hand, their customary marriage was celebrated like a State event. The occasion featured such indigenous customs as the couple dressing up traditionally and Mandela's elders negotiating the bride's price with the bride's kin, according to customary laws and traditions (Haffajee, 2005). Haffajee (2005) observes (Online):

> The event was significant for many reasons, yet above all, it moved traditional customs and laws from the fringes to the center of South African society. It signaled a shift in power for customary law which the apartheid state treated as common law's "poor cousin". A groundswell of innovation is underway to instill new authority, resources and dignity to customary law. Not only is the aim to correct historical injustice, but to rebuild trust in the criminal justice system and respect for the rule of law. The challenge lies in building a legal system which integrates common and customary law in line with the new constitution, enshrining such fundamental principles as gender equality. "The old, unequal relationship between common law as the big brother and customary law as the poor cousin is gone," says Professor Thandabantu Nhlapo of the South African Law Commission. "Both have to be judged in terms of the constitution."

President Mandela's example is commendable in the age in which many educated and/or privileged Africans unfortunately view their traditions, customs, and native laws (customary law) contemptuously. Such people thoughtlessly and inexplicably regard customary law as inferior and/or useless compared to European laws. South African customary law, in many ways like other African customary laws, continues its efforts to emerge from the shackles placed upon it by the defunct European colonizing powers.

Chapter Summary and Conclusion

Like most constitutions, the respective constitutions of Brazil, Kenya, Nigeria, and South Africa are superior to all other laws of each country. A law, such as customary law, inconsistent with any of these constitutions is invalid to the extent of the inconsistency and the constitution shall prevail. As expected, the specific constitutional provisions on customary law in each country vary. The Nigerian Constitution 1999, for example, expressly assigns jurisdictions and judicial roles to the country's Customary Courts (including Native Courts, Area Courts, and Customary Courts of Appeal) and the court officials. Thus, the Nigerian constitution acknowledges the important role of Nigerian traditions, customs, and native laws (customary law) in the country's social control. However, the Nigerian Customary, Area, and Native Courts are largely subject to the country's English-style courts, which dispense justice based mainly on the English common law, the so-called statutes of general application, and Nigerian local legislation. Certainly, Nigerian Customary, Area, and Native Courts cannot apply or enforce a customary law or tradition that contradicts the Nigerian constitution or a written law.

The South African constitution recognizes and champions the country's customary law. Although it does not specifically create a Customary Court, the South African constitution expressly empowers Parliament to establish such a court if Parliament deems it necessary. The Brazilian constitution expressly recognizes the country's indigenous law and justice by affirming the traditions and customs of the country's indigenous populations. Thus, their traditions, customs, and native laws are enforceable in Brazil's official courts. The Kenyan constitution recognizes the country's customary law, even though this appears to be restricted to civil matters. However, the Kenyan constitution establishes only Western-style courts (High Court and Court of Appeal inclusive). Although the constitution does not establish a Customary Court, it authorizes the Kenyan legislature to create other necessary courts. Overall, the Kenyan constitution requires all Kenyan courts applying customary law to a case to comply with Chapter V of the constitution, which provides for the "Protection of Fundamental Rights and Freedoms of the Individual." A customary law provision that violates a guaranteed right will be declared void.

In the final analysis, the constitution of each of Brazil, Kenya, Nigeria, and South Africa, which constitution mainly supports foreign-style law and justice systems, subjects the customary law of each country to the relevant constitution.

References

Black Administration Act, 1986 (South Africa).
"Brazil" (2009) *The World Factbook*, Central Intelligence Agency, USA (Online). https://www.cia.gov/library/publications/the-world-factbook/geos/br.html; Internet; accessed March 2009.
Constitution of Brazil, 1988 (Online; Retrieved on December 19, 2006).
Constitution of the Federal Republic of Nigeria, 1999.
Constitution of the Republic of Kenya.
Constitution of the Republic of South Africa, 1996 (effective February 3, 1997).
Elechi, O. Oko (2006) *Doing Justice Without the State: The Afikpo (Ehugbo) Nigeria Model*. New York, New York, USA: Routledge.
Ezeanya and Others v. Okeke and Others (1995) 4 Supreme Court of Nigeria Judgments 60.
Haffajee, F. (2005) "South Africa: Blending Tradition and Change" in *The UNESCO Courier* (Online; Retrieved on November 7, 2005). See http://www.unesco.org.courier/1999_11/uk/dossier/txt23.htm; Internet.
"Kenya" (2009) *The World Factbook*, Central Intelligence Agency, USA (Online). https://www.cia.gov/library/publications/the-world-factbook/geos/ke.html; Internet; accessed March 2009.
Native Administration Act (South Africa).
Okonkwo v. Okagbue and 2 Others (1994) 12 Supreme Court of Nigeria Judgments 89.
Okereafọezeke [a.k.a. Okafọ], N. (1996) *The Relationship Between Informal and Formal Strategies of Social Control: An Analysis of the Contemporary Methods of Dispute Processing Among the Igbos of Nigeria*. UMI Number 9638581. Ann Arbor, Michigan, USA: University Microfilms.
Okereafọezeke [a.k.a. Okafọ], N. (2000) "Repugnancy Test (Policy) and the Impact of Colonially Imposed Laws on the Growth of Nigeria's Native Justice Systems" in *The Journal of African Policy Studies*, Volume 6, Number 1, pp. 55-74.
Okereafọezeke [a.k.a. Okafọ], N. (2002) *Law and Justice in Post-British Nigeria: Conflicts and Interactions Between Native and Foreign Systems of Social Control in Igbo*. Westport, Connecticut, USA: Greenwood Press.
Okereafọezeke [a.k.a. Okafọ], N. (2003) "Traditional Social Control in an Ethnic Society: Law Enforcement in a Nigerian Community" in *Police Practice & Research: An International Journal*, Volume 4, Number 1, pp. 21-33.
Onagoruwa, O. (2009, March 17 and 18) "Law-Making Process in Nigeria" (1) and (2) in *The Guardian*, http://www.ngrguardiannews.com/editorial_opinion/article04//indexn2_html?pdate=17030...;Internet.http://www.ngrguardiannews.com/editorial_/article03//indexn2_html?pdate=18030...; Internet.
Proclamation No. 6 of 1900 (Nigeria).
Recognition of Customary Marriages Act, 2004 (South Africa).

Saleh-Hanna, V. (2008) *Colonial Systems of Control: Criminal Justice in Nigeria.* Ottawa, Ontario, Canada: University of Ottawa Press.

Shaidi, L. P. (1992) "Traditional, Colonial and Present-Day Administration of Criminal Justice" in *Criminology in Africa* Rome: United Nations Interregional Crime and Justice Research Institute ("UNICRI"), Publication No. 47.

Snyder, F. G. (1982) "Colonialism and Legal Form: The Creation of Customary Law in Senegal" in C. Sumner, ed., *Crime, Justice and Underdevelopment.* London, UK: Heinemann.

Chapter 4
Indigenous Versus Foreign Controls in Selected Countries: Australia, Canada, Japan, United States of America

Chapter 4 concludes Part 2's analysis of the relationships between indigenous law and justice and colonially or occupationally introduced law and justice in selected countries. This Chapter examines the indigenous/foreign law and justice interactions in Australia, Canada, Japan, and United States of America. As in all three chapters of Part 2 (Chapters 2, 3, and 4), each country is discussed separately under these two subheadings: "History, Constitutionalism, Law, and Government" and "Critique of the Colonial and Postcolonial Interactions Between Indigenous and Foreign Controls."

Australia

History, Constitutionalism, Law, and Government

As the only country in the world that is also a continent by itself, Australia is large and small at the same time. It is the world's sixth largest country, but also the smallest continent. Contemporary Australia is a mixed society, including Native Aborigines and Europeans, but with European settlers dominating the country. However, before the European settlers arrived in Australia, Aborigines had lived there for over 40,000 years. In the 17th Century, the first Europeans began exploring the country. In 1770, Captain James Cook took over the country for Britain. The late 18th and 19th Centuries saw the creation of six colonies, which in 1901 amalgamated into the Commonwealth of Australia. On January 1, 1901, Australia received political independence from Britain. Australia is made up of six states and two territories. The country has federal parliamentary democracy. A Prime Minister as the head of government rules contemporary Australia, while the British monarch remains Australia's head of state.

A United States Central Intelligence Agency estimate puts the Australian population at over 21 million (see "Australia" USA CIA Estimate, 2009). That estimate includes the following ethnic distribution of the country's population: White 92%, Asian 7%, Aboriginal and Others 1%. It is surprising that Native Australians (Aborigines) are so few. In any case, Europeans now dominate every aspect of Australian life, including its languages (English), religions (Christianity), and law and justice (English common law). A survey of the country's basic source of laws – the *Constitution of the Commonwealth of Australia, 1901* (Australian Constitution) – bears out the striking similarities between the Australian government, law, and justice, on the one hand, and the government, law, and justice of England, Australia's former colonizer. But, how does the Australian Constitution address indigenous law and justice *vis-à-vis* the European law and justice brought to Australia by European colonizers?

Critique of the Colonial and Postcolonial Interactions Between Indigenous and Foreign Controls

The USA CIA Estimate (2009) puts the Australian "Aboriginal and Others" population size at 1% of the Australian population. The percentage belies this author's expectation prior to this study. Judging by how long the Aborigines had inhabited Australia before the European immigrants, it seemed logical that the Aborigines would constitute a substantially larger portion of the Australian population. A review of the racial make-up of contemporary Australia reveals a near-inexistent or fast disappearing Aboriginal subpopulation. Nonetheless, it is somewhat surprising, even if not out of the character a colonizer and the colonizing instrument, that the Australian Constitution pays little, even if negative, attention to the country's Native Aboriginal population. Before closely examining the Australian Constitution, I was under the impression that modern Australia would officially allow wide latitude to the Natives, especially through the Australian Constitution. A closer study of the constitution reveals that the dominant European immigrant population has historically and contemporarily sought to suppress the Native Australians.

The size and role of Native Australians in the country's scheme of things deserve further scrutiny. Australian official accounts of the Native population presents a picture of a small Aboriginal population (1%) relative to the colonial/postcolonial European immigrants (92%). If these percentages are accurate, they would represent sad consequences of colonial Europe's hallmark rampage and destruction of things non-European in every society they colonize. By its provisions, the Australian Constitution seems to precisely capture the attitude of the dominant colonial and postcolonial European Australians towards the country's indigenous populations and their law, justice, and way of life. Typically, this attitude is negative, hostile, and aims at suppressing the indigenes.

At its enactment in 1901, the Australian Constitution regarded Australian Aborigines as inferior to the immigrant Europeans. This negative constitutional attitude is well evidenced in section 127 of the constitution, thus: "In reckoning the numbers of the people of the Commonwealth, or of a State or other part of the Commonwealth, aboriginal natives shall not be counted." In effect, according to the Australian Constitution, the country's Aborigines were not sufficiently, if at all, human to be identified and acknowledged as such. Although the section 127 provision was repealed in 1967 [see *Constitution Alteration (Aboriginals)*

1967], the whole public policy attitude towards the Aborigines, especially via the Australian Constitution, remains essentially the same. A survey of the amended constitution reveals virtually no acknowledgement of, nor recognition for, Australia's Aboriginal law, justice, or the system for their application.

Moreover, the Australian government's opposition to the 2007 United Nations Charter on the rights of indigenous peoples (the document was designed to protect the human rights of native peoples, and their lands and resources) further evidences Australia's official low regard for its indigenous population. Australia was one of only four countries (others are Canada, New Zealand, and USA), out of some 154 countries in the world, to oppose the Charter (see "Indigenous Rights Outlined by UN," 2007). See also "United Nations Declaration on the Rights of Indigenous Peoples" (2007) for the Charter protections. However, it is heartening to note that the government of Australia may be having a change of heart in its attitudes and treatment of its Aborigines. In February 2008, the Australian Prime Minister (PM), Kevin Rudd, apologized in parliament for laws and other policies that imposed overwhelming misery, suffering, and damage on the Aborigines. In particular, the PM identified the "stolen generations," which refers to the thousands of Aboriginal children compulsorily removed from their families and forced to grow up away from their homes. The "stolen generations" resulted from the twisted colonial policy of assimilation, which endured in Australia from the 19th Century to the late 1960s (see "Australia Apology to Aborigines," 2008; see also "Aborigines Open Canberra Session," 2008). Whether the announced change of heart translates to positive and necessary transformation of Australia's official policy towards the indigenous population remains to be determined. Only concrete changes to the relevant laws and other public policies to acknowledge and ensure, in practical terms, the equality of the Aborigines to their European counterparts will authenticate the government's apology.

Canada

History, Constitutionalism, Law, and Government

Canada's over 33 million inhabitants (see "Canada" USA CIA Estimate, 2009) live in the world's second largest country after Russia. Most of Canada was a British colony until July 1, 1867, when it became Union of British North American Colonies. Later on December 11, 1931, Canada's independence was recognized. Postcolonial Canada is a federated constitutional monarchy with parliamentary democracy. Whereas the royal head of England remains Canada's head of State, Canada is organized on the basis of a federal system that grants rights and responsibilities to the federating provinces and territories.

In many instances, the constitution of a country is a single document made up of the most important statements guaranteeing and allocating rights and duties to the citizens, the government, and its agencies. For Canada, the constitution consists of written and unwritten acts, customs, traditions, and case law. The *Constitution Act* of March 29, 1867 (an Act of the British parliament establishing a Canadian federation of four provinces) and the *Constitution Act* of April 17, 1982 (transferring formal control over the constitution from Britain to Canada while adding a charter of rights and freedoms together with constitutional amendment procedures) make up the written component of the Constitution of Canada.

Contemporary Canada consists of English-speaking and French-speaking postcolonies. Specifically, Quebec province, one of Canada's ten provinces and three territories, is a former French colony, whereas the remaining provinces and territories are former English colonies. Quebec has sometimes demanded increased autonomy and self-determination from English Canada. The colonial forces and philosophies of England and France operating in the same country (Canada) have caused Canada to compromise on many policy issues to accommodate the often opposing English and French ideas of politics, government, and society. Thus, the Constitution of Canada declares that English and French versions of the Constitution Act "are equally authoritative" (section 57, Part VII of the Schedules to the *Constitution Act 1867*). Further, section 22 of the Act acknowledges that a person may officially use a language other than English or French even if the "legal or customary right or privilege [relating to that language was] acquired or enjoyed either before or after the coming into force of [the Charter of rights]". On law and justice, Canada's legal system is based on English common law, with the exception of Quebec province where civil law system based on French law dominates.

The co-existence of English and French systems in Canada has undoubtedly added another dimension to the need and demand for Canada to fashion ways to integrate its indigenous and foreign systems for a more efficient society. Instead of postcolonial Canada working to synthesize one foreign justice system (English or French) with its indigenous justice systems, the country has to work to synthesize two prominent foreign justice systems (English and French) with its indigenous justice systems. The situation probably increases the difficulty level for postcolonial Canada. However, even though this could be especially problematic, there is no doubt that Canada could benefit from a meaningful merger of its indigenous, English, and French law and justice ideas for improved social control. Thus, the co-existence of diverse, competing law and justice systems in a society is not necessarily a negative attribute for that society.

Critique of the Colonial and Postcolonial Interactions Between Indigenous and Foreign Controls

The Constitution of Canada is the country's supreme law. Any law inconsistent with a provision of the constitution is, to the extent of the inconsistency, of no force or effect (section 52, Part VII of the Schedules). The constitution recognizes Canada's indigenous systems and the rights based on them, even though it restricts those systems and rights by subjecting them to the constitutional provisions.

However, the "indigenous systems and rights" should include traditional methods and organs of law, order, and social control. Thus, the Constitution of Canada, at least by implication, protects the country's indigenous law and justice systems. Under Section 25, Part I of the Schedules to the constitution, "the guarantee in this [Constitution's] Charter of certain rights and freedoms shall not be construed so as to abrogate or derogate from any aboriginal, treaty or other rights or freedoms that pertain to the aboriginal peoples of Canada...." Also, Part II of the Schedules to the constitution titled "Rights of the Aboriginal Peoples of Canada – Recognition of Existing Aboriginal and Treaty Rights" provides that "The existing aboriginal and treaty rights of the aboriginal peoples of Canada are hereby recognized and affirmed" [section 35 (1)]. Further, the same Part II of the Schedules to the Constitution commits the government of Canada and the provincial governments to the following principle. Prior to any amendment to a constitutional provision guaranteeing Aboriginal peoples' rights under indigenous law, Aboriginal representatives will be invited to participate in the discussions leading up to a change.

These constitutional provisions illustrate the importance with which the Constitution of Canada regards the country's indigenous law and justice for social control. However, despite appearing to promote indigenous rights, the Canadian government (along with Australia, New Zealand, and the USA) opposed the 2007 United Nations Charter on the rights of indigenous peoples (the document was designed to protect the human rights of native peoples, and their lands and resources) (see "Indigenous Rights Outlined by UN," 2007; "United Nations Declaration on the Rights of Indigenous Peoples," 2007). This opposition undercuts the government's claim to the advancement of indigenous rights. Furthermore, the Constitution of Canada limits the indigenous laws and rights of Aboriginal Canadians by subjecting them to the constitution. Where an indigenous law, custom, or practice is repugnant to, or inconsistent with, a constitutional provision, the constitution prevails to the extent of the contradiction. Thus, the Constitution of Canada serves to check the country's indigenous systems and processes.

Japan

History, Constitutionalism, Law, and Government

Japan is a modern country with largely continuous historical ties to its ancient societies. Although the country has changed substantially in many ways, in other ways (including religion, culture, language, societal and organizational norms, and social control) modern Japan bears remarkable semblance to its pre-modern variety. Japan's ability to "develop" while grounded in its indigenous roots is noteworthy. That is a commendable combination even if the country has necessarily redefined the roles of its institutions of State. Regardless, the continuous ties that the country has maintained with its rich past probably provide more positive than negative perspectives for the Japanese. Without doubt, there are Japanese national endeavors for which many Japanese are not proud, such as the country's role in the World War II (WWII). However, the country has taken steps to redefine itself more positively and reintegrated itself into the community of nations post-WWII. Moreover, Japan has proved its resilience over the centuries and millennia by surviving and progressing nicely in a rather harsh environment.

Consistent with its character for survival, Japan has transformed itself as necessary to overcome challenges to the nation. Japan's standings during and after the WWII accurately capture its ability, willingness, effectiveness, and efficiency in adapting its national orientation to changing circumstances. In the WWII, Japan partnered with Germany to wage war on many countries in the world. Following its defeat in the war, Japan accepted the conditions imposed on it by the victorious countries, including the USA, and reformed its national orientation and focus. It renounced war in its post-WWII constitution and substantially limited the powers of its Emperor. In the post-WWII world, Japan is one of the most potent economic forces. So, even in the face of its constitutional declaration that "land, sea, and air forces, as well as other war potential, will never be maintained," and that "the right of belligerency of the state will not be recognized" (Article 9, Chapter II of the *Constitution of Japan, 1946*), post-WWII Japan wields substantial influence in world affairs.

Contemporary Japan is respected for its economic prosperity as well as for its largely independent (from the West) socio-cultural and religious lives. It is worth noting that this independence is traceable mainly to the 250-year period preceding 1854, when *Tokugawa Shogunate*, or military dictatorship, led the country in an isolation period from overseas influence beginning in 1603. The 250-year period enabled Japan to become more stable and allowed its indigenous culture to grow without foreign interferences. Another factor that informs Japan's native-based development is the country's homogeneity. Even in 2009, Japan's estimated population of over one hundred and twenty-seven million people (see "Japan" USA CIA Estimate, 2009) consists of 98.50% "Japanese," while the remaining 1.50% is made up of Koreans, Chinese, Brazilians, etc. Whatever the differences among the 98.50% "Japanese" pales in comparison with what obtains in other countries, which tend to be far more diverse. Relative to other countries, the Japanese appear to share enough similar social, cultural, religious, social control, and other characteristics to be a largely homogenous nation. The national language (Japanese) is nearly universal among the citizens while most Japanese (84%) adhere to Shinto, an indigenous Japanese religion, and Japanese Buddhism.

Japan's strong indigenous foundation has in effect facilitated its adjustments for life in the modern world without abdicating or substantially dislocating the nation's essence. As an example, Japan's history is traceable to 660 B.C., when Emperor Jimmu founded the country. Post-WWII Japan is a constitutional monarchy in which the Emperor remains the head of State. The victorious WWII countries, including the USA and Britain, wrote Japan's 1946 Constitution after rejecting what the victors regarded as an inadequate attempt to change the preexisting *Constitution of the Empire of Japan, 1889* (the Meiji or Imperial Constitution), which, it appeared, facilitated the imperial warring nation that Japan had become and exhibited in WWII. Although Douglas MacArthur, the Supreme Commander for the Allied Powers (the post-WWII colonists of Japan), claimed that neither he nor his superiors in the USA planned to compel a new political system on Japan unilaterally, he selected the drafters of a new constitution for Japan. The new constitution was designed to include the following main provisions: a substantially whittled down power for the Emperor, a provision that the Emperor is not the source of Japan's laws, and a provision renouncing war,[1] among others. The Emperor signed the draft constitution on November 3, 1946, to take effect from May 3, 1947. By the new *Constitution of Japan, 1946* (Constitution of Japan), Japan's imperial power has declined substantially regarding day-to-day government. Daily government is in the hands of a Prime Minister chosen on the basis of periodic elections. However, the Emperor continues to symbolize national unity and heritage. The Emperor's role in government is mostly based on the advice of elected officials and the electorate.

Critique of the Colonial and Postcolonial Interactions Between Indigenous and Foreign Controls

As already alluded to, there is substantial evidence to conclude that the Constitution of Japan contains indigenous Japanese systems and principles as well as American and European versions. In spite of Japan's advertised allegiance to its traditional roots, the country's legal system, which the Constitution of Japan guarantees, is modeled after European civil law system with English-American influence. The country's Supreme Court, which is the highest court, has the power of judicial review of legislations. The Supreme Court and the other courts (High Court, District Court, Family Court, and Summary Court) are official State creations. All the courts are bound to apply the constitution, other State legislations, and to the extent possible Japan's customary law. However, the constitution is the supreme law. Where a customary law, legislation, or other act contradicts an aspect of the constitution, the customary law, etc. shall have no legal force or validity (Article 98). Also, in an attempt to depart from Japan's pre-WWII stance, Article 99 expressly enjoins the Emperor, Regent, Ministers, members of the Diet (parliament), judges, and all other public officials to respect and uphold the constitution. Thus, by the *Constitution of Japan, 1946*, the rule of law prevails in Japan.

Although the *Constitution of Japan, 1946* is the supreme law of the land, the country's traditions, customs, and native laws (customary law) play invaluable roles in the country's social control. The constitution does not appear to guarantee a constitutional role for customary law. This is perhaps because such customary law role is so entrenched and widespread that it is assumed. Alternatively, the absence of a constitutionally guaranteed role for Japanese customary law could be

---

1 Recently, there have been clamor and efforts by some internal powers within Japan to reverse aspects of the non-militarization undertaking.

interpreted as a design to discourage adherence to Japan's pre-WWII principles. In any case, the role that Japan's customary law plays in case management and law and order maintenance, especially through unofficial or out-of-court processes, is unquestionable. In this connection, there is substantial literature suggesting that the Japanese deeply loathe altering their society's interrelationships and thus, unlike United States citizens and Western Europeans, for examples, avoid going to official courts to settle disputes. But this view should be considered more carefully. Thus, according to Dolan and Worden (1994), the correct view is that the Japanese may be every bit as litigious as Westerners; however, their reluctance to resort to official processes to manage disputes stems from the dearth of lawyers in Japan.

Therefore, Dolan and Worden (1994) take the position that the well-known Japanese preference for informal, unofficial means of case management derives from factors other than purely altruistic qualities. The Japanese, according to Dolan and Worden (1994), are capable of being every bit as individualistic as an American or European, by resorting to official, formal courts and processes for case management. Specifically, the relative unavailability of lawyers to assist with case prosecution in courts restrains Japanese from resorting to formal processes. Dolan and Worden (1994) explain (Online):

> Factors other than a cultural preference for social harmony, however, explain the court-shy behavior of the Japanese. The Ministry of Justice closely screens university law faculty graduates and others who wish to practice law or serve as judges. Only about 2 percent of the approximately 25,000 persons who applied annually to the Ministry's Legal Training and Research Institute two-year required course were admitted in the late 1980s. The institute graduates only a few hundred new lawyers each year. Plagued by shortages of attorneys, judges, clerks, and other personnel, the [official] court system is severely overburdened. Presiding judges often strongly advise plaintiffs to seek out-of-court settlements. The progress of cases through even the lower courts is agonizingly slow, and appeals carried to the Supreme Court can take decades. Faced with such obstacles, most individuals choose not to seek legal remedies. If legal personnel are dramatically increased, which seems unlikely, use of the courts might approach rates found in the United States and other Western countries.

The Japanese system appears designed to discourage officialism (formal roles of State institutions and personnel) in justice and social control (see Okereafoezeke, 1996; 2002a). Comparatively, the approximately "few hundred new lawyers" graduated in a year in Japan (Dolan and Worden, 1994) would be fewer than the number of lawyers practicing in one big US city, such as New York, Los Angeles, or Chicago.

Thus, perhaps, faced with a shortage of lawyers, Japanese, in the overwhelming majority of cases, resort to unofficial processes under customary law, to manage their civil and criminal grievances, conflicts, and disputes. Despite Dolan and Worden's (1994) skepticism, what is undeniable is that the Japanese frequently use their customary laws and indigenous systems to manage disagreements, rather than resort to official courts. The citizens' reasons for doing so are subject to different interpretations. In any case, taking responsible steps to discourage over-litigiousness in a society is positive, provided that aggrieved citizens receive satisfactory considerations and resolutions of their grievances, conflicts, and disputes. Such steps in Japan are credible features of Japanese law and justice. There is nothing wrong with the Japanese system that encourages the citizens to utilize and receive satisfactory resolution of cases through their indigenous laws and systems.

United States of America

History, Constitutionalism, Law, and Government

For centuries, "Native Americans" of various ethnic groupings inhabited North America. The Native American domination of the North American continent continued until the 15th Century when European colonists invaded North America. Christopher Columbus was a prominent member of the European colonizing ventures. His reputation as the "discoverer" of America persists to this day despite the fact that Native Americans inhabited the continent long before Columbus and his team reached America. However, over time, Britain, in its then position as the world's dominant economic and military power, took possession of, and imposed its rule over, much of North America. The British colonial rule over North America continued until 1776 when 13 North American colonial territories (later to become states) declared themselves independent of Britain. The 13 colonies christened themselves the United States of America. The former colonies making up the new country united into a common force and challenged the British colonization and subjugation of the territories.

By 1782, Britain had made informal peace overtures to the rebellious 13 colonies. Britain would provide the 13 colonies with some autonomy within the British Empire. The 13 ex-colonies rejected this overture and would not accept any peace separate from France, the ex-colonies' loyal ally. On September 3, 1783, seven years after the declaration of independence, the new nation was recognized as the United States of America following the *Treaty of Paris, 1783*. Among other provisions, the treaty, which the Congress of the Confederation of America later ratified on January 14, 1784, recognized the 13 colonies as free and sovereign states and established the boundaries between the USA and the British North America (later called Canada). In the 19th and 20th Centuries, 37 new North American states joined the original 13 to form a 50-state USA. In 2009, the country's population is about three hundred and four million residents (see "United States of America" USA CIA Estimate, 2009).

The USA is built on constitutionalism and federal republicanism with a president in charge at the federal level while a governor runs each of the 50 states. At the federal level, the president, elected indirectly (through the "electoral college" system) every four years, is the head of State and the head of government. The *Constitution of the United States of America*, with all the Amendments thereto, provides for division of powers, responsibilities, and checks and balances among the branches of government: Executive, Judiciary, and Legislature. In the US arrangement, each branch of government checks and is checked by another branch. This discourages a government branch from dominating the others – the constitution treats all the branches as co-equals. In particular, the US Supreme Court, which is the highest court in the country, plays a critical role in stabilizing the country's constitutional arrangement. The Supreme Court decided in *Marbury v. Madison* (1803) that it has the power of "judicial review" (power to examine and decide whether or not a legislative or executive act is lawful). The Supreme Court more or less assumed the power and has kept it since *Marbury*. The power of judicial review allows the Supreme Court and other courts to determine the constitutionality of a legislative or other act. Over time, this evaluative judicial power has grown and been strengthened such that the executive and the legislature are conscious of the fact that the Supreme Court may strike down their acts. Therefore, it is reasonable to expect these government branches to take what the courts would do into consideration in making and implementing legislative and executive acts. What obtains at the federal level is mostly found in all the states.

In addition to its 50 states, the USA has forcefully acquired, possesses, and dominates overseas lands and peoples. In its over 232 years as an independent postcolony, the US has transformed itself from a strong, exemplary opponent of colonization (see for examples the US alliances with revolutionary France and the US revolutionary war of independence against Britain in the late 18th Century) to a colonizer (see for instances the US unjust invasion of, and war against, Vietnam in the 1960s-70s, as well as the US immoral and illegal invasion of, and war against, Iraq beginning in 2003). The US 21st Century colonial adventure in Iraq is particularly disturbing because the US went ahead with its plan to invade independent Iraq in spite of the overwhelming opposition to the idea among member countries of the United Nations Organization (UN), the headquarters of which the US hosts. I have had occasion to condemn in strong terms this US irresponsible, hegemonic, anti-diplomacy action (see Okafọ, 2003a). In the same article, I warned that, like all colonizers before the US, the negative consequences of the US invasion of Iraq would be far greater than the bad that they violently overthrew in President Saddam Hussein. Events in Iraq have since confirmed the prediction in that June 2003 publication.

In addition to the unjust US wars, the country has regrettably formed and implemented other colonialist policies and programs around the world. The US routinely uses its armed forces to threaten and regulate relations with other countries. In the 20th and 21st Centuries, the US maintains military bases and outposts in more than two-thirds of the countries of the world. Even now, the US seeks ways to expand and/or initiate military presence in many other countries, including Poland, Nigeria, Japan, and Spain, among others. This is worrisome because often intimidation, bribery, and other coercive methods secure the illegitimate US military presence in a country. The leases of the US Naval Base in Guantanamo Bay, Cuba and the strategic Panama Canal, Panama, almost in perpetuity to the US, strongly illustrate US highhandedness in its dealings with other, weaker countries. These unduly long contractual arrangements seem unfair and intended to subjugate the host nations (Cuba and Panama, as examples) to the powerful USA. In each instance, the contract establishes the US and its agents as a nation within the host nation, for decades. These US actions evidence the country's colonial mindset. The actions run counter to 21st Century behavior expectations by the civilized world. Also, the colonial actions of the USA contradict the moral democratic ideal that the founding fathers of the country espoused especially in their declaration of independence and revolutionary struggle against colonial Britain. Eventually, it seems that these US colonizing ventures around the world will end when the country loses the economic advantage it has enjoyed for decades over other countries. Then, it will no longer be able to support these colonizing settlements.

Critique of the Colonial and Postcolonial Interactions Between Indigenous and Foreign Controls

The US justice system is based on federal and state subsystems founded on English common law. The federation and each of the 50 states have separate legal systems all of which, except Louisiana State,[2] are common law-based. The *Constitution of the United States of America* (US Constitution) proclaims its superiority to all state constitutions and laws, and all state and federal judges are bound by the US Constitution. Thus, any state constitutional provision or law contrary to the US Constitution is void (Article VI). Since the arrival of Europeans in the Native lands now called the USA, the European settlers have sought to either dominate or exclude the Natives from their long-held lands. As an example, by the post-independence US Constitution, "representatives shall be apportioned among the several States according to their respective numbers, counting the whole number of persons in each State, excluding Indians not taxed" (Article XIV, Section 2). See also Article I, Section 2 for a similar provision. These and analogous provisions were designed to define and treat the American Natives as unwanted foreigners in their own lands. Article I, Section 8 manifests this by the fact that it groups Native Americans with "foreign nations." It seems evident that what the European settlers in the Native lands sought to do, and substantially succeeded in doing, was to replace meaningful or threatening Native ideas and ways of life with European versions. This is an example of system and/or idea supplanting by a dominant force. This form of displacement has been expressed as "Substitutive Interaction" (Okereafọezeke, 2002a, pp. 18-19).

---

2 Louisiana state's law and justice are based on the French, German, and Spanish codes of law and by extension Roman law, rather than the English common law.

Substitutive Interaction is a colonial characteristic. It is not an attribute of equal relations. It is a form of interaction in which a dominant party seeks to replace (substitute) another's values, ideas, processes, systems, etc. with those of the dominant party (Okereafǫezeke, 2002a, pp. 18-19). Domination, emasculation, and replacement of the virtues of the colonized are hallmarks of colonization. As already mentioned, colonial USA follows the same pattern in its relationships with many countries. Also, within the USA, relative to its Native populations, postcolonial USA exhibits many characteristics of the colonizing personality. Long after the British colonization of the US and in the US revolutionary and post-revolutionary era (after the war against British colonization and domination), the US continued its efforts to subjugate the Native Americans. To the extent that this failed, the US decided to separate the Native Americans from the dominant European Americans by creating "reservations," within which allegedly the Native Americans are autonomous. This separation is curious. The fact that the Native American tribes remain within the confines and physical land space of the USA highlights the policy's absurdity. Even in the 21st Century – over 232 years post-US independence from Britain – there are legitimate questions about the validity of the "reservations" jurisdictions of Native American justice systems. The questions emanate from the fact that "reservations" justice systems operate within, and are confined by, the dominant official English common law-based system.

The ambivalent separation of the Native American reservations justice systems from the official US system notwithstanding, it is noteworthy that the string of individual rights guaranteed by the "Bill of Rights" provisions (the first ten Amendments to the US Constitution) may protect individual and group rights of the indigenous populations. The Bill of Rights provisions include freedom of expression and prohibition of State religion (Amendment I), prohibition of unreasonable searches and seizures of person and property (Amendment IV), prohibition of double jeopardy, that is two or more trials for the same offense (Amendment V), right to speedy and public trial (Amendment VI), and prohibition of cruel and unusual punishment (Amendment VIII). It seems that whether or not the Bill of Rights protections are extensible to a Native American party to a case depends on whether a case involving a determination of fundamental rights is in a US (federal or state) criminal justice system or a Tribal justice system. For example, a party before an official state or federal court is entitled to the relevant constitutional protections, while a party before a tribal court may not enjoy the safeguards.

However, it seems absurd that a judicial body – whether an official government court or a Tribal court – within the USA could try, judge, or punish a person in a way that violates any of the fundamental guarantees of justice in the country as stipulated in the Bill of Rights. The half-hearted attempt in the US system to grant jurisdictional autonomy to Native American tribes means, at least in theory, that a Tribal court is independent of the official, English common law-based justice system. Such a Tribal court seems to be vested with the power to hear and determine a case by following a process that might be illegal under the US Constitution. In any case, the US opposition (along with Australia, Canada, and New Zealand) to the 2007 United Nations Charter on the rights of indigenous peoples confirms the official US instituted obstacles to the expansion of the country's indigenous institutions and processes. The US opposed the 2007 Charter, which was designed to protect the human rights of native peoples along with their lands and resources. See "Indigenous Rights Outlined by UN" (2007) and "United Nations Declaration on the Rights of Indigenous Peoples" (2007).

The US Constitution – which is superior to all other sources of laws in the country (Article VI) – trumps every law that opposes the constitution. Thus, indigenous traditions, customs, and native laws that offend the constitution will likely be rejected, at least by the official courts and agencies of law and social control. In this connection, the fact that the European cultures, particularly the Christian religion and English language, dominate law and justice in the USA is significant. In the US setup, the English common law or its derivative dominates the Native American law and justice systems as well as the systems of other immigrant groups that have since entered the USA. That the USA is the world's most immigration-induced, diverse population is hardly disputable. More than any other country, the USA has for long maintained an official policy that attracts many of the best citizens of other world societies. These immigrants enter the USA with the immigrants' cultures and native laws. However, the English common law-based US justice system soon renders the immigrants' native systems nugatory. The US courts have routinely shown their willingness to uphold the US English common law-based laws over alternative socio-cultural defenses to crimes. A court could treat a socio-cultural defense as a mitigating factor in punishment but not as a complete defense to a crime, however compelling the socio-cultural defense might be (Okereafǫezeke, 2000; Renteln, 2004). In the final analysis, the indigenous law and justice systems in the USA are subjected to the official English-style system.

Chapter Summary and Conclusion

This chapter (the last of Part 2 of this book) analyzed the indigenous/foreign law and justice systems relationships in Australia, Canada, Japan, and the USA. Deliberations on the four countries reveal a common feature: the official constitution in each country is the supreme law of the land and trumps all other laws including each country's indigenous laws. In view of Australia's strong pre-colonial Aboriginal population, it is surprising that the country's indigenous population has been substantially reduced. A 2009 estimate of Australian Aborigines puts their population at 1% of the country's population. Modern Australia's low regard for the Aborigines can be found in the 1901 Australian Constitution, according to which Australian Aborigines are inferior to the immigrant Europeans. Under section 127 of the constitution, Aborigines should not to be counted in determining the country's population. Although section 127 was later repealed, the new official policy lacks meaningful, if any, recognition or protection for the Aborigines, their justice system, or other lifestyle. In 2008, the Australian Prime Minister apologized to the Aborigines for decades of destructive colonial policies and programs by the immigrant Europeans against the Aborigines. It remains to be seen whether his apology results in meaningful ameliorative actions.

In Canada, the *Constitution of Canada* is the supreme law of the country. Thus, indigenous laws are constitutionally limited. To this extent, the Australian and Canadian situations are similar. However, the two countries differ because the Canadian constitution provides for a stronger recognition and acceptance of Canada's indigenous systems than does the Australian constitution. The combined effects of section 25, Part I and section 35 (1), Part II of the Schedules to the Canadian Constitution are that the constitution recognizes the existing and treaty rights of Canadian Aborigines and expressly provides that other Aboriginal rights not guaranteed by the constitution are nonetheless protected. Also, the participation of the Aboriginal peoples' representatives in discussions of any planned amendment of their rights is a condition precedent to such a change. These provisions, which should apply to Aboriginal rights under Canada's indigenous law and justice, can be quite expansive depending on the interpretation placed on them.

Post-WWII Japan is a constitutional monarchy based on the rule of law. This differs starkly from the pre-WWII Japan in which the Emperor was viewed as the source of Japanese laws. Thus, Japan's 1946 Constitution is superior to all other laws, including the country's customary law. However, all Japanese courts shall apply the country's customary law. But a customary law provision that offends the constitution shall be unenforceable. Regardless of the prominence of its constitution, Japan's customary law is highly regarded in the country's social control. In general, the Japanese appear to prefer traditional, out-of-court management of civil and criminal cases over going to the official courts. This leads to the conclusion that Japanese are non-confrontational, community-oriented, and seek and emphasize collective peace over individual rights. However, there is a contrary view that Japanese would be every bit as litigious as say United States citizens if only the Japanese had available to them as many lawyers, judges, courts, etc. as do US citizens. What is undeniable, however, is that Japanese resort to far more unofficial, than official, processes for case management, whatever their reasons for doing so.

The US claim to being a nation of laws is strengthened by the country's constitution, especially the Bill of Rights component, which guarantees an array of individual rights, including life, expression, liberty, public trial, property, and fair hearing. The Bill of Rights protections are important elements of the US constitution, which is the supreme law of the country. However, one of the most prominent contradictions of the US society is the idea of "reservations," which purports to give control of land areas to Native Americans for their tribal affairs. The relevant tribal customary law is mandated to regulate relations in each reserved area. The reservation arrangement is intended to grant "independence" to the Natives. However, the extent of the resulting independence remains unclear. The reserved areas remain within the jurisdictional boundaries of the USA. Regardless of the jurisdictions of the reservations, the US constitution, with its English common law foundation, is the overriding source of laws. It seems that in the final analysis, the overwhelming powers of the official state and federal governments will apply and enforce an applicable English common law over an opposing customary law, except perhaps where the dominant state or federal authority perceives an issue as minor. Thus, tradition- and culture-based explanations of crimes, such as criminal defenses based on Native American cultures and practices, are usually rejected in the US state and federal courts. Where they are accepted at all, they serve only to mitigate punishment, rather than exculpate the accused. It is clear that English law and justice, as expressed in the US Constitution and other laws, dominate the Native American and all other systems of law and justice in the country.

In spite of local variations in each country, Australia, Canada, New Zealand, and the USA appear to have a common nonchalance, if not contempt, for indigenous rights. The four countries respectively opposed the 2007 United Nations Charter on the rights of indigenous peoples, which was created to protect the human rights of native groups, and their lands and resources (see "Indigenous Rights Outlined by UN," 2007; "United Nations Declaration on the Rights of Indigenous Peoples," 2007). The Charter provides that countries should allow more control to indigenous peoples over the lands and resources the indigenes traditionally controlled. Countries should also return seized lands to their rightful owners or pay compensations for those properties. Out of 154 countries in the world, only Australia, Canada, New Zealand, and the USA opposed the Charter rights, because of alleged incompatibility with the local laws of each of the opposing countries.

Australia, for example, justified its opposition to the Charter by claiming that the country could not allow tribes' customary laws to have precedence over national laws. According to the country's Indigenous Affairs Minister, "There should only be one law for all Australians and we should not enshrine in law practices that are not acceptable in the modern world" ("Indigenous Rights Outlined by UN", 2007, at p. 2). Of course, the Minister's claim is based on the assumption that indigenous laws and rights are incompatible with modernity. The Minister's claim is misguided and misleading. As I have demonstrated in Chapter 1 of this book, indigenous traditions, customs, and native laws are not necessarily incompatible with a modern State. Indeed, most laws, rules, and regulations of a modern State are rooted in indigenous communities. Specific indigenous law provisions that affront modernity should, through negotiated democratic processes, be brought in line with contemporary times to ensure increased freedom for the citizens. Curtailing the citizens' freedom by rejecting their indigenous-based rights, such as Australia and the other three countries have done, is a wrong justice course. However, the Minister's claim seems to be an excuse for continuing the exploitation of the oppressed indigenous populations in the four countries that opposed the Charter.

It is quite instructive that the four opposing countries are in the forefront of countries in which immigrant European populations have dominated, oppressed, and overwhelmed the respective indigenous populations in the last several hundred years. Perhaps it should not surprise any objective student of world history that these four countries insist on maintaining the European domination of indigenous peoples. What is perplexing, however, is the fact that the four countries are widely, even if inaccurately, labeled "developed First World" countries (see Okereafoezeke, 2002b; Okafo, 2003a). Despite the obvious contradiction between their respective international standings as advanced nations and the deliberate suppression of their citizens, Australia, Canada, New Zealand, and the USA are comfortable with opposing a Charter designed to advance the rights of oppressed and cheated peoples in their respective countries.

References

"Aborigines Open Canberra Session" (2008, February 12) in *BBC NEWS* online. See http://news.bbc.co.uk/2/hi/asia-pacific/7240382.stm; Internet.
"Australia" (2009) *The World Factbook*, Central Intelligence Agency, USA (Online). https://www.cia.gov/library/publications/the-world-factbook/geos/as.html; Internet; accessed March 2009.
"Australia Apology to Aborigines" (2008, February 13) in *BBC NEWS* online. See http://news.bbc.co.uk/2/hi/asia-pacific/7241965.stm; Internet.
"Canada" (2009) *The World Factbook*, Central Intelligence Agency, USA (Online). https://www.cia.gov/library/publications/the-world-factbook/geos/ca.html; Internet; accessed March 2009.
Constitution Act, 1867 (Canada).
Constitution Act, 1982 (Canada).
Constitution Alteration (Aboriginals), 1967 (Australia).
Constitution of Japan, 1946.
Constitution of the Commonwealth of Australia, 1901.
Constitution of the Empire of Japan, 1889 (the Meiji or Imperial Constitution).
Constitution of the United States of America.
Dolan, R. E. and Worden, R. L., eds. (1994) "Japan - The Judicial System" in *Japan: A Country Study*. Washington, D. C., USA: GPD for the Library of Congress. See http://countrystudies.us/japan/ (Online; Retrieved March 6, 2007).
"Indigenous Rights Outlined by UN" (2007, September 13) in *BBC NEWS* online. See http://news.bbc.co.uk/1/hi/world/6993776.stm; Internet.
"Japan" (2009) *The World Factbook*, Central Intelligence Agency, USA (Online). https://www.cia.gov/library/publications/the-world-factbook/geos/ja.html; Internet; accessed March 2009.
Marbury v. Madison (1803) 1 Cranch 137 (USA).
Okafo, N. (2003a) "Developed Atavism – 21st Century Colonial USA" in *NigeriaWorld*, June 12, 2003. See http://nigeriaworld.com/articles/2003/jun/121.html; Internet.
Okereafoezeke [a.k.a. Okafo], N. (1996) *The Relationship Between Informal and Formal Strategies of Social Control: An Analysis of the Contemporary*

Methods of Dispute Processing Among the Igbos of Nigeria. UMI Number 9638581. Ann Arbor, Michigan, USA: University Microfilms, Inc.

Okereafọezeke [a.k.a. Okafọ], N. (2000) "The Immigrant Offender and the Dynamics of Socio-Cultural Defenses to Crimes in the United States of America" in *Phi Beta Delta International Review*, Volume X, Spring 2000, pp. 173-189.

Okereafọezeke [a.k.a. Okafọ], N. (2002a) *Law and Justice in Post-British Nigeria: Conflicts and Interactions Between Native and Foreign Systems of Social Control in Igbo*. Westport, Connecticut, USA: Greenwood Press.

Okereafọezeke [a.k.a. Okafọ] N. (2002b) "Yoruba Hometowns: Community, Identity, and Development in Nigeria" (Book Review) in *Africa Today*, Volume 49, Number 1, Spring, pp. 115-118.

Renteln, A. D. (2004) *The Cultural Defense*. Oxford, England: Oxford University Press.

Treaty of Paris, 1783 (United States of America).

"United Nations Declaration on the Rights of Indigenous Peoples" (2007) United Nations General Assembly Sixty-first Session, Agenda Item 68, Report of the Human Rights Council.

"United States of America" (2009) *The World Factbook*, Central Intelligence Agency, USA (Online). https://www.cia.gov/library/publications/the-world-factbook/geos/us.html; Internet; accessed March 2009.

Part 2 Summary and Conclusion: Lessons from the Countries Surveyed

Two common threads are apparent among the twelve countries comparatively surveyed in this Part 2 of the book. One, the countries differ in the types of the foreign control systems applicable within them. The differences derive from the variety of erstwhile and current colonizers and occupiers of the different countries as well as the postcolonial changes that each country has made to its system. Two, in many of the countries surveyed, the native systems are officially relegated to inferior roles relative to the foreign systems, especially on important substantive and procedural issues. While recognizing the unique dynamics found in each of the countries, relevant modifications to each country's law and other social control systems and processes are necessary to make them more useful in a postcolony.

Surveys and comparative analyses of the twelve countries provide ideas of dos and don'ts in each country. With necessary modifications, some of these ideas are transferrable to other postcolonies. Nigeria, the primary case study nation, like each of the other postcolonies, can gain several ideas from the other countries on how to reconstruct its postcolonial law and justice system. A few examples are useful here.

One, the Afghan, Iraqi, and Saudi Arabian constitutions declare their respective countries Islamic States. Consequently, all laws are subject to Islam, which is the grundnorm. These constitutional provisions may work for the three countries due to their respective overwhelming Islamic populations. The countries respectively have Muslim populations of 99% for Afghanistan, 97% for Iraq, and 100% for Saudi Arabia (see USA CIA Estimate, 2009). The homogeneous or near-homogeneous religious affiliation among its citizens allows each country to elevate Islam to a State religion and basic source of laws. However, such a provision is unlikely to succeed in a country whose citizens claim a wide variety of religions. In Nigeria, for example, the widely diverse citizen beliefs and faiths mean that no one religion has the capacity (numerical or otherwise) to dominate the other groups in the country. Official religious distribution figures reported for Nigeria by the USA CIA Estimate (2009) are Muslim 50%, Christian 40%, and Indigenous Beliefs 10%. I strongly suspect that far more Nigerians than reported hold Indigenous Beliefs. Unfortunately, many Nigerians habitually label themselves either "Muslim" or "Christian" to appear virtuous. It is fashionable in Nigeria to equate a "Muslim" or "Christian" label with righteousness with little, if any, regard for the quality of the bearer's acts and omissions (Okafọ, 2003b). The frontal brandishing of a privileged religious label (mainly Christianity and Islam) as evidence of piousness is a common fraud found in "developing" postcolonies, such as Nigeria, as well as in their "developed" counterparts, such as the USA.

However, even if one believes the official USA CIA Estimate (2009) figures for Nigeria, it is clear that none of the numerous organized religions in the country has the numerical advantage enjoyed by Islam in Afghanistan, Iraq, or Saudi Arabia. Consequently, an attempt to use official policy to elevate a particular religious category above all the other religious groups in Nigeria will fail due to such a policy's exclusion of a majority of the citizens. Therefore, the *criminal shari'ah* policy in twelve northern states of Nigeria, by which the states have sought to elevate *shari'ah* criminal law above the Nigerian constitution, is not viable. Those twelve states remain parts of the Nigerian federation of thirty-six states. The *Constitution of the Federal Republic of Nigeria, 1999*, apparently in recognition of the diversity of the country's citizens, guarantees every citizen from every part of the country the freedom to move to, live in, and work in, another state and remain protected by the Nigerian constitution. This universal protection for all citizens must be retained in a reconstructed law and justice system.

Two, among the 12 countries surveyed in this Part of the book, Afghanistan, Iraq, and Saudi Arabia subject their respective constitutions to Islam. On the other hand, each of the remaining nine countries (Australia, Brazil, Canada, India, Japan, Kenya, Nigeria, South Africa, and USA) has a supreme constitution, which means that the country's constitution trumps all other laws. A superior constitution makes sense in recognition of the constitution as the national document that binds together all the diverse peoples of a country. This is critical especially for the nation-building and growth of a postcolony. Nigeria, with its three hundred ethnic nations, should emulate the nine countries' secular stand by defining Nigeria as a secular State, in writing and in practice. The Nigerian government should avail itself of every opportunity to reemphasize the secularity of the country and the supremacy of the constitution. It is unfortunate that the defunct President Olusegun Obasanjo government (May 1999-May 2007) shied away from taking steps to enforce the secular mandates of the *Constitution of the Federal Republic of Nigeria, 1999* against Zamfara and the other eleven northern states that implemented *criminal shari'ah* in Nigeria. No one of Nigeria's ethnic nations or religions has the capacity to dominate the other groups in the country, whether socially, culturally, religiously, politically, or otherwise. Well defined, generally accepted constitutional guarantees and duties are vital for justice in a postcolony. Of course, while advocating for a secular constitution, it is important to also consider the totality of the guarantees provided by such a constitution. Even a secular constitution may fail to guarantee enough freedoms and rights.

Three, Kenya offers an example of attempts to reconcile a postcolony's traditions, customs, and native laws (customary law) with its modern constitutional State status and the attendant fundamental rights. The Kenyan constitution requires all the country's courts applying customary law to comply with the constitutional provisions for the "protection of fundamental rights and freedoms of the individual" (Chapter V of the *Constitution of the Republic of Kenya*). By this provision, Kenya appears to understand the need to uphold proper rights standards in a postcolony, even while advancing customary law. However, modern State constitutional rights need not oppose customary law rights and processes. Constitutional rights and customary rights and processes should complement, not conflict with, each other. A postcolony will be positioned to avoid such conflict by taking the following two steps. Step 1, create a truly citizen-driven and citizen-centered constitution. By this, citizens participate in making the constitution and indeed make and give it to themselves or at least consent to it. Also, the constitutional provisions are tailored to the needs and interests of the majority of the citizens, rather than designed to serve the narrow interests and preferences of the privileged class. Step 2, incorporate customary law rights, duties, and processes into the reconstructed postcolonial law and justice system. This action will be carried out with the recognition that customary law rights, duties, and processes are not static; rather they change or should change according to the needs and wishes of the citizens. Steps 1 and 2 would facilitate the removal of outdated, unpopular and anti-human rights customary principles and processes, thus ensuring that the applicable customary law principles and processes are in accord with the contemporary aspirations of the citizens.

In this connection, the lesson from Japan is instructive. Analysis of Japanese social control reveals that neither Nigeria nor any other country needs to abandon its roots (indigenous traditions, customs, and native laws) to develop. The Japanese example shows that the country has maintained its indigenous roots, mainly through its national symbols and citizens' connections to their common heritage, while at the same time pursuing, acquiring, and perfecting various forms of Western technology to improve the lives of Japanese. Thus, a country can make proper and sensible compromises to develop and thrive as a modern State without losing its distinct character, identity, or purpose. Currently, China, to some extent, is following the Japanese model to expand the life options of the immense Chinese population, again without giving up the essential Chinese character.

Four, surveys of Australia, Canada, and the USA reveal that although each country is contemporarily dominated by Westerners, it includes indigenous peoples. Often, the interests of the indigenes are at variance with those of the dominant European immigrants who control each country. One of the stark realities in each of the three countries is the continuing need to recognize, enforce, and protect the rights and processes of the indigenous peoples. The negative implication of the Australian, Canadian, and USA rejection of the 2007 United Nations Charter on the rights of indigenous peoples ("Indigenous Rights Outlined by UN," 2007; "United Nations Declaration on the Rights of Indigenous Peoples," 2007) is that these countries do not regard the indigenous peoples' rights as deserving protection in the modern State. It is important to stress that this is a wrong attitude to have for solving the issues confronting a postcolony. Thus, Nigeria and other postcolonies should avoid reconstructing law and justice or developing at the expense of less powerful, smaller ethnic nations within the country. A policy that neglects or suppresses the freedoms and rights of some ethnic groups in a postcolony is antithetical to growth, advancement, and peace.

Contemporary Nigeria is grappling with the negative consequences of ignoring, marginalizing, and exploiting its Niger Delta region. Crude oil was first discovered in commercial quantity in Nigeria in Oloibiri (a Niger Delta community), in the present Bayelsa State, over 50 years ago. Oil discoveries in other parts of the Niger Delta region soon followed. In time, the region's oil made Nigeria Africa's largest and world's sixth largest producer of crude oil as well as a prominent member of the Organization of Petroleum Exporting Countries (OPEC). Today, crude oil accounts for more than 90% of Nigeria's export revenue. Nonetheless, successive Nigerian leaders have ignored or fought against persuasions to treat the Niger Deltans equitably. The governments have shunned, harassed, imprisoned, and killed many Niger Deltans, including Adaka Boro and Kenule Saro Wiwa, for agitating for their ownership rights and freedoms over their lands. For the Niger Deltans, not much has improved despite their losses.

At present, the Niger Deltans continue to pay the heavy price of oil exploration in their lands and communities, but without the benefit of the proceeds from these explorations. Rather, the proceeds are controlled by outsiders, including non-Nigerians (especially Americans, British, French, Dutch, and other Westerners) that the Nigerian governments have licensed to do so. The proceeds from the oil explorations are diverted to other foreign and Nigerian destinations to be shared. The Nigerian State's share is largely wasted. Considering the obscene amount of money Nigeria has realized from the oil riches, the State has made no meaningful improvement in the citizens' lives since independence in 1960. So, having endured their relegation for decades, Niger Deltans decided to protest and demand to be treated fairly. Nonetheless, the Nigerian State retains its negative attitude to the Deltans' sufferings. The fallouts of these negative State attitudes are lack of peace and breakdown of law and order in the region because the Deltans have resorted to violence to demand fair treatment in their country. A postcolonial national policy that recognizes and enforces the natural rights of the Niger Deltans over their properties, gives the citizens access to, and participation in, government, and generally allows them to control their destiny, will promote the peace, stability, and development of the area and other parts of Nigeria.

The four ideas identified in this section and others discovered in the surveys of the twelve countries in Part II of this book contributed to the law and justice reconstruction recommendations proffered in this book. In the final analysis, what is needed is for each postcolony to *look inward first, look to its neighbors second*, and *look further outward third* to identify, synthesize, and properly use the best systems and elements of law and justice for its social control.

References

Constitution of the Federal Republic of Nigeria, 1999.
Constitution of the Republic of Kenya.
"Indigenous Rights Outlined by UN" (September 13, 2007) in *BBC NEWS* online. See http://news.bbc.co.uk/1/hi/world/6993776.stm; Internet.
Okafọ, N. (2003b) "Religious Labels and Conduct Norms in Government" in *NigeriaWorld* (March 13). See http://nigeriaworld.com/articles/2003/mar/132.html; Internet.
"United Nations Declaration on the Rights of Indigenous Peoples" (2007) United Nations General Assembly Sixty-first Session, Agenda Item 68, Report of the Human Rights Council.
USA CIA Estimate (2009). See https://www.cia.gov/library/publications/the-world-factbook/index.html; Internet.

PART 3
Elements in Law and Justice Reconstruction

Introduction to Part 3

With Nigeria as a case study, Chapters 5, 6, and 7, which constitute Part 3 of this book, offer a critical appraisal of postcolonial law and justice. The chapters examine the challenges of creating a credible, effective, and efficient social control system for a postcolony and recommend solutions to nagging law and justice problems facing the emerging nation. Part 3 examines the following Nigerian component subsystems of law and justice: legislature, law enforcement, courts and tribunals, and correctional institutions. The discussions dwell mainly on *criminal* justice. However, many of the reconstruction elements identified and explained in this Part 3, as in other divisions of this book, apply to *civil* justice as well. Also, recommendations are offered for policy initiatives, changes, programs, and other actions to redesign law and justice in view of the prevailing circumstances. If implemented, the recommendations are expected to alter the focus of law and justice in the relevant country by looking primarily inwards to indigenize law and justice, to create a more effective and efficient social control system. The recommendations offered in this book derive from relevant historical and contemporary experiences. For Nigeria, a proper consideration of the experiences offers a good guide for addressing the present social control problems confronting the country.

In the area of law and justice, the British colonizing authority (mid-19th Century to October 1, 1960) imported the English common law system and made it the "general law" of the new nation, Nigeria. The colonizers did this in spite of the fact that the English common law was alien to Nigerians. The conquerors went further to officially brand the hitherto Nigerian general law "customary law". The new, colonial label ("customary law") was designed to portray the previous general law of the nations of Nigeria as an inadequate, handicapped, and atavistic collection of moral exhortations, loose guidelines, and generally weak norms, which lack the requisite authority and force to regulate relationships in a sophisticated society. Since then, the colonists have consistently interpreted "customary" law as that "other" law-like set of societal regulations (not quite law, certainly not at the level of Western law). Thus, colonial Britain assumed that it was entitled to civilize Nigerians by giving them the "modern" English common law. Despite the British efforts, the English common law remains alien to Nigerians.

The life circumstances in contemporary Nigeria differ markedly from the circumstances before and during the British colonization of Nigeria. Beyond that, however, faced with the English system imposed on them, Nigerians have had to adjust substantially to accord with colonial and postcolonial State demands. Decades after political independence from Britain, Nigerians are still adjusting to the alien commands of English law. The result is that although the lifestyle of the average contemporary Nigerian is mostly indigenous African-based, successive colonial and postcolonial Nigerian governments have regulated that African-based life by means of foreign, English or English-based law and standard. This occurs often without the citizen's consent. Notwithstanding, considerations of the diverse and often conflicting social, cultural, economic, political, and other dynamics in present-day Nigeria require that scientific efforts to restructure the country's law and justice system, such as this book recommends, make necessary compromises to achieve the most reasonably balanced system for effective and efficient social control.

Chapter 5 identifies and analyzes various hindrances (obstacles) to proper law and justice reconstruction in Nigeria. Proper law and justice restoration would yield an indigenized postcolonial system in which the age-old indigenous systems are synthesized and blended with appropriate elements of the foreign systems, exemplified by the English-based common law system, to maximize social control. Further, in the remaining chapters of Part 3, the essential characteristics of law making and law enforcement (Chapter 6), and law application and judgment execution (Chapter 7) in a reconstructed postcolonial law and justice system are considered, and necessary changes are recommended for improved social control.

Chapter 5
Obstacles to Indigenizing Law and Justice: A Case Study of Post-British Nigeria[1]

Chapter Introduction

On October 1, 1960, Nigeria received political independence from Britain. Nonetheless, the British monarchy retained its privileged colonial status by remaining at the helm of Nigeria's government and public affairs. On October 1, 1963, Nigeria declared itself a republic, removed the British monarch as Nigeria's head, and thus severed an important political cord between Nigeria and Britain. Five decades later, and despite "independence" and "republicanism," Nigeria's official law and justice remain largely extensions of British models. Scientific data support the view that Nigeria's indigenous justice and law systems remain viable and effective social control instruments that can be officially discovered and strengthened for modern Nigeria. Based on a mix of the author's personal observations, interviews, and archival information, this chapter analyzes post-independence Nigeria to explain the failure to reform and indigenize the country's law and justice. There is ample evidence to conclude that Nigeria's post-independence leaders and other citizens are not sufficiently committed, if at all, to indigenizing the country's law and justice. The leaders and citizens tend to pursue or support the continuation of colonially imposed policies and programs that strengthen the English law and justice system, while weakening Nigeria's indigenous justice and law systems. A variety of explanations ("obstacles") are identified and scrutinized for the leaders' and citizens' respective idiosyncrasies.

Nigeria: Profile and Issues

Numerous postcolonies in the world continue to grapple with integrating their indigenous (home-grown) systems of law and justice with the foreign counterparts imposed by colonialism and/or occupation (see example, Comaroff and Comaroff, 2006). Nigeria provides a good example of such societies. Even while studying

---

[1] An earlier version of this Chapter was presented by the author at the American Society of Criminology conference, Denver, Colorado, USA, November 18-22, 2003 (see Okereafọezeke, 2003b). Also, an abridged adaptation of the research reported in this Chapter was published as Okereafọezeke (2005) in Fields and Moore's *Comparative and International Criminal Justice: Traditional and Nontraditional Systems of Law and Control.*

the impositions by colonists and occupiers, it is essential to appreciate the role a society may play in continuing to colonize itself, by perpetuating the colonizing policies and programs of their defunct oppressors. It is wondrous that a country fights to be independent and, after receiving it, remands itself to its erstwhile tyrant. For decades, Britain terrorized Nigerians and other Africans through colonization. After a long struggle, Nigeria gained "independence" in 1960. Then, Nigerian leaders decided to stick with Britain in the "British Commonwealth," which in reality extends the British colonizing enterprise beyond the touted 1960 independence exercise. It seems reasonable to conclude that the fundamental British goal (domination) of Nigeria, through colonial or postcolonial policies, remains intact (Okafọ, 2004).

However, in considering the obstacles to managing the conflicting indigenous and foreign systems in Nigeria, the respective roles of the country's successive civilian and military regimes, as well as the functions of the country's educational and other institutions, private sector groups (including professional organizations, such as the Nigerian Bar Association), communities, and individuals, among others, are relevant. It is reasonable to argue that the role of the government in law and justice reform and indigenization trumps the roles of the other stakeholders. This is mainly because the government commands high profile presence and controls the coercive institutions of State as well as the resources that drive their activities. Thus, more than any other stakeholder, the government is strategically positioned to design, implement, and enforce public policies, including those affecting law and justice reform. Consistent with its overwhelming command position and superior control of resources, the government is expected to do more towards law and justice reform and indigenization. However, the relative roles of the civilian and military governments in Nigeria ought also to be considered. But, Nigerians and other observers may be justified to have different expectation levels for the civilian *vis-à-vis* the military regimes.

Postcolonial Nigerian civilian governments owe greater responsibility for law and justice indigenization than do the military juntas. As a result, this chapter focuses on the role of the country's post-independence civilian governments more than that of the military regimes. With eight military governments against four civilian governments, the Nigerian Armed Forces have dominated politics and leadership in the country. The military domination of Nigerian politics and government notwithstanding, the country's civilian governments should be held to a higher standard of responsibility to the citizens than the military. Post-independence Nigerian civilian governments and their leaders are: Prime Minister Tafawa Balewa (1960-1966), President Shehu Shagari (1979-1983), President Olusegun Obasanjo (1999-2007), and President Umaru Yar'Adua (2007-). The following are the country's military regimes and the main actors: Generals Aguiyi Ironsi (1966), Yakubu Gowon (1966-1975), Murtala Mohammed (1975-1976), Olusegun Obasanjo (1976-1979), Muhammadu Buhari (1984-1985), Ibrahim

Babangida (1985-1993),[2] Sani Abacha (1993-1998), and Abdulsalami Abubakar (1998-1999). Even with the legendary thievery, frauds, and imperfections besetting elections in Nigeria, the country's civilian governments may be able to claim marginally greater citizen consent as justification for the governments. Conversely, the military governments were dictatorships always overtly imposed by forces of arms, with many of the power usurpations occurring through bloody coups d'etat. The civilian governments' claim to greater citizen consent entitles Nigerians to expect more responsibility and accountability from these governments in various aspects of the country's life, including law and justice transformation.

The subject matter of this chapter – the obstacles to reconstructing and indigenizing law and justice in Nigeria and strategies for overcoming the obstacles – relates directly to the position of Nigeria's indigenous justice and law systems in the country's post-independence structure. The status of Nigeria's native justice and law systems has been an issue since the British colonization of Nigeria. Decades after Nigeria attained political independence from Britain, the status question has remained critical, even if Nigerian post-independence leaders have swept it under the proverbial carpet. During its colonization of Nigeria, Britain sought to entrench the British ideas and standards of law and justice in Nigeria. They succeeded, at least officially. Thus, post-independence official Nigerian ideas and principles of law and justice are little more than extensions of their British precursors. This is despite the irrefutable scientific conclusion by many researchers that most Nigerians, privately, unofficially, or informally regulate their lives and manage grievances, conflicts, and disputes through their indigenous systems of justice, social control, and law, rather than through the imposed English system (see as examples, Okereafǫezeke, 1996; 2002; Elechi, 2006). After carefully evaluating scientific data, Okereafǫezeke (2002) concludes, *inter alia* (at p. 188):

> ... Nigeria's native justice systems work. Based on the illustrations that the Igbo[3] system provides, Nigeria's native systems are effective and efficient partners in the administration of justice in the country. The greatest obstacles to the native systems' assumption of their deserved and rightful position of primacy in Nigerian justice, law, and social control are negative official policies and attitudes. Since British colonial rule over Nigeria and up to the present post-independence government, there has been no meaningful effort to rescue and indigenize Nigeria's systems of justice and law. In particular, Nigerian post-independence leaders have lacked the nation-building vision, the intelligence, and the political will to reverse the present duplicate judicial path instituted for us by colonial Britain. Are we supposed to ignore or relegate our native and long-practiced systems of justice, social control, and law and continue to play

---

2   General Babangida imposed Ernest Shonekan's "interim" government on Nigeria in 1993 before being forced from power.

3   The Igbos (or Ibos) are located mainly in the southeast of Nigeria. With a population of roughly 30 million, they are one of the country's three largest ethnic nations.

by the rules imposed on us by our defunct colonizer? The British imposition of the English legal and justice system on Nigeria happened by means of political expedience. Thus, the reversal of the obnoxious British policy will involve Nigeria's contemporary political climate and the players.

This chapter is based on data and conclusions that show that average Nigerians tend to rely on their traditions, customs, and indigenous laws more than the British-imposed English law and justice, which Nigeria's post-independence governments have sustained and emphasized over Nigeria's native systems. It is safe to conclude that Nigerians would not rely so heavily on their traditions, customs, and native laws to manage cases if they did not believe in their indigenous systems and processes. And, Oli (1994), after comparing the relative effectiveness of "Traditional" and "Christianized" Igbo control systems on behavior, concludes: "Information tends to support the original hypothesis that traditional Igbo social control systems are more compelling [than Christian social control systems] on behavior" (at p. 29). At this juncture, it should be asked: What types of grievances, conflicts, and disputes do Nigerian indigenous law and justice systems manage?

Nigerians' reliance on their traditions, customs, and native laws to manage cases is not limited to minor grievances, conflicts, or disputes. It extends to very serious, complex cases, as demonstrated in Okereafoezeke (1996; 2002; Elechi 2006). The case studies contributing to this chapter range from those dealing with relatively minor issues, such as ostracism, to those concerning more serious violations like assault, theft, land and land-related issues, breach of contract, trespass, rape, incest, and homicide, among others (Okereafoezeke, 1996; 2002). In short, the data demonstrate that any case – civil or criminal, major or minor – may be satisfactorily managed unofficially (that is, outside the law and justice systems of the official federal and state governments) *via* a Nigerian indigenous justice and law system. Also, there are many avenues for case management in the indigenous Nigerian system. The case management paths are often hierarchical, evidencing sophistication and organization in these systems.

The research activities leading to this chapter were based on a combination of methods: face-to-face interviews of indigenous, unofficial as well as official government justice personnel, such as judges, lawyers, and other actors in the native and official government justice systems in parts of Nigeria. Other available persons, that is non-personnel in either justice system, whom the author believed could provide useful information, were also interviewed. Other research methods employed include archival searches of related documents, personal observations of the native and official government justice systems by the author, and the administration of a written questionnaire to law students at a prominent Nigerian university, located in the southeast of the country.

On the strength of the findings, along with the conclusions from previous and current research on the hindrances to indigenizing Nigerian law and justice, the following four main questions guide the discussions in this and the remaining chapters of this book. One, why has official postcolonial Nigeria retained and emphasized the British ideas and principles of law and justice (English law) at the expense of Nigeria's native justice and law systems, even though the native justice and law systems, unlike the English law and justice system, are based on Nigerians' experiences, lifestyles, practices, and aspirations? Two, why does this situation persist despite the official declarations of law reforms by several commissions, both *ad hoc* and standing, at the state and national levels? Three, what changes (systemic, substantive, procedural, etc.) should be made to Nigerian law and justice to transform the system for contemporary and future uses? Four, what roles have average Nigerians, as individuals and in groups, played or should play to ensure the indigenization of Nigerian law and justice to bring them in line with Nigerians' needs and expectations? Some of the analyses and answers to these questions emphasize the structural dislocations engendered by the British impositions on Nigeria, while other assessments and responses demonstrate the critical roles of the idiosyncrasies of Nigerian post-independence leaders on this issue.

Identifying and Analyzing the Obstacles to Indigenizing Law and Justice in Nigeria

There are varied issues (or "obstacles") contributing to the continuing lack of appropriate reform for law and justice indigenization in post-independence Nigeria. "Appropriate reform for law and justice indigenization in post-independence Nigeria" refers to designing and effecting needed changes to the British-inflicted substantive and procedural law and justice in Nigeria. Appropriate changes should reflect Nigerians' post-British needs, preferences, and aspirations. The necessary law and justice indigenizing transformation efforts should be based on, and exude, in theory and in practice, Nigerians' origins, cultures, languages, beliefs, customs, traditions, historical circumstances, preferences, and aspirations. These essential home-grown ingredients ought to be entrenched both in the substantive and procedural aspects of post-independence Nigerian justice and law. Thus, the essential ingredients should form the foundation for post-independence Nigerian law and justice. However, post-independence law and justice reconstruction should be planned and executed with sufficient broad-mindedness to borrow from other societies to supplement the indigenous Nigerian systems. Anything less is not good enough (see Okereafọezeke, 2002, pp. 18-20).

Research shows that the law and justice situation in contemporary Nigeria does not reflect the appropriate level of indigenization needed in this post-independence era. The following issues or "obstacles" account for this situation. For clarity, the obstacles are categorized into three broad groups: Government-Centered Obstacles, Profession-Centered Obstacles, and Citizen-Centered Obstacles. Some of the obstacles tend to overlap. However, each obstacle is categorized and discussed in only one group in which, based on the data, the obstacle appears to be most commonly located.

Government-Centered Obstacles

The following eight obstacles are found mostly among the official Local, State, and Federal governments and their personnel.

One, Unpatriotic political leadership/Lack of proper nation-building vision The data show this impediment to be one of the most notorious reasons for Nigeria's inability to effect appropriate reform to indigenize the country's law and justice five decades after political independence from Britain. A survey of the post-independence history of Nigeria shows that the importance of the patriotism and nation-building phenomena cannot be overstated. I have had occasion in another publication to analyze the patriotism and nation-building credentials of some Nigerian leaders, particularly President Olusegun Obasanjo, May 1999-May 2007 (Okafọ, 2003a). The indigenization issue under consideration in this book gives rise to the same elements as those addressed in Okafọ (2003a). Thus, relevant portions of that publication are reproduced as follows. The article titled "Burden of Patriotism: Obasanjo, Leadership, and Nigerian Nation-Building," states in part:

> ... a patriot in President Obasanjo's position at this critical stage of Nigeria's existence would have led Nigerians much more purposefully and with a view to attaining nationhood. The way to do so is to be and remain faithful to [the] crucial characteristics of a patriot. To be patriotic is to be devoted. Regarding a country – especially a country like Nigeria that purports to be building toward a nation – a patriot is a person that is loyal and unwavering toward that country's overall best interests. Thus, a patriot recognizes and accepts that there are, and will be, many circumstances in which a person's or sub-group's well-being may conflict with the collective good. Even in such prevalent situations, a patriot resolves each inconsistency in favor of the collective interests of the country. The patriot renders individual and subgroup's advantages or perceived gains, however attractive they may be, subservient to the collective national welfare.

> From the perspective of political leadership, it seems that on every issue that confronts Nigeria a straightforward way to determine what is in the country's overall best interests is to ask: What official response will strengthen rather than weaken Nigeria? Associated with this question are other related, equally important questions, such as: What response will increase the citizens' sense of belonging and confidence in the country? What response will most encourage the citizens to make their best individual and collective contributions toward nation-building? What response will demonstrate to the citizens that the country's leaders have a purposeful vision of the country's future and that these leaders are honestly pursuing that vision?

... Patriotism is burdensome. It requires passionate and honest observance of, and adherence to, the innate (self) and societal control mechanisms to resist the temptations of behaving shortsightedly to serve personal or subgroup interests. Instead, patriotism evokes steadfast focus on the long-term positive goals and overriding interests of the country. In Nigeria, patriotism should capture the great need to establish strong foundations for building the country into a nation. Such structures are embarrassingly lacking in this country that has so much and yet offers its citizens so little. In the present state of affairs, even hope in the Nigerian enterprise is in short supply because the leaders are very good at pontificating about the need for hope without giving the average citizen concrete reasons for hope. President Obasanjo in particular is good at exhorting the citizens to pray and to hope for a greater Nigeria. But, as Martin Luther put it, "prayer is a necessary supplement to human effort, but a very dangerous alternative". Unless Obasanjo takes the necessary practical steps to strengthen Nigeria by laying strong foundations for nationhood, Nigeria will remain an ad hoc contraption, which the British colonists created to serve their desires and which now serves the desires of Nigeria's post-independence predatory leaders.

President Obasanjo exemplifies the dearth of post-independence patriotic and visionary leadership necessary to midwife proper reforms to indigenize law and justice in Nigeria. Through his eight-year presidency, Obasanjo took numerous steps, including ignoring judicial decisions and directives, usurping judicial powers, misusing and abusing police powers, and illegally protecting his friends, acquaintances, and political associates suspected or accused of corruption and other crimes. Obasanjo's handling of the 2007 general elections in Nigeria, which he infamously dubbed "a do or die affair" for him and his ruling PDP political party highlights his lack of patriotism and nation-building vision. Obasanjo disgracefully and criminally presided over a massive robbery of the citizens' votes to entrench his incompetent PDP candidates despite Nigerians' preferences and the best interest of the country (Okafọ, 2007). A leader who was so entrenched in destroying or bending the rule of law could neither be trusted nor expected to strengthen law and justice by reforming the system (Okafọ, 2007). Such leadership deficiency is rampant at all of Nigeria's three levels of official government: local, state, and federal. President Umaru Yar'Adua, whom Obasanjo illegally installed as the former's replacement in 2007, has largely continued with the Obasanjo ways despite promises to the contrary. But, the strategic position of the president's office makes presidential participation in such unpatriotic activities particularly dangerous and antithetical to nation-building. It should also be pointed out that the few leaders that appear to be aware of the need to indigenize law and justice in Nigeria continue with the *status quo* ostensibly because of the advantages they derive from it, some of which are discussed below.

Two, Lack of political will to change the status quo The data show that another common feature of Nigeria's post-independence leadership, regarding the need to indigenize Nigerian law and justice, is the leaders' unwillingness to formulate and execute an indigenization policy for fear that such a policy would be unpopular among powerful and influential Nigerians. The indigenization policy at issue would retrace, adopt, modify as necessary, and use indigenous Nigerian law and justice for social control rather than continue with the prevailing system imposed by colonial Britain. Fear of losing political power is a key reason for avoiding such a policy, even though research shows that it would be very popular among average Nigerians. The Nigerian elite's control, albeit illegitimate, of the country's politics and government is well documented. Since independence, both the civilian and military elite in the country have succeeded in taking and keeping power, often by force of arms or election rigging, and excluding average Nigerians from the process of choosing the country's leaders. But, why would indigenization of Nigerian law and justice be unpopular among powerful and influential Nigerians? The answer lies partly in the advantages accruing to the country's leaders and other powerful and influential persons, and the widespread ineffectiveness of English law and justice in Nigeria.

Three, Widespread ineffectiveness of English law and justice   As in much of Africa, social control among Nigerians who subscribe to the country's indigenous systems is predicated on the strong beliefs in the omniscience and omnipresence of God, worshipped through various traditional media. Most believers in the indigenous systems accept that God is all-knowing. Thus, God will identify and punish a transgressor even if mortals are unaware of the transgression or unable to identify the culprit or prove the wrongdoing. This is because God is present everywhere, at all times. And so, based on this conviction, there is no escape from accountability for one's conduct. A guilty person would voluntarily identify himself or herself as responsible for a wrongdoing without waiting for the system to do so, and would come forward even if humans are unable to make the identification. For those citizens faithful to the indigenous systems, these beliefs discourage the believers from committing crimes. Therefore, all these lead to increased social control by crime and deviance avoidance. And, where crime or deviance occurs, there is a high likelihood that it would be solved.

Oli (1994) tests the effects of indigenous Nigerian beliefs on social control. The test compares the following two groups of Igbos (a southeast Nigerian nation): "Traditional Igbos" (that is, Igbos that believe in the indigenous religions, customs, and traditions) and "Christianized Igbos" (Igbos that subscribe to the Christian belief). The study also compares the social control elements of the Traditional system and the Christian system. While pointing out that the official Christian-based law and justice system (English system) is emphasized over the indigenous system, the study concludes:

> The fear of spirits is gradually replaced by belief in expiation of sins, and an increased resort to devious means for achieving greatness. Control by tradition is replaced by police control. The English legal system notion that one is presumed

innocent until detected and proven guilty, replaces fear of the omnipresence of spirits, admission of guilt and certainty of punishment ... Information tends to support the original hypothesis that traditional Igbo social control systems are more compelling [than Christian social control systems] on behavior" (Oli, 1994, at pp. 26 and 29).

Thus, it seems good policy to place greater value on indigenous law and social control systems and processes to allow them credible and deserved roles in contemporary Nigeria. Without a comprehensive social control mechanism for Nigeria, such as the country's indigenous systems offered before British colonization, crime is likely to increase among the Christianized Igbos and other Nigerians (see Okafor, 1978; also Ogbalu, 1979).

Thus, Oli (1994) demonstrates that many, perhaps most, Nigerians follow their traditions, customs, and native laws in their private and public endeavors. This point is supported by previous research, such as Okereafoezeke (1996). See also Okereafoezeke (2002; 2005); Elechi (2006); and Okafo (2006). However, many elite Nigerians, who dominate the country's politics and leadership, prefer to maintain the existing British-compelled English law and justice system because, under the English system, the elite escape punishment easier for crimes than under the indigenous justice and law systems. There are generally held perceptions that justice under the English system is slow or unavailable to numerous Nigerians, that it is often inaccurate because it may be visited on an innocent person while the guilty escapes sanction, that it is not stiff enough and as such a person contemplating a crime or deviance can afford to take the risk of being identified and punished if the reward accruing from the crime or deviance outweighs the punishment.[4]

Nigerian leaders and elite are good at concealing crimes and deviances. Where privileged criminal suspects are identified and tried under the prevailing English system, many escape with little or no punishment, while being left to enjoy the fruits of their transgressions. The endless deluge of former and current public office holders suspected or accused of stealing mind-boggling amounts of public funds but who have escaped punishment inevitably leads average Nigerians to conclude that the official justice system is incapable of advancing the interests of the generality of Nigerians. Thus, the English law and justice system is perceived as an ineffective social control mechanism in the country. It is perceived, for good

---

4 The issue of "stiffness" of punishment in this circumstance refers to a punishment's direct reach. That is, the extent to which a criminal and/or the persons around the criminal suffer as a direct consequence of his/her crime. Thus, punishment by an official, English-style court has limited reach and is therefore less stiff because only the offender is punished directly. On the other hand, punishment imposed by an indigenous justice process has wider and farther reach and is thus stiffer. It is generally understood that the supernatural is capable of visiting, and often visits, punishment on the individual offender *as well as* his/her family members and close relatives, and may extend the punishment to the other members of the offender's community.

reason, as a justice system designed to protect the privileged, well-off at the expense of the others. Many Nigerians, especially those who believe in the superior efficacy of the indigenous systems, are convinced that the country's leaders would not get away with their crimes and deviances if the country's law and justice system was based on the native institutions, rather than on English institutions.

Four, Lack of accountability   There is generally a very low level of responsibility by Nigerian public officials towards the citizens. Were it not so, the leaders would not be able to get away with a fraction of the things with which they have been able to get away since independence. Analysis of Nigerian politics and government since independence shows that most of the country's elite and government leaders do not regard the average citizens as deserving of sufficient consideration or influence. Thus, the elite and leaders do not answer to the citizens. Nor do the leaders and elite believe that the average citizens can hold the former liable for bad public policies. In a true democracy, in which citizens have the electoral capacity to unseat a government or leader pursuing unpopular policies, the leaders usually try to formulate policies and programs consistent with the citizens' wishes. That has not been the situation in Nigeria which, since independence, has not experienced a true democratic government.

Rather, all of the country's governments since then have been military and civilian dictatorships. The military regimes have been results of *coups d'etat*. Although the civilian governments have purported to be democracies, in reality they have been imposed on Nigerians through rigged elections, such that the citizens' votes have not counted for much, if anything, in choosing the country's leaders. To illustrate, in the 2007 general elections, President Olusegun Obasanjo and his corrupt acolytes (Maurice Iwu, Chairman of INEC and Sunday Ehindero, Inspector-General of Police, among others) depraved the nation's democratic efforts and resources to a personal power elongation enterprise for Obasanjo. In doing so, these perverse occupants of positions of trust contemptuously ignored the citizens and their votes, thus illustrating the leaders' impunity (Okafọ, 2007). Two years after their crimes against Nigerians, Obasanjo, Iwu, Ehindero, and others carry on as if they did nothing wrong. None of them has been made to answer for his/her crimes. As a matter of fact, Iwu remains in office as the nation's "chief electoral officer," because those he installed in offices in 2007 continue to allow him to operate with impunity.

It bears recognition that the Nigerian society is not alone in feeding the postcolonial Nigerian leaders' lack of accountability. These leaders operate with such impunity partly because the international community overlooks or glosses over the bankrupt leaders' iniquities. The international oversights and misrepresentations are not limited to so-called rogue regimes. Instead, otherwise respected countries and international institutions encourage the Nigerian leaders' transgressions. It is startling that the United Nations (UN) Secretary General, Ban Ki Moon, appointed the same Obasanjo who raped the rule of law and democracy in Nigeria to be the UN special envoy to the Great Lakes of Africa, to negotiate peace and reconcile the warring parties. Obasanjo has since taken the position and jets across the world parroting constitutionality, the rule of law, peaceful coexistence, and compromise as essential ingredients of a stable and progressive society. But, it must be asked: How do Obasanjo's antecedents qualify him for this UN position? Ban Ki Moon appointed Obasanjo to lead the international efforts to build and strengthen the rule of law despite his notorious perversion of the rule of law in Nigeria between 1999 and 2007 (Okafọ, 2007), the consequences of which remain with us. No wonder then that Nigerians and other Africans in London, England, protested against Obasanjo and held him hostage when he delivered a speech at the London School of Economics in March 2009 (see "Obasanjo is Smuggled into LSE Event Through Back Door" 2009).

Five, Inadequate knowledge of the efficacy and potentials of the indigenous justice and law systems   Some of the Government-Centered Obstacles identified in this research, such as the absence of political will to change the status quo and taking advantage of the ineffectiveness of Nigeria's official English law and justice system, assume that the protagonists (government officials and other elite) recognize the relative disadvantage to which Nigeria's indigenous justice systems are subjected in the country's official structure. This assumption is highly questionable, if not false. The data strongly suggest that some of the leaders and elite are unaware or only minimally aware of the relative strength and effectiveness of the indigenous justice and law systems in general social control. Also, the leaders and elite seem unaware that despite the strength of the indigenous systems, they are officially subjected to the English-style law and justice system. The limited knowledge by the leaders and elite partly informs their lack of action to indigenize law and justice in Nigeria.

Many contemporary Nigerian leaders and elite – indeed many contemporary Nigerians – whether educated in the country or abroad, have not been sufficiently informed about the indigenous systems and processes, especially concerning law and justice. In Nigeria, pre-primary, primary, secondary, and tertiary schools curricula are embarrassingly devoid of indigenous ideas and solutions to local problems. Instead, the designers and the implementers of the curricula usually focus primarily or exclusively on foreign (usually British, American, and other Western) ideas and ideals for solutions to local issues (Okereafọezeke, 2002). The drought of knowledge about indigenous justice and law, in particular, and the unwillingness to advance the indigenous systems and processes is astonishing. Even well educated Nigerian leaders and elite fare no better than the less educated. In fact, a strong case can be made that the educated and elite deserve more blame for the official degradation of Nigeria's indigenous law and justice. The educated and elite often feel more comfortable promoting the foreign ideas as way of demonstrating their superior intelligence and knowledge over the less educated (Okafọ, 2004).

Six, Neocolonialist craving for foreign ideas and ideals Consider the following two factors. One, there is insufficient education in Nigeria about the availability and efficacy of the country's native justice and law systems. Two, there are imperialist teachings that the native systems are outdated and irrelevant while the imposed British models represent modernity. The two factors have combined to give rise to neocolonialist reasoning, action, and omission by many Nigerian leaders and elite. These leaders and elite demonstrate little or no original thought (Onyechi, 1975, at p. 270). Rather, they support and encourage what I have described elsewhere as "Substitutive Interaction" (Okereafoezeke, 2002, at p. 19). Substitutive Interaction results in the supplanting of a preexisting system or process with another, usually foreign, system or process. The supplanting may be done by a foreign or domestic power, with or without force. However, colonization provides a prominent example of Substitutive Interaction. By this, a colonizing or occupying foreign power substitutes a colonized population's native laws and customs with the colonizer's legal system, such as Britain did in Nigeria and many other societies. Substitutive Interaction would also happen where a domestic government supersedes an indigenous system of justice and law with a foreign system.[5] Thus, with the prevailing Substitutive official policies and programs, Nigeria's indigenous law and justice systems are neglected while the foreign, English system is promoted (see Okereafoezeke, 2002, pp. 18-20).

Seven, Anomic leadership and a confused society Anomie equals absence of norm, or confusion about proper conduct rules. The prevailing situation in Nigeria where the country's leaders pursue and emphasize an alien law and justice system even though, as research shows, most Nigerians think primarily of managing their cases traditionally according to their customs and native laws, creates confusion in the country. It is difficult to be certain of the guiding rules of conduct when the official governments' laws and rules of conduct differ substantially from the citizens' traditions, customs, and indigenous laws. In this situation, what are officially proscribed conflict with accepted and expected practices among the people. Thus, a citizen who complies with an indigenous law may be arrested, tried, convicted, and punished under the official English system without regard to the actor's traditions, customs, and native laws. Apart from confusing the population, the situation ensures disrespect and contempt for the official system. The anomic condition, unless corrected, could destabilize the country to a point where neither the English nor indigenous system would be capable of controlling the population.

Eight, Lack of continuity in governments, public policies, and programs Since the end of British colonial rule over Nigeria, Nigeria has consistently failed to establish stability in its governments and public affairs. Several attempts to streamline

---

5 Contrast two other kinds of interaction: Cooperative Interaction and Pluralistic Interaction (Okereafoezeke, 2002, pp. 18-20).

election procedures have failed woefully. Almost all elections organized in Nigeria to choose presidents, governors, senators, representatives, etc. have ended in chaos, with one or more political parties rigging the elections and installing its candidates into offices regardless of the votes. The widely publicized travesty called the 2007 general elections is instructive. This and similar bastardizations of electoral processes have led to coups d'etat in postcolonial Nigeria. Thus, it has been impossible to know with reasonable certainty how long a particular government will be in power. Also, in most cases, the incoming government removes all the major impressions that the previous regime made on the population and replaces those imprints with the current government's preferences.

The following is an example of ill-advised and ill-considered changes in public affairs. The elected Governor of Osun State (one of Nigeria's 36 states), *by decree*, scrapped all the customary courts in the state "with immediate effect ... as the governor's *pronouncement* means that they have been scrapped completely" (Adeoye, 2003, p. 1).[6] Of course state law had created the customary courts, yet the governor was able to annul them by simply pronouncing accordingly. There is no evidence that the governor consulted with, or relied on the recommendation of, the state legislature, nor is there indication that the governor sought and received the citizens' support for scrapping the courts. An important matter like that should first have been submitted to the state legislature for debate and vote or to the citizens for debate and referendum. Considering the manner in which the customary courts were scrapped, what will prevent a future government in Osun State from restoring the scrapped courts? Imagine the resources that would be expended to develop a new customary court structure and personnel.

To be sure, even stable democracies experience shifts in policies and programs between governments, especially where a different political party or group takes over the government. However, there are three main factors that distinguish Nigeria's experiences. One, as mentioned, because of the unstable political culture, it is impossible to predict with reasonable certainty when a change of government will happen in Nigeria. Two, an incoming government usually does not derive its power from the citizens. In fact, widespread electoral malpractices ensure that the incoming regime takes over power in spite of Nigerians' expressed wishes. Three, when a new government changes preexisting policies and programs, the leadership hardly abides by the rule of law as a controlling standard. In a stable democracy, a new government that seeks to change a policy or program of a previous government has to ensure that the rule of law is maintained because the procedures for getting into and remaining in public offices contain basic guarantees for the citizens, no matter who occupies a public office. In a stable democracy, the citizens' constitutional and legal rights against the government and its officials are guaranteed and reasonably enforced.

All these add up to the importance of the citizens' interests and the need for the government of formulate policies and execute programs to address those interests.

---

6   Italics added by this author for emphasis.

Specifically, in a stable democracy, government officials always have to be wary of the citizens because of the latter's voting power that could be used against the incumbent administration. Such basic guarantees are pitifully absent in Nigeria. Example, the country's basic document (the *Constitution of the Federal Republic of Nigeria, 1999*) was really created by a few military and civilian power usurpers led by General Abdulsalami Abubakar and foisted on the rest of the country. Because the constitution-making process has already weakened the citizens, it is easy for the government of the day to ignore or abuse those aspects of the constitution it does not like with little or no consequence. Thus, the citizens are not in a (strong) position to force the government to develop and implement sound policies and programs.

Profession-Centered Obstacle

This obstacle is found mainly in the professional groups, especially law professional bodies and their members.

Intellectual and professional inadequacies of lawyers and judges This impediment captures a shortfall in the levels of intellectualism and professionalism exhibited by many Nigerian lawyers and judges, especially those that make and implement policies and standards. Many Nigerian lawyers and judges, in the practice of law and education of prospective lawyers, defer too much to the English legal system, such that in fundamental terms Nigeria's official law is little more than an extension of the British model. There is grossly insufficient effort to build a legal system, and practice law, based on Nigeria's indigenous systems and unique circumstances. Gower (cited in Onyechi, 1975, at p. 270) describes this shortage of creativity as a "besetting sin" of legal education and practice, thus:

> … the British trained African lawyer appears to believe that English law is the embodiment of everything that is excellent even when applied to totally different social and economic conditions. Certain it is that no one who studies criminal law from Mr. Seidman's Casebook is likely to continue to believe that English criminal law makes complete sense when applied to African conditions. [African lawyers] merely substitute for a study of English law, a study of Nigerian, Ghanaian, Tanzanian, Zambian or Malawi law. The received criminal law of all these countries is basically English criminal law. The statutory provisions in any of them closely resemble those in others. Yet at present relevant decisions in one are rarely cited in the others because the lawyers know English decisions best, their local decisions next best, and those of African states not at all.

Gower's statement remains a substantially accurate reflection of the Nigerian situation. The country's leaders' and elite's limited knowledge of the efficacy of Nigeria's indigenous justice and law systems in turn fertilizes the country's unbridled craving for foreign ideas and ideals.

In the warped belief "that English law is the embodiment of everything that is excellent even when applied to totally different social and economic conditions" (Gower, cited in Onyechi, 1975, at p. 270), many Nigerian lawyers and judges routinely rely on and cite English laws and decisions to decide even cases that Nigeria's indigenous customs and traditions exhaustively cover. And, it is unacceptable to claim that the Nigerian customs and traditions are not known. Most of them are widely known and available. What is required of a law teacher or practitioner is to make reasonable effort to identify those relevant provisions and offer them as guides in deciding cases. To do so, however, the law teacher or practitioner has to first overcome the self-condemnatory belief and attitude that instructs them to look to England for solutions to problems in Nigeria.

Much like their reliance on English laws and decisions, these Nigerian lawyers and judges dress like English lawyers and judges even in the generally unfriendly Nigerian hot climate. The respective dress codes for Nigerian lawyers and judges and their English counterparts are strikingly similar: black trousers, black shoes, white shirt, black tie, black suit, with wig and gown (for men), black skirt and black suit on top of white blouse, black shoes, with wig and gown (for women). These layers of clothes are bound to generate more heat and make the Nigerian lawyer or judge uncomfortable. Contrast the Nigerian lawyers and judges' dress code with the much simpler, less strict dressing styles for lawyers and judges in the USA. Note that, like Nigeria, the USA is a former British colony. Yet, lawyers and judges in the USA are not required to wear wig and gown even though the USA generally has much colder weather conditions than Nigeria.

It is fitting to add a personal anecdote here. While I was a law student at the University of Nigeria, many of the lecturers in law strongly admonished law students to "dress appropriately," meaning dress up in suit and tie to lectures, school events, and other public activities. Some lecturers went as far as threatening the students with sanction for "inappropriate dressing." On one occasion, shortly after graduation, I went to the University with a colleague. As we walked from our car to a building, "dressed appropriately," a student who saw us in suits and ties in the blazing tropical sun, lamented in Igbo language: "Hei, na anwụ a n'ine!" ("Hey, even in this blazing sun!"). The student felt sorry for us because it was too hot for us to be dressed in suit and tie. Note that that day's weather condition was typical in the Nigerian environment, at least for the season. The student's expression of concern summed it up for my colleague and me. We felt foolish and tried to laugh it off. The larger point is that it is at least unwise for a person to make himself or herself so uncomfortable by dressing up in foreign attire, which bears little, if any, relationship with the borrower's local environment. Yet, lawyers and judges in Nigeria do this everyday. An important question to be asked in this connection is: Will a good law student, lawyer, or judge cease to be so if he or she dresses in indigenous Nigerian attire?

Citizen-Centered Obstacles

The following two obstacles arise from the general citizens' actions and omissions, rather than the conducts of governments and other groups.

One, Citizens' acquiescence   There is an insidious acquiescent culture in Nigeria. It is such that the average citizen does not want, or is not sufficiently enlightened, to ask questions about who runs the country and how public policies are made and implemented. Asking such questions should be every citizen's business, rather than the responsibility of a few "critics". Unfortunately, however, Nigerian leaders and elite have mostly alienated the citizens from the public processes, and the citizens have generally imbibed the exclusion and, strangely enough, accepted it. The absorption and acceptance have led to a largely passive citizenry, even among the educated. There subsists in Nigeria a negative culture in which the average citizens do not sufficiently demand and insist on the best policies and programs from their leaders. Most governments, especially those that are corrupt – as most of Nigeria's governments have been – would take advantage of an acquiescent citizenry. That is exactly what happens in Nigeria. Policies and programs that would open up the system for greater citizen participation, benefit the citizens, and strengthen the country – such as the indigenization of Nigerian law and justice – are not pursued partly because the citizens do not demand that their leaders and elite actualize such ideas.

Two, Uninformed logics of "education," "native customs and traditions," and "modernity"   Data show that many Nigerians, not just the leaders and other elite, hold the view that a person cannot be educated or modern if he or she believes in, or practices, Nigeria's traditions, customs, and native laws. As mentioned earlier, it is particularly troubling to note that this view is commonly found among the educated citizens, probably even more so than among the uneducated population. The following example is noteworthy. At the November 2003 American Society of Criminology Conference in Denver, Colorado, USA, where I presented an earlier version of this chapter, a Nigerian-born, US-based Ph.D. holder and university lecturer of criminal justice co-presented another paper. In his contribution, he argued that Nigeria's traditions, customs, and indigenous laws should be discarded because they impede efforts to build a united, progressive, and modern nation. In their place, he suggested, the English law and justice system should be used exclusively for social control in Nigeria. I challenged his idea by pointing out that there is abundant scientific evidence that Nigeria's traditions, customs, and native laws are working quite well and effectively for social control in the country, and that it is safe to state that most Nigerians follow their indigenous systems, rather than the English system, and that on those bases, it would be most irresponsible and counterproductive to seek to do away with the native systems and pretend that they no longer exist. Nonetheless, he was obstinate in his position.

I am baffled that I have to defend Nigeria's traditions, customs, and native laws, especially to an educated Nigerian. However, that happens fairly frequently. Persons who generate the need for such defense have somehow reached the warped conclusion that an "educated" person living in a "modern" society cannot also believe in, or practice, his or her traditions, customs, and indigenous laws. That is a false and unfortunate belief. Even the so-called major law and justice civilizations of the world, such as the "common law," which is the basis of English law and justice, originated from the traditions, customs, and native laws of English tribes. There is therefore the need for a rethink in the way many Nigerians look at the role of the country's indigenous systems and institutions *vis-à-vis* their foreign counterparts. At present, the foreign systems and institutions enjoy too many advantages over their indigenous (Nigerian) equivalents.

Chapter Summary and Conclusion

Five decades after political independence from Britain, there has been no meaningful effort to effect appropriate reform to indigenize law and justice in Nigeria. Appropriate law and justice restructuring would officially acknowledge, encourage, and strengthen Nigeria's traditions, customs, and indigenous laws as th primary means of regulating relationships, thus indigenizing law and justice in the country. The argument that Nigeria's law and justice should be reorganized to ensure the primacy of the country's traditions, customs, and native laws is based on scientific research activities, which show the efficacy of the country's customary laws. Research also shows that the citizens tend to regulate their affairs more on the basis of their customary laws than the English law imposed by colonial Britain. Despite the widely documented effectiveness and efficiency of Nigeria's indigenous laws and customs, the country's successive post-independence governments and leaders have failed to adequately support the home-grown systems. Instead, these governments and leaders faithfully continue with the British colonial policies and programs that entrenched English law and justice as the dominant system in Nigeria.

The data studied for this chapter reveal several explanations for the continuation of the British colonial policies and programs in Nigeria. The explanations ("obstacles"), as presented in this chapter, were categorized into three: Government-Centered, Profession-Centered, and Citizen-Centered Obstacles. Altogether, eleven obstacles were identified. They were distributed among the three identified categories, depending on where research shows each obstacle to be concentrated. Without downplaying the respective roles of the other two categories of hindrances, the Government-Centered Obstacles should be treated as the most consequential because of the enormous powers and resources that the Nigerian governments at the local, state, and national levels command. With their overwhelming powers and resources, the governments can make or break an issue, such as law and justice indigenization, depending on how they choose to respond to the subject. However, it seems that any meaningful effort to reform and indigenize Nigerian law and justice as discussed in this chapter must begin with a full recognition of the need for such action. Thus, Nigerian leaders' understanding of this need and the leaders' willingness to develop and carry out such a revolutionary venture are central variables necessary to effect indigenization.

Finally, the importance of reforming and indigenizing law and justice for post-independence Nigeria cannot be overstated. For more effective and efficient social control in Nigeria, the country's official governments need to preach the same things that are important to the citizens and that the people follow. Since British colonial rule and up to the present, there has existed in Nigeria a deep chasm between the officially certified, encouraged, and financed system of law and justice (the British imposed English system) and the more relevant, more meaningful, and more commonly practiced systems of justice and law (the indigenous systems). The gulf will remain – and may get wider – unless the official methods and procedures for managing grievances, conflicts, and disputes are brought in line with the citizens' experiences and preferences, which research shows to be the indigenous law and justice systems and processes. There is no doubt that the proposed law and justice indigenization will improve social control in Nigeria because it will be an official statement that the people should continue to regulate their lives in ways that most of them already do.

References

Adeoye, S. (September 8, 2003) "Osun scraps customary courts" in *The Guardian*. See http://odili.net/news/source/2003/sep/8/8.html; Internet.
Comaroff, J. and Comaroff, J. L., eds. (2006) *Law and Disorder in the Postcolony*. Chicago, Illinois, USA: The University of Chicago Press.
Constitution of the Federal Republic of Nigeria, 1999 (effective May 29, 1999).
"Obasanjo is Smuggled into LSE Event Through Back Door" in *SaharaReporters* at http://www.saharareporters.com/index.php?option=com_content&view=article&id=1832:obasanjo-is-.
Ogbalu, F. (1979) *Igbo Institutions and Customs*. Onitsha, Nigeria: University Publishing Co.
Okafọ, N. (2003a) "Burden of Patriotism: Obasanjo, Leadership, and Nigerian Nation-Building" in *NigeriaWorld* (February 6). See http://nigeriaworld.com/articles/2003/feb/061.html; Internet.
Okafọ, N. (2004) "British Commonwealth as Colonization by Consent", in *NigeriaWorld* (January 21). See http://nigeriaworld.com/articles/2004/jan/212.html; Internet.

Okafọ, N. (2006) "Relevance of African Traditional Jurisprudence on Control, Justice, and Law: A Critique of the Igbo Experience" in *African Journal of Criminology and Justice Studies*, Vol. 2, No. 1, June, pp. 36-62.

Okafọ, N. (2007) "Rule of Law, Political Leadership, and Nobel Peace Prize: Analysis of the Obasanjo Presidency 1999-2007" in *NigeriaWorld* (January 12). See http://nigeriaworld.com/articles/2007/jan/122.html; Internet. See also "Analysis of the OBJ's Presidency" in *SaharaReporters* at http://www.saharareporters.com/da001.php?daid=204; Internet. See further "Analysis of the OBJ's Presidency" in *Daily Triumph* at http://www.triumphnewspapers.com/archive/DT19012007/ana19107.html; Internet. http://www.triumphnewspapers.com/archive/DT22012007/any22107.html#; Internet.

Okafor, F. (1978) *Africa At The Crossroads*. New York, USA: Vintage Press.

Okereafọezeke [a.k.a. Okafọ], N. (1996) *The Relationship Between Informal and Formal Strategies of Social Control: An Analysis of the Contemporary Methods of Dispute Processing Among the Igbos of Nigeria*. UMI Number 9638581. Ann Arbor, Michigan, USA: University Microfilms.

Okereafọezeke [a.k.a. Okafọ], N. (2002) *Law and Justice in Post-British Nigeria: Conflicts and Interactions Between Native and Foreign Systems of Social Control in Igbo*. Westport, Connecticut, USA: Greenwood Press.

Okereafọezeke [a.k.a. Okafọ], N. (2003b) "Civilian Leadership and Law Reform in Nigeria." Paper presented at the American Society of Criminology Conference, Denver, Colorado, USA, November 19-22, 2003.

Okereafọezeke [a.k.a. Okafọ], N. (2005) "Political Challenges to Indigenizing Justice in Post-British Nigeria" in C. B. Fields and R. H. Moore, Jr., eds. *Comparative and International Criminal Justice: Traditional and Nontraditional Systems of Law and Control*, Second Edition, Waveland Press, pp. 339-351.

Oli, S. I. (1994) "A Dichotomization: Crime and Criminality Among Traditional and Christianized Igbo", in A. T. Sulton, ed. *African-American Perspectives On: Crime Causation, Criminal Justice Administration and Crime Prevention*. Englewood, Colorado, USA: Sulton Books.

Onyechi, N. M. (1975) "A Problem of Assimilation or Dominance" in T. O. Elias, et al., eds., *African Indigenous Laws: Proceedings of Workshop (7-9 August, 1974)*. Enugu, Nigeria: The Government Printer.

Chapter 6

Model Law and Justice: Legislation and Enforcement

Chapter Introduction

The model ingredients of a reconstructed postcolonial law and justice system in this chapter are discussed under two subheadings or components, as follows: Rule and Law Making, and Rule and Law Enforcement. The subheadings address two of the four critical components and agencies of a postcolonial justice system, such as Nigeria's. The remaining two components (Case Processing and Adjudication, and Corrections and Other Post-trial Actions) are discussed in Chapter 7. Collectively, the four components facilitate the critical examination and understanding of the model ingredients of justice in a postcolony.

Rule and Law Making

It is essential to distinguish relevant "repugnancy test" characteristics from the essential ingredients of home-grown laws and law making recommended in this book for a postcolony. Repugnancy test in Nigeria, for instance, represents the colonial British view that an indigenous tradition, custom, or law is not to be applied or enforced by the court if the court interprets the tradition, custom, or law as repugnant to natural justice, equity, or good conscience, or contrary to an official law (Okereafǫezeke, 2000). In the colonial era, the interpreting judges were invariably English citizens. In today's Nigeria, a judge is typically trained in English traditions, customs, and laws, usually at the expense of the Nigerian models. The repugnancy test colonial policy in Nigeria, which began during British colonization, remains viable in various forms and influences throughout Nigeria.

The limited, if any, accommodation the British colonial personnel and their successors are willing to grant Nigerian indigenous traditions, customs, and laws cannot reasonably be defined as indigenization (Cunneen, 2002). Indigenization of law and justice should mean the rediscovery and development of the indigenous systems and processes of justice, law, and control for use in the modern State. The rediscovery and use, of course, recognize the need to modify or discard outdated indigenous provisions and principles, as necessary. Such changes will ensure that indigenous social control rules and laws are consistent with modern State realities. On the other hand, the repugnancy test, in conception and practice, seeks to destroy, emasculate, or subjugate Nigeria's indigenous principles of law, justice, and social control to their British counterparts. Whereas the repugnancy test seeks to replace or fundamentally alter the indigenous systems, the law making aspect of justice reconstruction advanced in this book is intended to indigenize law and social control by strengthening the home-grown systems and processes. Thus, efforts at justice reconstruction in contemporary Nigeria should overthrow the negative aspects of the repugnancy test.

Regarding model law making for a postcolony, such as Nigeria, the following two broad questions are important. One: What are the essential characteristics of the processes for making rules and laws for a society to reconstruct its justice following colonization?[1] Two: What are the necessary substantive changes to the rules and laws of such a postcolony? The first question emphasizes law making procedure, while the second question raises issues of substantive contents of laws. The two *procedural* and *substantive* queries are based on recognitions of the "how" and "what" aspects of a society's laws – how the laws are made and what they provide. For the purposes of this discussion, the "how" (procedural) question is more important. Once the key ingredients constituting the proper process for law making in a society are identified, it will be easier to predict the nature, form, and the more important substantive contents of the laws that will follow. Thus, this section will emphasize the relevant procedural considerations in law making for postcolonial justice reconstruction. The appropriate responses to the relevant issues depend on the circumstances of each society. In the Nigerian example, the country's local and foreign experiences, diversity of peoples, groups, and other constituent parts, and availability of verifiable and credible indigenous systems are some of the important considerations in compiling a range of procedural characteristics, and substantive reflections, of the country's reconstructed law and justice system.

On the procedural question, the following important actions, for the reasons given, ought to be incorporated in Nigerian postcolonial law and justice reconstruction.

One, *Change the Nigerian Justice System to Reposition Indigenous Law and Justice*: One of the two main objects of the proposed justice reconstruction in Nigeria is to reassert the country's indigenous systems of justice and law as the basic means of social control (grundnorm). This will mean a change of the prevailing postcolonial legacy based on the English law and justice system, misnamed "general law," which the British colonists foisted on Nigerians without their consent. Rediscovering the long-emasculated indigenous systems will likely give Nigerians a greater sense of belonging in their country and improve social control among them. In response to Question 21, Appendix A ("Which is more acceptable to you: the English Justice System as practiced in Nigeria or Your

---

1 As a reminder to the reader, throughout this book, "colonization" includes conquest and occupation. A colonized, colonial, occupied, conquered, etc. society is one whose indigenous citizens and/or their descendants are (or were) subjected to foreign authority, usually by force.

Native Justice System, why?"), one of the Survey Reaction Participants[2] in the study to elicit reactions for this book opines as follows:

> My native justice system is more acceptable to me because our native norms and customs are more respected and obeyed. The English justice system is an imported system in Nigeria. People obey native justice system because they feel that their forefathers will give them instant justice if they offend the gods (statement by a Survey Reaction Participant, a Justice of the Peace, Customary Court Judge, and Retired Court Registrar).

The quoted statement cites the alien character of English law in Nigeria as one of the system's handicaps. Another Survey Reaction Participant expresses the same sentiment, thus: "The native justice system is more acceptable because it is better understood by the people it affects." Yet a third Survey Reaction Participant describes English law and justice in Nigeria as "a strange grundnorm" to emphasize its foreignness. To the first participant, another advantage of indigenous justice over English justice is the view, which is widely held, that justice is swifter under the indigenous system than under the English system. Thus, in identifying and responding to wrongdoers, the indigenous system avoids the lengthy delays prevalent in English law. For these and other reasons, Nigeria's indigenous systems of justice and law should be repositioned as the basic social control means.

However, the argument to restore the prominence of indigenous traditions, customs, and laws should not mean the end of every foreign idea of law or justice in Nigeria. What it means is that the indigenous systems will feature primarily and prominently. And, every useful, credible foreign idea for improved justice in Nigeria will be explored to add to, and improve, the indigenous Nigerian system. But indigenous Nigerian justice and law systems should constitute the grundnorm or basic law of the country. However, the following caveat should be noted:

> While urging the proper Nigerian authorities to reinforce the country's indigenous traditions, customs, and laws (customary law) over English law, it is equally important to point out that unreasonable, unpopular, and outdated customary law should be discarded and replaced with more progressive principles. Like every postcolonial society, Nigeria should strive to achieve a modern society that maintains a reasonable balance between the welfare and freedom of its citizens and the progress and orderliness of the State (Okafọ, 2008, p. 61).

Former President Olusegun Obasanjo once proposed a mandatory ten-year interval for the review of *all* laws in Nigeria (Ogbu, 2004). But, all the country's laws need not be reviewed at the same time. That may even prove to be extremely difficult, if not impossible. Thus, the precise interval for reviewing *all* the country's laws seems negotiable. Regardless, that should not take away from the need to continuously

---

2 See the Prologue to this book for the definition of "Survey Reaction Participant."

review the country's laws to determine their currency, consistency with the citizens' beliefs, norms, and expectations, and suitability for up-to-date social control. The laws and changes thereto should reflect the citizens' socialization and modes of social relations. In any case, the importance of periodically evaluating existing laws to determine the needed changes, if any, cannot be overemphasized.

In response to Question 21, Appendix A, a Survey Reaction Participant prefers the English justice system to the Nigerian indigenous justice system because the English justice system "gives one great opportunity to defend one's self. It is fair and just." Assuming that the Survey Reaction Participant accurately characterizes the English justice system *vis-à-vis* the Nigerian counterpart, this comment should motivate and challenge policy makers and justice officials implementing reconstructed indigenous-based justice to strengthen accused persons' abilities to defend themselves. This will, in turn, portray indigenous justice more positively.

Two, *Change the Nigerian Justice System to Expand Indigenous Law and Justice*: The second main object of the proposed law and justice reconstruction in Nigeria is to develop and expand the indigenous systems. The development and expansion will come with official governments' encouragement, increased use, as well as aggressive governmental and non-governmental efforts to promote and streamline the varied indigenous systems. It is expected that these efforts will in time culminate in a Nigerian common law much like the English common law. In response to Question 5, Appendix A ["Do you believe that Nigeria's justice and legal system should be fundamentally changed to reposition the native systems in the country as the grundnorm(s) ...?"], one Survey Reaction Participant, gives an affirmative answer but goes on to state that "this can only be done when and where we have a common native legal and justice system applicable throughout the country." See also Kolajo (2000), who shares the view that no single uniform set of customs prevails throughout Nigeria. But, if we wait for Nigeria to first have "a common native legal and justice system applicable throughout the country," as the Survey Reaction Participant suggests, we will never make the needed changes to Nigerian law and justice. The preferred procedure is to first reposition or affirm the country's indigenous law and justice as the grundnorm and then work to unify them as much as necessary and possible. In time, increased emphasis of the common features and potentials of Nigeria's many customs, traditions, and native laws will help to minimize the present real and imagined diversities and conflicts among the different groups and their respective systems.

England offers a good example of a successful policy and procedure to expand indigenous law and justice. English common law was developed post the Norman Conquest of England when circuit judges were sent to different English tribal communities to settle disputes. Although the applicable customs varied from one community to another, over time the judges were able to identify, emphasize, and apply the common rules to cases in different communities. Eventually, the differences paled and the generally accepted and generally applied principles and laws became the English common law. Today's common law is more universal and easier to administer, at least within England, than the preceding English tribal laws. The common law also became predictable. This characteristic grew out of codification, case law, and other forms of writing. Clearly defined legal principles lead to judicial precedent (*stare decisis*), which is one of the key anchors of contemporary English justice.

Thus, according to a Survey Reaction Participant in response to Question 21, Appendix A, English common law emerged as a "purely scientific" system. The participant grossly overstates the measurability and objectivity of the English common law by describing it as "purely scientific." However, regardless of the accuracy of the legal system's characterization as purely scientific, the road to the present English common law has been long but deliberate. The result is a unifying and generalizing set of verifiable and commonly used norms for the English. Regarding Nigeria's indigenous traditions, customs, and laws, some of those characteristics found in the English common law system (codification and other forms of writing, universality, etc.) are absent or uncoordinated. There is no reason that the English experience cannot be replicated in Nigeria, over time. However, this has to begin with official acceptance, affirmation, and reassertion of Nigeria's indigenous traditions, customs, and laws as the basic principles for regulating relations in Nigeria.

Three, *Consult Extensively With, and Involve, Stakeholder Groups in Law Making*: As all modern societies are increasingly more complex than their primogenitors, it is impossible or impractical for all the members of a political entity, such as a Local Government Area, State, or Federation in Nigeria, to participate directly in law making. An attempt to get the citizens to exercise their law making powers directly would be cumbersome, extremely tedious, and inefficient. Thus, a reasonable option for citizen participation in law making in a modern society is through freely elected representatives. However, any reasonable effort to reconstruct law and justice for a postcolony should include wide consultation with all federating stakeholders, including ethnic, religious, gender, and professional groups. Further, the authority responsible for law and justice reconstruction should ensure that the stakeholders are given reasonable opportunities to participate in the discussions and negotiations leading to the makings of new laws and the revisions of existing laws.

Understandably, many of the stakeholder groups seek to advance peculiar agendas for the betterment of the lives of their respective members. Thus, all such groups are partisan, sometimes extremely so. Ethnic groups across Nigeria offer good examples of partisanship or sectionalism. For various reasons, ethnic nations are wont to protect their respective turfs. It would be foolish for an effort at law and justice reconstruction to ignore this historical and contemporary reality. Therefore, consultations involving such groups should aim to assure the members that they are an important part of the State and would neither be emasculated nor compromised to give advantage to any of the other groups. Such consultations should preferably be done in public allowing the general citizenry to verify the transparency of the process. Consulting with the various competing constituencies and involving them in the law making process gives the stakeholders a sense of worth and belonging in the society. The likelihood of achieving this can be increased by providing the groups with a credible process for freely choosing their representatives in periodic elections. Those representatives should speak and act for the group in State affairs. Moreover, the final product of such consultation and negotiation, such as a new or revised law or other policy, is more likely to inspire acceptance and compliance from stakeholders who have participated in the process than those who have not been so involved. Participation in the law making process increases the likelihood that a stakeholder group would identify with the resulting law and have a sense of co-ownership of the law.

Four, *Include Persons With Strong Knowledge and Understanding of Indigenous Traditions, Customs, and Laws in Law Making Institutions*: This procedural quality emphasizes the importance of traditions, customs, and native laws in the overall scheme of justice reconstruction. By this, all law making institutions will be reconstituted to include persons with thorough knowledge and understanding of the substantive and procedural rules, regulations, and laws of the relevant ethnic constituencies represented in the modern political entity. Thus, as examples, every Nigerian Local Government Area's legislative authority will be reconstituted to include persons with proven knowledge and understanding of the applicable traditions, customs, and native laws (customary law). Typically, such persons are older community members with substantial experiences in indigenous procedural and substantive laws, including traditional rulers, respected traditional chiefs, and other credible community leaders who could be viewed as custodians of customary law. For example at the state level, including these knowledgeable and experienced persons in the law making institutions can take the form of reconstituting and expanding the role of the erstwhile "House of Chiefs" in some parts of Nigeria, to emphasize customary law in state law making.

According to this recommendation, persons with strong knowledge and understanding of indigenous traditions, customs, and laws may be appointed, rather than elected, to serve in the law making institutions at the Local, State, and Federal levels of government. The appointment is necessary because elected persons may not possess the desired customary law knowledge. Therefore, the membership of each legislative assembly will consist of elected and appointed individuals. The ratio of the appointed to the elected members may be determined by negotiated law. But the vast majority of the law makers at each level should be elected, rather than appointed, in line with democracy. Democracy is perhaps the best guarantor of broad participation by the citizens. However, the critical customary law role of the appointed legislators should offset any seeming undemocratic character of their memberships of the various legislatures. Under the proposed arrangement, every constituent part of a political entity (Local Government Area, State, or Federal Government) will elect its representative. Additionally, the experts on the applicable traditions, customs, and indigenous laws will be appointed. To avoid having bloated legislative houses, it will be necessary to merge constituencies, so as to reduce the number of constituencies by half with a view to deriving a total number of elected and appointed legislators that equals the current total.

This model is proposed for use at the Local Government, State, and Federal levels in the Nigerian federal structure. A negotiated and set number of the appointed law makers will be chosen for each ethnic group to eliminate or minimize any charge of domination or official preference for an ethnic group. The appointed legislators will have the same voting powers as their elected counterparts to avoid being treated as inconsequential in the law making process. The appointees will fill a major need in the country's law and justice reconstruction efforts. They will serve as experts on indigenous traditions, customs, and laws, allowing the experts to identify areas of agreement as well as disagreement between the country's indigenous laws and other legal models. As a part of enacting a law, the appointed and elected legislators will be expected to address this question: "How do the relevant indigenous Nigerian traditions, customs, and laws address the issue under consideration?" The answer will determine the legal provision, if any, to be enacted.

In the proposed arrangement, the expert law makers will advise the other legislators and the public at large on how best to proceed in making a new law or amending an existing one. If there is an applicable, verifiable, and effective indigenous law or provision for dealing with the issue concerned, the indigenous provision should be adopted and enacted, with changes as necessary. In a situation where a useful indigenous provision exists, it would be utterly unnecessary to create a new, probably alien, law to regulate the citizens who are already used to a different standard. Rather, the proper procedure should be that the existing, indigenous law or provision should be enacted by the relevant Local, State, or Federal legislature for future use. This procedure will strengthen the proposed indigenous-based essence of Nigerian law and justice. Only where preexisting indigenous laws and provisions are inexistent or clearly insufficient should novel laws be contemplated and enacted. In such a vacuous situation (my guess is that they are few and far between), useful laws from other jurisdictions, within and outside Nigeria, should be considered to create a fitting law. This approach will help to avoid the unfortunate situations where otherwise useful, credible, and verifiable indigenous laws, which the citizens widely use, are willy-nilly emasculated by legislative houses allegedly in pursuit of modernity.

Five, *Publicize Proposed and Recent Laws*: Every law needs publicity to justify its wide application. Publicity increases the citizens' awareness of the rules governing their affairs along with periodic changes to those rules. Thus, publicity has the capacity to increase citizens' compliance. Law that is not (sufficiently) publicized is thereby limited in its effectiveness. Moreover, such law is unfair and unjust to the uninformed citizens. To be fair and just, a new or recent law needs to be publicized to the citizens by means of the most appropriate media. The circumstances of the citizens will determine the appropriateness of a publicity strategy used in each situation. The typical method of publicizing official laws in Nigeria is the issuing of government gazette containing the law sought to be publicized. In time, such law is included in the Volume of Laws of the jurisdiction for the relevant year. Occasionally, for laws on high profile issues, formal ceremonies are held to mark the signing into law of the approved legislative bills. However, these manners of publicizing laws are limited because the majority of the citizens either are not aware of the new laws or are insufficiently informed about the provisions. There is insufficient media coverage of such events. In any case, the overwhelming majority of media coverage is done in the English language, which is Nigeria's official language, despite the fact that most Nigerians are illiterate or at least English-illiterate. This means that these citizens are unable to read and write effectively in English.[3] Far more Nigerians thus fail to appreciate the ingredients of the country's laws.

In contemporary Nigeria, the appropriate means of publicizing new and recent laws will involve official government and unofficial, community efforts, both using a combination of the relevant indigenous languages and English. Publicity will be achieved through such media outlets as national, state, and private television stations, radio stations, newspapers, newsletters, pamphlets, posters, etc. However, since the overwhelming majority of TVs, radios, and newspapers are published in English, the Local, State, and Federal governments owe duties to make conscientious efforts to publicize the laws equally, if not more, in the respective indigenous languages. The Local and State governments, in particular, can work closely with traditional leaders and agencies, as well as various community and other cultural groups, to disseminate the provisions of the proposed and recent laws, in the respective indigenous languages, to the citizens. In addition to publicity through the various media, electronic and printed paper copies of the laws should be readily available, in the indigenous languages, and free to the citizens.

The erstwhile General Ibrahim Babangida regime's (1985-1993) "Mass Mobilization Program," MAMSER, offers, at least as the program was defined, an instance of grassroots efforts to raise the consciousness of Nigerians. The program was intended to increase the citizens' awareness of the various government policies and programs and to get the citizens to understand the roles they could play to create a better society. The program's expressed anchor on the masses' support could be central to educating Nigerians on proposed and recent laws. Altogether, if the combined official (governmental) and unofficial (non-governmental) publicity strategies recommended here are adopted, they will likely increase the citizens' awareness and understanding of proposed and recent laws.

Six, *Provide Simple, Easily Interpretable Statements of the Laws*: A reconstructed law and justice system should include simple legal provisions to allow the average citizen to read, understand, and properly interpret the provisions of the laws. In Nigeria, as in many other postcolonies, it has been fashionable to view legal provisions as necessarily beyond the reach of the average person. Thus, a non-"learned person" is not expected to read and properly interpret legal provisions. As

---

3 This disconnect (official government insistence on the use of the English language in official businesses in Nigeria despite the fact that most Nigerians either cannot communicate well in English or prefer to speak their indigenous languages) is important enough to be raised more than once in this book.

a Nigerian-trained lawyer, I have observed this attitude firsthand. But, this line of thinking should be seen as a by-product of a slavish mentality, which imperialism wrought on Nigeria. The colonial importation of alien English law into Nigeria led to a citizenry that accepted and later advanced the misguided notion that legal provisions are beyond the average citizen's capacity to understand. The erroneous reckoning is that the mystery of law adds to its utility. This thinking is mistaken. Laws that are made to apply to citizens should be reasonably understandable and interpretable, such that a citizen of average mental capacity and exposure should be able to appreciate those laws and their provisions. Therefore, law and justice reconstruction ought to include re-writing unnecessarily complicated and confusing laws to make them simpler and within the reach of the average citizen. Otherwise, with time, most citizens would become so alienated from the laws applied to them that the citizens would search for alternative ways to manage their grievances, conflicts, and disputes.

Seven, *De-Emphasize "Ignorance of the Law is No excuse" Maxim*: It is necessary to underline the need for a postcolony to place less emphasis on the "Ignorance of the law is no excuse" aphorism. In a postcolony, this truism is easily asserted to apply laws and punish persons who do not know or do not sufficiently, if at all, understand the legal obligations placed on them. But, it is unfair for a society to punish its members who have not been (sufficiently) informed and educated about their obligations. Punishments and other adverse actions should be preceded by reasonable communication of the expected obligations to the citizens. Only where a citizen disregards or ignores the known obligations can the society legitimately impose sanction. Moreover, simple, easily interpretable postcolonial laws that are based on extensive consultations with, and involvement of, stakeholders will likely reduce the number of citizens in the society who are ignorant of the law, thus resulting in greater social control. Having an ignorant population works against effective social control. On the other hand, a knowledgeable and understanding population increases the likelihood of effective social control. Finally, curtailing the use of the "Ignorance of the law is no excuse" maxim will remind the State of its obligation to inform, educate, and expose its citizens to the laws the State seeks to apply to the citizens.

Eight, *Account for a Contemporary, Cosmopolitan Society*: The core argument against reconstructing the justice system of a postcolony to reposition indigenous law as the grundnorm is that indigenous law and justice belong to a by-gone era when society was simple, rather than sophisticated, and homogenous, rather than today's heterogeneous society. The argument is that indigenous law and justice will not be able to regulate relations among the contemporary mixed and advanced citizenry. However, it is reasonably hypothesized that adequate education and orientation of Nigerians, for example, will assuage the difficulties posed by the contemporary cosmopolitan society. Thus, a blending or synthesis of the indigenous and postcolonial ideas is necessary. On this issue, two of the procedural recommendations already discussed are relevant. One is combining elected representatives and appointed indigenous systems expert representatives to make laws at the Local, State, and Federal levels. The other is adequately publicizing proposed and recent laws. The recommendations, if implemented, will afford opportunity for reasonable participation to all citizens so that they can help to change or amend laws that do not accord with the citizens' contemporary preferences.

Nine, *Change the Following Aspects of the Law of Evidence*: The importance of evidence in the justice process cannot be overemphasized. It is the foundation of judicial decisions. Whereas traditionally Nigeria's indigenous justice systems have relied on verified, objective as well as unverified, subjective pieces of evidence to decide criminal and civil cases, the English law in Nigeria claims to use verified, objective evidence only. "Verified, objective evidence" refers to important, relevant, credible facts about a case in point which facts help the presiding authority, such as a judge, to hear and decide a case fairly. The facts should be understandable by a reasonable person. They should also be convincing to such a person. It seems that some of the evidence practices in indigenous law and justice that allowed the traditional court judge to hear and decide a case based, for instance, on impressions of what God, gods, or a deity might do or intends to do are outdated. The trend under a reconstructed justice system should be to emphasize objective, rather than subjective, evidence. In the reconstructed justice system, cases should be decided based on proven evidence.

Thus, a person who makes a claim against another will be required to prove it before judgment is entered for the claimant. This will apply to criminal as well as civil cases. In fact, a criminal allegation calls for a higher standard of proof. Under English law, the standard is "proof beyond all reasonable doubts." This standard of proof is higher than the standard (proof on a preponderance of the evidence) applied to civil cases. The high proof standard should be maintained in a reconstructed justice system. High, rigorous proof standard will be maintained, especially for criminal cases, as a way of emphasizing the importance of a citizen's guaranteed rights. A person facing the prospect of losing his/her life or freedom of movement through imprisonment will be able to insist that the accuser produces clear evidence of guilt. Also, the accused will be afforded all reasonable opportunities to challenge and test the evidence against him/her. Thus, the adversary process that allows opposing parties to contest evidence against them will be maintained.

Even while recommending the continued use of verifiable, objective evidence to decide cases, it is necessary to recognize the efficacy of the indigenous methods of proving disputed facts. In traditional Igbo (Nigeria), for example, a person who makes a claim in the indigenous system may, in the absence of objective, verified evidence, swear by a known and respected deity to assert the claim. It is generally believed that the deity knows the truth between the disputing parties. Thus, a party claiming falsely will suffer the deity's wrath. The punishment options include illness and death of the false claimant and/or a family member. The following is the greatest contribution of this approach to justice processing. Fear of the deity's wrath is reputed to encourage disputants to tell the truth rather than risk the deity's fury. Regardless, where a misfortune (illness or death) befalls a false claimant, there remains a valid question about the veracity of a connection made between the activities of the deity and the misfortune that the claimant suffers. It is very difficult, if not impossible, to prove such a link. Moreover, the modern citizen may be uncomfortable with what may be considered a variation of the medieval "trial by ordeal," which basically burdened accused persons to prove that they were innocent of the charges against them. Thus, a positivist observer, who prefers to rely on proven facts, may be unconvinced by the idea proffered here. Despite concerns and reservations, the indigenous methods of proving facts remain effective and in wide use in modern Nigeria. Sometimes, however, they are abused as appeared to have occurred with the Ogwugwu Isiula Shrine in Okija, Anambra State, Nigeria, in 2004 (see Okafọ, 2005).

But, it must be emphasized, trials and case management involving deities have served generations of Nigerians. This strongly suggests that case processing through deities works. The spiritual influence of this form of case management on law and justice is undeniable. The gods intervene where necessary to ensure justice. This aspect of indigenous justice should therefore not be dismissed flippantly. What is needed is a reconstructed law and justice system that co-opts and uses this indigenous method with necessary modern State adjustments. Unlike the medieval "trial by ordeal," parties to a dispute in a reconstructed law and justice system should freely choose between evidence-based trial and indigenous-based trial before a deity. It seems reasonable then to recommend that the citizens be expressly given a choice between having their case and evidence heard based on an objective, verifiable procedure, on the one hand, and swearing on a well-known and reputable deity, on the other hand. Supposedly, the deity will be located within the geographical jurisdiction where the oath is sought to be taken. A party who opposes swearing by such a deity will have the option of trying his/her case by presenting objective, verifiable evidence, which the opposing party can challenge by cross-examination.

The poser facing a postcolony in this regard is how to credibly reconcile indigenous evidence practices, which are sometimes subjective, with modern State principles, which profess and aspire to create an objective process. Specifically, how can a reconstructed law and justice system get the parties, witnesses, etc. to a case to tell the truth before a court or tribunal without ignoring the indigenous beliefs, systems, and practices? As demonstrated throughout this book, indigenous beliefs, systems, and practices remain formidable partners in Nigerian social control. And, in spite of the official law on perjury (giving false testimony under oath or affirmation), a person's belief is central to whether or not the person tells the truth to a court. Therefore, a procedure that taps into a party's conscience or belief will motivate the person to testify truthfully in a judicial proceeding. At present, the two available options (Oath and Affirmation) largely sideline indigenous beliefs and processes. Moreover, the two options encourage persons with beliefs not covered by those options to tell lies and escape legal punishment. In the circumstances, the following compromise solution has the potential to produce the best result.

These are the elements of the proposed solution. The court will determine the entity in which each party, witness, etc. believes. A party, witness, or other person before a court may believe in the land through a deity, shrine, sacred forest, etc. Alternatively, a party or witness may believe in God through the Christian religion. Another party or witness may believe in Allah through the Muslim religion. Of course, the identified beliefs do not exhaust the possibilities. However, in each case, the court will have the party or witness swear by the relevant subject of belief to tell the truth, the whole truth, and nothing but the truth. I am cognizant of the fact that it is impossible to be certain that a person believes in what he or she claims (Okafọ, 2003b). Nonetheless, directing a person to state his or her belief, with threat of legal sanction, will put most people on the spot to be truthful. Also, other citizens' testimonies will be admitted to establish a party's or witness's belief or faith. For example, evidence by other citizens may show that a party religiously participates in scheduled rituals before a deity. The party may even be identified as a member of the deity's staff. Such a person will be required to swear by the deity rather than get away with swearing or affirming to something else. It should also be noted that for a majority of the persons before a court, evidence pointing to their beliefs will be readily available among their friends, neighbors, acquaintances, co-workers, and community members. Again, by the proposed solution to the evidentiary issue, most people will feel pressure to truthfully declare their true belief so as to be accurately sworn or given an oath to speak the truth to the court.[4]

Ten, *Limit the Role of Religion in Official Law and Justice*: A reconstructed law and justice system has to properly address the role of religion as an official instrument for citizens' control. Consider this issue in Nigeria as follows. Nigeria is a complex, diverse population. Consequently, the country's successive post-independence constitutions have prohibited State religion, thus recognizing the private essence of religion. For example, section 10 of the *Constitution of the Federal Republic of Nigeria, 1999* prohibits State religion. However, at the same time, successive federal and state governments, by their policies and programs, have routinely ignored the constitutional injunction. The governments' financial and managerial sponsorships of the Christian and Muslim pilgrimages, usually to Jerusalem (Israel/Palestine) and Mecca (Saudi Arabia), respectively, exemplifies the governments' disregard for the constitutional provision. Of the numerous religions in Nigeria, the governments chose to spend public resources on only two. This has gone on for decades. The President Umaru Yar'Adua regime (May 2007 –) expressed a willingness to discontinue government sponsorship of pilgrimages. Implementation of the regime's declared policy shift is another matter. Previous governments had made the same promise but never delivered. A reconstructed law and justice system will reassert and enforce a constitutional prohibition of State religion. In this connection, citizens' education is necessary to sensitize them on their rights and obligations against a government that disregards its constitutional

---

4   Issues concerning Oath and Affirmation are discussed further in Chapter 7.

and other legal obligations. Education will encourage the citizens to challenge such a wayward regime.

It is important to remind the reader of the centrality of religion to indigenous and other forms of social control. Certainly in Nigeria, religion plays a fundamental role in indigenous law and justice. This critical role should be encouraged even under a reconstructed law and justice system, without prejudice to the application and enforcement of the constitution's "no State religion" policy. The recommended procedure for applying religion in indigenous justice within a reconstructed justice system will allow disputants to incorporate their religious beliefs to further or defend their cases, as the case may be. The involvement of religion in this process will be purely private, even if it is done within the processes of a public institution (official court). Because this religious involvement will be limited, it is not different from the way religion is already applied in oath taking and affirmation in the current judicial process. Either way, the practice essentially focuses on what the party making a declaration on the basis of a religion believes or declares to the world that he/she believes. The recommended process allows for a limited use of religion without adopting a State religion. Thus, the policies of a dozen[5] of Nigeria's 36 states drafting Islam and enacting *shari'ah*[6] as a criminal code violates the Nigerian constitution as well as the process recommended in this book.

Eleven, *Ensure a Credible Constitution Through Proper Constitution-Making*: Constitution-making in postcolonial Nigeria has been mostly a tortuous State secret, to put it mildly. In both procedure and substance, post-independence Nigerian constitutions have habitually lacked key essentials, particularly in the procedures for their creation and enactment. A country's constitution should be the outline of the general and some specific rules governing the society. The citizens, acting directly or through their freely chosen representatives, are to define and enact the rules. However, the impracticality of having all the citizens of a country participate in making their constitution makes it imperative that such constitution will be made and enacted by representatives. Even then, the general citizenry will have the final say on the nature and contents of their constitution. These essentials are expected in any society in which government officials profess to exercise State authority and power on behalf of the citizens. The essential ingredients of constitution-making are absent in Nigeria. Most of the numerous constitution-making processes in Nigeria's postcolonial life pervert true constitutionalism. In these instances, including the Nigerian Constitution 1999, citizen participation was substantially restrained, if not altogether shut out, by the ruling military dictators and their civilian collaborators.

The process that led to the Nigerian Constitution 1999 illustrates the pattern that excludes the citizens from the constitution-making process. The General

---

5 The 12 states are located in the northern, predominantly Hausa/Fulani, part of the country.

6 The subject of *shari'ah* as a basis for criminal law in Nigeria is discussed further in Chapter 7.

Abdulsalami Abubakar-led military junta (1998-1999) wrote and gave the constitution to Nigerians. In fact, the junta kept the document a secret until the civilian leaders who would govern the country on the basis of the constitution had emerged. Only then did the military regime publish the constitution (see Boda, 1999). In many respects, it is a misnomer to call the 1999 document a "constitution" considering the deliberate and unjustifiable exclusion of an overwhelming majority of the citizens from the constitution-making process. The same criticism applies to most other such documents in Nigerian history. A constitution-making process in which all Nigerians are given reasonable opportunities to participate directly or indirectly in drafting, debating, adopting, enacting, and amending their constitution will properly ground the desired reconstructed law and justice system envisaged in this book. In other words, a constitution made and owned by the citizens is the foundation of reconstructed law and justice. Moreover, this type of constitution is necessary for the continuity of the Nigerian State (see Soyinka, 2000; Enahoro, 2002; Okocha, 2003).

Therefore, it is not enough, for example, for holders of legislative and executive offices in Nigeria to arrogate to themselves the right and mandate to "review" an existing imposed constitution, such as the Nigerian Constitution 1999. In this connection, there is a difference between constitution "review" and "amendment." The amendment of a constitution follows specified steps and involves the State organs assigned by the constitution to carry out the function. It is a narrow function to change specific provision(s) of the constitution. Typically, elected legislators and executive office holders amend a constitution. On the other hand, constitution review, a much more comprehensive task, essentially seeks to create a new constitution on the ashes of the existing document. Of course, aspects of the existing constitution may be retained in the subsequent document, but that is after each provision is evaluated by the reviewers and determined to be useful for the future. Because constitution review entails such fundamental alteration of the existing constitution, the review should be performed by the citizens directly or indirectly through their elected representatives. The citizens hold (or should hold) ultimate authority and power in a State. Thus, Nigerian legislators and executive office holders who claim to be reviewing the country's constitution, such as the Nigerian Constitution 1999, do so without justification.

For one thing, these legislators and executive office holders were not elected to "review" the constitution. Moreover, regarding the 2007 general elections as an example, there is a widely held view that a vast majority of the legislators and executive office holders, at the local, state, and federal government levels, usurped their positions through doctored elections. As I have pointed out in this book, events on the ground in Nigeria before, during, and after the 2007 elections should convince the reader to view the mandates of the elections "winners" with suspicion. Nigerian voters, local and foreign human rights groups, elections watch groups, international governments and other associations, such as the USA and the European Union condemned the elections as loaded with fraud and incompetence. Therefore, the mandates of the "elected" government officials are at best questionable considering the flawed elections that produced the officials. Put simply, most of the legislative and executive office holders in Nigeria do not have the mandates of their respective constituents and thus do not represent the citizens.

The significance of proper process and genuine citizen representation in constitution-making should be obvious. However, to be sure, in a United States Institute of Peace Special Report on Democratic Constitution Making, Hart (2003) writes:

> How the constitution is made, as well as what it says, matters. *Process* has become equally as important as the content of the final document for the legitimacy of a new constitution ... Genuine public participation requires social inclusion, personal security, and freedom of speech and assembly. A strong civil society, civic education, and good channels of communication between all levels of society facilitate this process ... Participatory constitution making is today a fact of constitutional life as well as a good in itself. Despite challenging difficulties of definition and implementation, a democratic constitution-making *process* is, in the words of African observer Julius Ivonhbere, "critical to the strength, acceptability, and legitimacy of the final product."[7]

And, Madunagu (2002), writing on "The Nigerian State and Its Laws," states: "A student of scientific methods of social analysis would naturally expect the Constitution of a state to reflect, both generally and in some critical 'material particulars', the positions, interests, and character of the dominant social classes in the community over which it rules" (p.1). On the contrary, the situation in contemporary Nigeria is such that the Nigerian Constitution 1999, like most of the successive postcolonial constitutions, does not reflect the positions, interests, or character of most Nigerians. Rather, these constitutions unduly favor narrow interests and constituencies at the expense of the general citizenry.

Twelve, *Use Indigenous Language for Constitution*: The issue here is the language in which the constitution of Nigeria, the most important public document, should be written. Again, it seems obvious that to achieve the greatest citizen understanding and participation in the country's principles and policies, the constitution should be written in the country's indigenous languages, owned and understood by the citizens. Unfortunately, through history to the present, Nigerian constitutions have been written exclusively in English, which is mischievously and fraudulently labeled Nigeria's "official language." The "official language" tag reads like a code name for something the rulers do not want the average Nigerian to understand, let alone challenge. For avoidance of doubt, most Nigerians cannot speak, read, or write fluently in the official English language. Thus, it makes little, if any, sense to write the citizens' fundamental document (the constitution) in a language with which most of the citizens are not familiar.

---

7   Italics are in the original source.

A reconstructed law and justice system will do well to include a constitution written and published in as many of Nigeria's indigenous languages as possible (see Oyekanmi, 1999; see also "Legislator Wants Constitution in Nigerian Languages," 2000). If initially the constitution cannot be written and published in all the indigenous languages, in time the document should be translated into *all* of the country's languages as the federal government once committed to doing ("Nigeria Upgrades Main Local Languages," 2007). Therefore, it is insufficient to write the constitution in only some of the country's languages while excluding the other, usually "minority," languages (Akiri, 2004). Efforts should be made to write or translate the constitution into all of Nigeria's indigenous languages.

The remaining section of this discussion on Rule and Law Making is devoted to recommended substantive changes.

The range of substantive changes to be made to postcolonial Nigerian law and justice is wide. The changes are needed on a variety of life issues to put the justice system in a position to deliver more effective and efficient social control. Consistent with the theme of this book, such law and justice reconstruction will reflect the realities of the postcolonial life of the average Nigerian, but with a strong recognition of the preeminence of the applicable indigenous traditions, customs, and laws. Suffice it to cite the following sample areas for substantive considerations in the law and justice reconstruction of the postcolony.

One, *Reform Marriage Laws*: Conflicting laws and standards govern the marriage institution in Nigeria. The disagreements between the various indigenous laws and the English law in Nigeria are wide and breed unneeded anomie (Okafọ, 2008, p. 60):

> ... the contrasts between the official English law in Nigeria and the country's indigenous customs and traditions have created a confused or anomic condition in which Nigerians either do not know or do not accept the official rules governing the citizens. Often, the official English law imposes a behavior standard that contradicts the citizens' history, experiences, and preferences expressed through indigenous customs and traditions. A famous example can be found in the marriage institution. Indigenous traditions, customs, and laws permit a man to marry more than one wife. English law in Nigeria forbids it, and punishes it as a crime. No doubt, the anomie engendered by this disagreement negates effective social control.

Is there any wonder then that Nigerian prosecutors and official courts have little or no desire to prosecute or convict accused bigamists? Although the English law in Nigeria criminalizes bigamy, the country's indigenous systems provide for, protect, and encourage the practice. It should be noted that although the indigenous systems allow and protect bigamy, modern economic, social, and other realities have conspired to curtail this practice.[8] Regardless, a properly reconstructed law and justice system will do away with the fruitless attempt to impose an English practice on Nigerians.

Also, while trying matrimonial causes, Nigerian courts are often faced with double, if not multiple, marriages (indigenous as well as English marriages). A consequential question then is: which of the conflicting marriages is to govern the subsequent matrimonial dispute? Again, because of the State resources at the disposal of the English system, marriage under English law is often enforced over indigenous marriage, even if the parties intended differently. A credible, effective, and efficient postcolonial law and justice system will substantively recognize the indigenous and English forms of marriage equally, and not treat either as inferior. Indeed, qualified persons will be able to marry in the indigenous system, the English system, or any other verifiable system. Moreover, this will be consistent with the important constitutional provision prohibiting the adoption of a State religion.

Two, *Land Matters: Define "Land" to Accord With Indigenous Understanding*: "Land" has a more elastic meaning under English law than under Igbo law, for instance. Under English law, anything attached to land, such as a house or other improvement, is a part of the land. Thus, the landowner owns the land along with all that are affixed to it. This is popularly expressed in the Latin maxim, *quic quid plantatur solo solo cedit*. This English law doctrine flies in the face of Nigerian indigenous law. In the indigenous system, land is separate from the attachments to it. Thus, it is common for the indigenous system to recognize a person as the owner of a piece of land, while another person owns a house built on the land. Also, a landowner may loan his or her land to another person to farm, sometimes for many years. Whenever the land is to revert to the owner, the farmer is recognized as the owner of the crops on the land and must be given enough time to harvest the crops. Considering the strategic importance of land and land relations in the Nigerian economy, this disagreement between the country's indigenous law and English law is substantial. As in many such conflict areas, it makes little sense that successive post-independence Nigerian governments have continued to require the citizens to obscure or subject their age-old indigenous land law and principle to the English standard. This area of the law is in need of urgent change to recognize, reaffirm, and enforce the relevant indigenous law and principle as the proper standard in all cases involving land issues.

---

8 In late 2007, a few months into his four-year governorship term in Adamawa State (one of Nigeria's 36 states), Murtala Nyako, a husband to four women, was forced to deal publicly with the disagreements among his wives as to who among them should be the state's "first lady." The embarrassment and unneeded headache arising from such a useless public spectacle in a state (and country) where the average citizen is consumed by overwhelming poverty and want of intelligent, honest, and dedicated leadership caused the governor to quarrel with the Nigerian press who rightly called him out for irresponsibly placing his personally chosen burden on the downtrodden citizens.

Three, *Land Matters: Liberalize Land Inheritance and Transfer*: Under Igbo customary law, for example, a female does not own land. Thus, she cannot inherit, buy, sell, or otherwise dispose of land. The Igbos say that: "Nwanyi adighi enwe ana," and "Nwanyi adighi ekwu okwu ana." These mean: "A female does not own land," and "A female does not negotiate land sale, lease, gift, etc.," respectively. However, neither statement means that a female member of a landowning group, such as a family, has no right to the land. On the other hand, she is entitled to use the land to provide for her sustenance, such as by farming the land or harvesting cash crops on the land. Then again, she is expected to ask the male head of the household for permission to use the land. The male is not expected to refuse unreasonably. In the final analysis, any disposition of the land must be done by a male member of the landowning group.

Under English law, females, as well as males, can own and transfer land under the applicable laws. This English standard in Nigeria is an affront to the indigenous system. There is a need to remove this divide between indigenous law and English law in Nigeria. What is needed is a land policy that recognizes the Nigerian customary foundation, but is sensitive to the contemporary importance of free economic transactions involving both males and females. Perhaps, a reasonable way out of this conflict is to enact a law that will continue to allow individually-owned and held lands to be transferrable by those individuals, males and females. Also, the law should provide for family and other group-owned lands to be transferrable only by the group leader (preferably male or female), according to the applicable indigenous law.

Four, *Enforce Indigenous Standards in Succession and Inheritance Generally*: Another area of substantial disagreement between indigenous law and English law is general property inheritance. In addition to the discussion of land inheritance, general inheritance refers to customary law versus English law stipulations on the disposal of personal, rather than real, property on the death of a parent, for example. Under customary law, the first male child inherits a father's property, while the last child inherits the mother's property. This rule applies to the Igbo ethnic nation, but it extends to other parts of the country as well. See *Abudu v. Eguakun* (2003) in which the Supreme Court of Nigeria upheld a similar custom in Benin (Nigeria). On the contrary, under English law, Will determines the devolution of property where a person dies testate. In the case of intestacy, state law decides how relevant property is to be shared. It seems reasonable to respect and enforce the applicable customary law provisions even in a modern State. It is reasonable to conclude that the citizens understand the customary law provisions better than English law. Moreover, the customary law provisions are more consistent with age seniority and family organization, which are highly valued in Igbo and other Nigerian communities.

Further on *Land Matters: Liberalize Land Inheritance and Transfer*, and *Enforce Indigenous Standards in Succession and Inheritance Generally*, the proper role of the Nigerian Constitution 1999 should be pointed out. A discriminatory customary law or practice appears to violate section 42 of the constitution ("Right to Freedom from Discrimination"). Where, for instance, a customary law provision forbids females from inheriting the property of a deceased relative, section 42 of the constitution would seem to have been offended. Section 42 is apparently a progressive idea. Why then is it not commonly applied by the Nigerian courts and enforced by the country's law enforcement agencies? The answer lies in the gap between the Nigerian constitution and the citizens. I have pointed out elsewhere in this book that the bane of the successive Nigerian constitutions, such as the 1999 constitution, is the absence of meaningful citizen participation in constitution making. Even in the postcolonial era, practically every Nigerian constitution, including the 1999 constitution, has been imposed by the ruling military and civilian elite. Thus, constitutional provisions, such as section 42, which do not enjoy the support of the citizens and their practices, are not fully applied or enforced.

Although seemingly enacted with good intention, section 42 and similar provisions have sidelined and sought to overthrow the citizens' practices, wishes, customs, and traditions. Any wonder then that, even such a progressive idea (prohibition of discrimination) receives little support from the citizens? The general public widely views the constitution suspiciously, being an imposed document. In Okoli (2007, p. 1), a prominent Nigerian legal practitioner, noting that "laws should not be made by the dead for the living," urges the country's Supreme Court to resort to judicial activism and invoke section 42 of the constitution to free women from discrimination. But, as pointed out here, the resistance to constitutional provisions goes beyond the words of the constitution. The wide perception among Nigerians is that they have not been involved in constitution-making. Also, that the imposed provisions contradict the people's age-old practices, beliefs, customs, and traditions. These assessments tame the distinguished lawyer's argument. Sensible, citizen-grounded constitutional provisions, not forceful application or enforcement of rulers' fiat legal wishes and commands, will do more to advance social control.

Five, *Define Indigenous Rights as Partners in Fundamental Human Rights*: There is little doubt that individual and group rights are central to life in every modern society. Rights enhance the quality of life in a population. Western legal thoughts have contributed substantially to the ideas and interpretations of those rights. But the notion of "rights" is not an exclusive preserve of the West. Indigenous ideas, principles, and practices have helped substantially to build individual and group rights. Sometimes, however, some of the Western rights provisions and their interpretations contradict rights under indigenous laws (Baah, 2000; see also Okereafoezeke, 2003). Because of the overwhelming power of the modern State, conflicts between indigenous and modern rights provisions are usually resolved in favor of the State. Despite contradicting the valued indigenous provisions, the utility of many of the modern rights provisions lies in their ability to expand and nurture the choices available to the citizens of a modern society, such as Nigeria. Thus, even under a reconstructed law and justice system, all rights – those defined in the constitution as well as those defined in the indigenous systems – that recognize and strengthen the citizens' freedoms should be maintained and, if necessary, expanded. There is no reason that indigenous laws could not be reformed and updated to be consistent with relevant fundamental human rights. It may be necessary to add here that individual rights and indigenous laws do not necessarily oppose each other, nor should they.

Six, *Distinguish Between the Communal Character of Nigeria and Western Individualism*: In spite of my expressed support for the maintenance of fundamental human rights in a reconstructed law and justice system, it is necessary for efforts at justice reconstruction to avoid creating all postcolonial societies in the image of Western European or North America. A basic character distinction between indigenous Nigeria, for example, and the Western society is that the Nigerian society is mostly communal while the West is mostly individualistic. In response to Question 11 ("In which areas of justice and law, if any, do you see strong disagreements between native customary law and English law in Nigeria?"), Appendix A, a Survey Reaction Participant states: "English law or justice system preserves the right of individuals irrespective of the way the opponent or the rest of the community feels, but African justice system or law seeks to preserve the unity and harmony of the community as a whole." Put another way, to indigenous Nigeria, the community is generally more important than the individual (see also Nzimiro, 1972), while to the West, the individual is generally more important than the community. Thus, in many instances, a Western society is willing to enforce the rights of an individual even if the rights contradict the overall best interests of the public. On the other hand, for the indigenous Nigerian community, as in many indigenous communities, the overall best interests of the public take priority over individual rights.

The communal versus individualistic difference between Nigerian and English societies is reflected in the societies' public policies, such as laws, and their application and enforcement. The applicable characteristics of communalism and individualism have served the respective societies for millennia. There is little reason to attempt to overthrow these essences. An overthrow attempt would breed societal dislocation and anomie. Thus, the proper approach is that a reconstructed law and justice system, in Nigeria for example, will, as much as necessary and possible, maintain communalism as a basic ingredient of the society. However, the new law and justice system will also recognize that one of the central tenets of fundamental human rights application and enforcement in a society is individualism. Individualism in this sense affords individuals and groups the opportunities to pursue their specific claims within the law regardless of their claims' effects on the rest of the society. Therefore, what is called for in a reconstructed law and justice system is reasonable balancing of the competing dictates of Nigerian communalism and the demands of individual rights. With negotiation among the stakeholders, the proper balance can be achieved.

Seven, *Emphasize the Shaming Philosophy and Strategy of Indigenous Criminal Justice and Corrections*: Nigeria's indigenous justice and English justice in Nigeria differ in their modes of managing convicts. Whereas the English system is designed almost exclusively to punish convicts through jailing, imprisonment, death, etc., the indigenous system uses a mixture of corrections and punishment, with emphasis on corrections. At the immediate family, extended family, and other community levels, the indigenous methods are widely practiced. Offenders are primarily viewed as valuable partners in the society. Generally, the community regards the offender as a person who needs the support of the other community members. Often, this form of support is given because of the need to reform the offender and reintegrate him or her into the society even after shaming (see Braithwaite, 2005). Thus, one of the key driving forces in the community corrections process is shaming.

An offender shames, is shamed, and/or is ashamed. By an action taken or omission made, an offender shames his/her family members, friends, acquaintances, and the community. An offender is shamed by his/her family members, friends, etc. by the steps they take to condemn or disapprove of the offender's behavior. An offender is ashamed (feels guilty) of what he/she has done or failed to do. Such an offender is ashamed because the offender believes that he/she has lost face, prestige, or standing in the community as a result of the action or omission. Even in cosmopolitan centers or cities, such as those of Nigeria, where familial relationships are relatively weak, the otherwise isolated member is wary of shaming, being shamed, and being ashamed because it is generally believed that a transgression committed outside one's birthplace or home community will in time become known to the transgressor's kinfolk.

The strong unofficial social control undercurrent that drives the corrections process in Nigerian communities should be maintained and encouraged even in the modern State. Both rural and city dwellers can shame, be shamed, and be ashamed. Thus, shaming can serve as a veritable tool for social control if the modern State emphasizes the centrality of familial relationships in all State policies and programs. This will mean that both rural and city residents, wherever they may be, will continue to identify strongly with their family members, friends, neighbors, acquaintances, and communities.[9]

Eight, *Acknowledge and Promote the Critical Role of the Family in Social Control*: The social, cultural, religious, and other differences between the Nigerian society and the English society are manifested in the societies' differing family organizational set-ups, managements, and control styles. The English family is mainly unitary and based on strong emphasis on immediate family members, individual rights, and freedoms. Conversely, the Nigerian family is only a component of the larger "extended family," with emphasis on the interests of the larger group. The diverse and complicated Nigerian family and extended family result in vast interrelationships requiring compromises among the members. These compromises are both expected and required for the continued welfare of the group as well as the individual members.

---

9 The shaming correctional strategy is discussed further in the section of this chapter on Rule and Law Enforcement.

In Nigeria, the family is really the foundation of the society. And, as mentioned earlier, the group interest usually takes precedence over the interests of individual members, unlike the English system that gives primacy to individualism. Considering the critical role of the family in a society, a reconstructed law and justice system in Nigeria should be based on this central family role. This indigenous Nigerian family function should be maintained by allowing family and extended family organs and leaders to retain the primary responsibility of controlling their members (Okereafoezeke, 1996; 2002). English law should never be employed to wrest an otherwise family role in social control. Under a reconstructed law and justice system, the family and the extended family should be empowered to do more for social control, thus lessening the burden on State institutions, such as the police, the courts, and the corrections agencies.[10]

Nine, *De-Emphasize Punitive Laws*: Doubtless, a society's response to its offenders reveals the society's soul. Nigeria's postcolonial punitive justice system leads the objective observer to the conclusion that the society is reactionary to its citizens' conducts. Sadly, much of the country's punitive laws, such as those providing for the death penalty for murder, attempted treason, armed robbery (even if death does not result from robbery), etc., are modern State carry-overs from colonization. These laws authorizing violent punishments have been sustained in this postcolonial era, notwithstanding the fact that under Nigeria's indigenous justice systems most of the underlying violations would be managed differently – usually less severely to promote community peace and harmony (Nzimiro, 1972). Although capital punishment exists in indigenous laws, they are fewer than what obtains in the modern Nigerian State. Thus, at a time when the aspiration to modernize should cause Nigeria to move away from laws imposing extreme, irreversible punishments, such as the death penalty, Nigeria sustains laws providing for the most extreme forms of punishment. And the country appears to implement these laws even in secrecy ("Nigeria: Government Misleads World About Death Penalty Record," 2007; see also "Nigeria Confirms State Executions," 2007).

Many countries have outlawed the death penalty and the United Nations Organization (UN) is strenuously campaigning against this punishment. In December 2007, the UN General Assembly approved a proposal for a global freeze on executions ("UN Calls for Halt to Executions," 2007). These UN and other efforts to stop capital punishment are based on questions surrounding the quality of justice in capital cases. Sadly, Nigeria, along with many other "developing" and "developed" countries, retains the death penalty. The emphasis in a reconstructed Nigerian law and justice system should be on reforming, not punishing, the offender. As much as possible, the restorative justice principle of victim, offender, and community involvement to determine and implement the best corrective measure to, as much as practicable, restore the parties to their previous conditions (Van Ness, 2002), should be emphasized. This policy aligns with the Nigerian

---

10 Recommendations for empowering the family, extended family, community members, etc. in a reconstructed law and justice system are discussed further in Chapter 7.

indigenous sense of communalism in which the best interest of the society, rather than the best interest of the individual, is pursued (Nzimiro, 1972). The need to abolish capital punishment and minimize, if not eliminate, other punitive laws in a reconstructed law and justice system is explored further in Chapter 7.

Rule and Law Enforcement

As a consequence of their uniforms and other official paraphernalia, State law enforcement agents are perhaps the most visible justice officials. In Nigeria, for example, other than undercover assignments, official law enforcement actions are normally performed in distinctive attire. It is not uncommon for less educated, less informed members of society to determine the severity of a breach of society's norm by the presence or absence of State law enforcement agents. In the eyes of the ordinary Nigerian, law enforcement – especially the uniformed variety, such as the Nigeria Police Force (NPF) – is the most critical component of the country's criminal justice system. Therefore, there is no shortage of professional and lay opinions about the NPF and other law enforcement. The comments address such issues as police corruption, police-citizen relationship, police effectiveness, community role in law enforcement, as well as other problems of, and obstacles to, policing.

Justice system commentators and other stakeholders have identified some of the fundamental problems with the NPF, while others have proffered some solutions to the problems. For example, "Re-inventing the Nigeria Police" (2005) outlines the following as some of the fundamental problems of the NPF (at p. 2):

> Our historical antecedents portray a Nigeria Police that started as a colonial force not intended as a friend of the people but holding allegiance to the colonial masters to whip the erring natives into line. Forty-five years[11] after the departure of the colonisers, our independence has bred generations of subtle promoters of home-grown neo-colonialism, and transferred police allegiance largely to the leaders that manipulate their way to power. Independence has thus not changed the mindset of the Police as instruments of manipulative coercion and enforcers of the will of the leadership. Their training has not transformed them into a friendly civil Police but produced quasi-military operators with 'kill and go' anti-riot mentality. Nigerians have therefore not had the comfort of a police operating in peace-time with a high sense of civil order.

There lies a fundamental problem with the NPF – it is neither organized nor managed to *serve* Nigerians. Rather, it is, and has always been, created to force them to comply with government leaders' wishes.

---

11 As of the year of the cited source – 2005.

Regarding solutions to the numerous problems confronting the NPF, varied measures have been proffered by professionals and social commentators. Abati (2008), for instance, offers solutions to the NPF ills, thus (at p. 3):

> The entire police system needs to be overhauled. Corrupt police men must be identified and expelled. But this change of attitude must begin at the leadership level, beginning with Divisional Police Officers (DPOs), Crime Investigating Officers and their various bosses all the way to the top. Structural questions also have to be addressed, First, the Police must be decentralized and made accountable not to the President, but to the Nigerian people. Its work must also be de-politicized. Inspectors General of Police seem to be more interested in doing the bidding of the President and the ruling party rather than serving the Nigerian people. The police recruitment process must also become more transparent. A Police Force that throws its doors open to the flotsam and jetsam of the society certainly cannot provide security. There is also a Police Service Commission established under Section 153 of the 1999 Constitution which is supposed to provide civilian oversight. Why is that Commission so ineffectual?

Despite widespread evidence of the NPF ineffectiveness and inefficiency, fed by structural, procedural, and substantive errors of policing (Abati, 2008), the NPF Inspector-General of Police (IGP) in 2007 proclaimed Nigeria to be one of the safest countries in the world (Ganagana, 2007). This leads an objective observer to wonder about the IGP's indices of "one of the safest countries in the world." Or is he simply denying the obvious to portray his organization as something that it is not?

However, this section of this book identifies and discusses key law enforcement changes needed to reconstruct the Nigerian law and justice system for more effective and efficient performance. Thus, reconstructed law enforcement in postcolonial Nigeria should include the following characteristics.

One, *Create a Three-tier Police – Local, State, and Federal Police Systems*: Through the colonial era and up to the present, Nigeria has been under a colonially engineered, entrenched, and mostly centralized police system. Except for a brief period shortly after independence when Regional police organizations operated, the national government, more specifically the head of state or president, has controlled the NPF, which is the country's main official law enforcement agency. The president, through the IGP, whom the president appoints, controls the NPF. Again, the president, directly or through the IGP and the police service authorities, appoints and controls other top police managers, including the Deputy IGPs, Assistant IGPs, State Police Commissioners, etc. As the president and the IGP run the police for the entire country, little, if any, consideration is given to the preferences of the average citizens and their respective local communities.

If implemented, policing in a Nigerian reconstructed law and justice system will be a shared responsibility. Policing will begin at the grassroots level – in each town and the applicable smaller units. Officially, however, the main jurisdictional levels of policing will be the Local, State, and Federal jurisdictions. These official levels are in line with a reform idea recommended by a panel on police reform, thus: "The police should be restructured to reflect the principle of federalism. This may require the recognition of the states, and local governments as distinct political entities" ("The Panel on Police Reform," 2008). Each of the Local, State, and Federal jurisdictions will have a police force, controlled by the jurisdiction. Although a town will neither establish nor run a police organization, each town will be legally empowered to contribute to the management, monitoring, control, and discipline of police personnel operating in the town. This will allow the average citizen in each community to share in the responsibility for his/her police force. However, each of the Local, State, and Federal jurisdictions will be able to hire, control, and discipline its managers and personnel.

One of the main advantages of this three-tier police model is its capability to elevate the responsibility of the police to the citizens. The Local, State, and Federal police will thus become responsible and answerable to the citizens of the jurisdiction in which it operates. Hiring the bulk of its managers and personnel from the residents of its jurisdiction will likely increase police compliance with the wishes and needs of the constituents. At present, police officers in Nigeria generally view the NPF as an agent of, and answerable only to, the Government of Nigeria (Okereke, 1995). Okereke (1995) rightly concludes that, being that the police see themselves as answerable only to the government, the NPF personnel are thus likely to view the citizens' concerns and expectations as inconsequential to law enforcement. This is a negative attitude that operates against effective and efficient social control. Average citizens should play a strategic role in their law enforcement efforts. Likewise, these citizens should participate meaningfully in the control of their law enforcement organization and personnel. Further, the three-tier police model, which involves towns, communities, organizations, groups, and persons within each official jurisdiction, will create or reinforce the importance of *cooperative policing*. The cooperative policing concept, if properly implemented, will accommodate and allow all stakeholders in the society to contribute their respective dues for law enforcement. Through cooperation in personnel, management, ideas, strategies, materials, etc., the society will experience more complete law enforcement, and more effective and efficient social control.

I wish here to address a legitimate outgrowth of the three-tier police model recommended in this book. There is a legitimate concern that a state police force may operate to victimize or discriminate against non-indigenes or non-state residents. This fear is founded on some of the activities of some Regional police organizations in Nigeria's First Republic (1960-1966). To assuage this concern, under the proposed arrangement, the federal law and justice authorities (federal police, federal prosecutors, federal courts, etc.) will have the power to investigate, hear, determine, and sanction local and state violators of Nigerians' constitutional rights, wherever the citizens may reside. This model follows the United States style that authorizes the US federal justice system to investigate, prosecute, convict, and punish violators of citizens' civil rights even if the offender and the victim reside in different states. The model proposed for Nigeria does not suggest that federal police are exempt from abuse of authority. However, it seems that more prominent federal institutions, such as the Court of Appeal and the Supreme Court, will be more likely than relatively obscure local and state institutions, to protect a citizen's rights. Also, to minimize jurisdictional conflicts, each police force will be empowered to enforce the laws defined and enacted for its jurisdiction. The distinctions among these laws will generally follow the pattern of the constitutional distinctions among Exclusive (federal), Concurrent (state and federal), and Residual (state) matters of government.

In recommending the three-tier police, it is recognized that a further balkanization of policing will not solve the law enforcement problem in Nigeria. This means that creating alternative nationwide police organizations whose subject matter jurisdictions are too narrow and insignificant will impede efforts to improve law enforcement. Such compartmentalization unnecessarily duplicates the functions of the NPF and complicates law enforcement generally. The focus should be on reforming the NPF and other law enforcement organizations to improve policing (see "Arms for the Civil Defence Corps?" 2008; see also Usigbe and Salem, 2008). The Nigeria Security and Civil Defense Corps (NSCDC) illustrate the waste and danger of duplicating policing organizations in this way.

Prior to 2004, the NSCDC was private and voluntary and operated behind the scenes of the NPF to assist with such duties as crowd control. The *Nigeria Security and Civil Defence Corps Act, 2003* established the corps as a government agency. A 2007 Amendment Act (No. 6) expanded the NSCDC powers allowing it to establish a special squad to bear arms. How, if at all, will the new NSCDC improve law enforcement in Nigeria? If anything, it is more likely to further complicate the already unwieldy, ineffective, and inefficient law enforcement system. Also, the resources that should go to improve the NPF are diverted to the new NSCDC unnecessarily. Further, there is a legitimate concern that the NSCDC armed personnel may not be sufficiently trained in weapons bearing and use. There is a strong chance that the situation may increase the already unacceptably high rate of law enforcement misuse of weapons resulting in "accidental discharges," which kill or injure unarmed civilians. Thus, the NSCDC expansion is inconsistent with the three-tier police model recommended in this book. Also, the expansion is far from the desired law enforcement restructuring Nigeria needs.

Two, *Ensure Quick, Rather Than Delayed, Law Enforcement*: Nigeria's official postcolonial justice system is reputed to be slow and often unjust. This citizens' perception spans the entire system. In particular, the NPF is generally viewed as incapable or unwilling to accelerate the law enforcement function to solve crimes quickly unless an interested party offers inducement to an influential NPF official. The "justice delayed, is justice denied" maxim is notoriously present in Nigerian law enforcement. One of the attractive characteristics of indigenous law enforcement in various parts of Nigeria is its ability to deliver "instant justice," such as by the *Bakassi Boys* (a Survey Reaction Participant in response to Question 12, Appendix A). Generally, "instant justice" connotes reckless vigilantism – a negative quality.

However, a comprehensive reading of the Survey Reaction Participant's overall response shows that "instant justice" is used instead to portray the positive quality of the indigenous justice process to take up and respond decidedly to a case in a short period of time. Parties in the indigenous process generally regard the time required in the process as shorter than what the English system commands. However, in a reconstructed Nigerian justice system, law enforcement need not be as quick and as unchecked as it may have been under the *Bakassi Boys*. This is because the *Bakassi Boys* are sometimes perceived as willing to compromise accuracy for quickness in adjudication and enforcement. Quick injustice should always be avoided, particularly in a reconstructed Nigerian system.

Additionally, the speed, efficiency, and accountability of postcolonial law enforcement should be increased. One way to do so is to change the policy statements regarding official law enforcement with a view to decentralizing police work, command, and control. The policy statements are contained in the constitution, *Police Act*, and other laws. A decentralization of the police organization, command, and responsibilities will obligate the police in each jurisdiction to respond to, and address, the same problems and issues that concern the citizens in that jurisdiction. The police will be made to answer to the citizens in the jurisdiction. Such local-based obligation will strongly challenge the police to address the citizens' needs and to do so efficiently. To retain their jobs, the police leaders in each jurisdiction will be greatly interested in working consistently with their citizens' interests. This will be further enhanced by an adoption of the recommended three-tier police system.

Three, *Re-Emphasize Shaming*: Nigerian reconstructed law enforcement, like much of the entire law and justice system, should espouse the important role of shaming in behavior modification and prevention. This will acknowledge and promote the idea that a reasonable human being is likely to avoid conduct or circumstance that will reflect badly on him or her. A reasonable person with a positive reputation or image to protect in society is likely to avoid any conduct that threatens the image. Thus, with this standard in mind, criminal offenders in a reconstructed law and justice system will be processed, tried and, if convicted, shamed (through society's reaction) for their violations of societal norms consistent with the gravity of each violation. Society's reaction toward a criminal offender will be expected to discourage that specific offender as well as potential offenders and other members of society. Shaming, when properly and consistently applied to offenders, is an effective means of social control (Braithwaite, 2005).

Many pre-colonial Nigerian communities widely used shaming as an authentic instrument of social control. Some communities employ this method, through varied strategies, even in this postcolonial era. The method has worked well for generations for these communities and works well in their efforts at social control. In Igbo, for example, shaming by *igba ekpe* (public shaming by humiliating display of convict) (Okereafoezeke, 2002, pp. 154-155, 181-182) is popular. The offender, relatives, friends, and others closely connected to the offender dread the public display in *igba ekpe*. This is because *igba ekpe* does not only shame the convict, it also reflects negatively on the offender's relatives, friends, and other close associates. Thus, where shaming is applied to control behavior through *igba ekpe*, for example, the community would have *shamed* the offender, the offender thus becomes *ashamed*[12] of his/her conduct, and the offender also *shames* his/her family, friends, etc. by the conduct and public spectacle. The interconnectedness in the shaming process and participants means that a single offender transgression can affect, and often affects, a large group of people. As a result, a person should consider the implications of a planned act or omission.

Even in this modern, postcolonial era, law enforcement predicated on an appropriate form of shaming can be very effective in social control (Braithwaite, 2005). Law enforcement as well as other components of a law and justice system should aim to shame criminal law violators. The method and extent of shaming must be as appropriate in each case. The object will be to coerce citizens to self-regulate and regulate one another to avoid receiving shame, avoid being ashamed, and to prevent shaming their significant others, including family members, on account of illegal behavior. Therefore, it seems reasonable to advocate a heightened use of shaming, whatever the specific differences in methods, because of its potential to contribute to more effective social control. The nature of shaming in the modern era probably needs to be altered to accommodate changes in society. This means that the substance and procedure of a society's shaming policy will reflect the shaming options available in the society as well as the relevant guidelines to forestall abuse. Again, the strength of shaming as a control factor is that most humans tend to be wary of actions (and omissions) that are likely to portray the actors negatively before their significant others, such as parents, guardians, siblings, friends, acquaintances, neighbors, co-workers, community members, etc. Hirschi (1969, p. 3), for example, theorizes that "a person is free to commit delinquent acts because his ties to the conventional order have somehow been broken." Hirschi's (1969) thesis is extensible beyond delinquency to crimes and other deviances.

In view of the strategic roles of the persons, groups, and institutions that constitute an individual's "conventional order" (Hirschi, 1969, p. 3) or significant others, a restoration of a sense of shame in an individual will likely deter the specific person from indulging in prohibited behavior (specific deterrence) as well as help to discourage other members of the society (general deterrence) (Brown, Esbensen, and Geis, 1991, p. 91; Lanier and Henry, 1998, p. 69). Therefore, the critical roles that a citizen's "conventional order" or significant others can play in law enforcement in the modern society cannot be overemphasized. These most important or influential others, who are most attached or closest to each offender and potential offender, are most familiar with the pushes and pulls on the citizen concerning society's norms and how best to respond to temptations to violate the norms. The influential others are strategically positioned to analyze and help

---

12 Note that an offense or other violation can cause a violator to become *ashamed*, even if the community cannot or does not identify the violator as the person responsible for the conduct.

to appropriately address each norm violation, whether formally or informally (Okereafoezeke, 2002, pp. 156-157):

> People who are closest to the community members preside over and manage the traditional, unofficial case management and law enforcement organs. The members of these organs are thus better positioned to understand the traditions, customs, and laws of their communities, as well as the best ways to enforce judgments on them. On the other hand, judges of the official courts and the state law enforcement personnel are far removed from the communities whose laws the judges and law enforcement personnel are called upon to enforce. Recognition of this fact would reduce the tendency of Nigerian officials to impose laws and means of enforcing them from the top.

Thus, in the traditional society setup, the "conventional order" or significant others run the law and justice system, including law enforcement. The new setup in a reconstructed law and justice system should incorporate this idea to take advantage of the connectedness among law and justice personnel, the system within which they function, and the citizens being served.

Consistent with the idea of empowering the citizens and groups closest to an offender is the need to employ and allow more local discretion even in official court sentencing and the enforcement of those sentences. From case to case, state law enforcement personnel, working together with their indigenous-based, community counterparts should be allowed reasonable latitude to determine and enforce the most appropriate response to each transgression, such as community-supervised work instead of jail term, within the permissible boundaries of a truly citizen-centered Nigerian constitution.

Four, *Build and Maintain Strong Police-Citizen Partnership*: The critical role of accurate information gathering in law enforcement should be obvious. Since the police and other law enforcement bodies are not present at the scenes of all law violations, their personnel need the cooperation of the public to properly investigate and solve legal infractions. Citizens have to be confident in, and feel comfortable with, their law enforcement agencies to provide useful information for more effective and efficient law enforcement. Even after the police complete investigation and evidence-gathering, they need witnesses to appear in court and to testify truthfully. Again, it helps a great deal if the citizens view the police positively, perhaps as "friends," rather than "enemies." In recognition of this, the NPF has previously adopted such slogans as "The Police are Your Friends" to help portray the police more positively to the citizens. Nevertheless, the activities of the NPF personnel leave much to be desired, to the extent that Abati (2005) prefers to call the law enforcement organization "Ehindero's"[13] Police ... because to dignify the police with the name Nigeria is becoming an insult to the average Nigerian who is daily assaulted, insulted and dehumanised by the men in black" (at p. 1).

---

13 "Ehindero" refers to the then Inspector-General of Police, Sunday Ehindero.

Beyond slogans, however, law enforcement in a reconstructed Nigerian law and justice system should incorporate the citizens and the communities as vital players in law enforcement. In the new arrangement, the emphasis will be on gathering relevant information to forestall crimes and other violations and, where they occur, to solve them as quickly and as thoroughly as possible. A police-citizen partnership encouraging the citizens to confidently provide the police with useful, relevant information will greatly help the law enforcement effort. Ensuring the following two conditions and steps will strengthen this strategy and improve the quality of law enforcement in a reconstructed law and justice system.

One, formal and informal citizen involvement at the grassroots community level in police management, monitoring, and accountability is needed. To directly and/or indirectly manage, monitor, and ensure the accountability of the police, the citizens must be able to exercise reasonable ownership over the police. At present, the citizens own the police only to the extent that the police are a public organization, financed with citizens' taxes. The police do not account to the citizens. They do not even have to listen to the citizens. They need only comply with the wishes and commands of the authority controlling them: the government in power. Two, the police must convince the citizens that it is safe, not dangerous, to cooperate with the police. The police must treat their citizen sources as confidential and anonymous to avoid any type of harm to information providers. Those who provide the police with vital information to prevent and solve crimes should be comfortable that they have performed their civic duties, and not made to feel like they have acted wrongly.

Five, *Reduce Politicians' Control Over Police*: The professional political class has almost complete control of law enforcement in Nigeria, particularly the NPF. The country's postcolonial life is replete with instances of politicians at the state (or regional) and federal levels using various police organizations to prosecute their agendas. In the 1960s, 1983, and 2007 national elections in the country, for examples, the politicians shamelessly manipulated and used the NPF personnel and equipment to rig themselves into various offices or retain their positions illegally. It is clear that Nigerian politicians are incapable of protecting, and/or unwilling to protect, police integrity and professionalism. Therefore, the politicians alone cannot honestly control the country's police organizations. To ensure law enforcement independence, representatives of the political class in each jurisdiction, along with other citizens, civil society groups, and indigenous community authorities, should control, monitor, and regulate police personnel within the bounds of the country's constitution and other relevant laws.

Six, *Support and Promote Constructive Vigilante Law Enforcement*: Vigilantism typically connotes negative action. Vigilante law enforcement is often perceived as disordered and subjective law and justice exploit, a variant of anarchy. It seems that discomfort with this negative vigilante implication resulted in the following statement. In response to Question 17, Appendix A ["Do you believe that local communities (or those to whom each community delegates the function) should be responsible for order and law maintenance in their part of the country?"], one of the Survey Reaction Participants answered: "No. Most of these people [local communities and their agents] harbor prejudices, hatred and animosities – they miscarry justice." In as much as this is true in some indigenous processes, the opposite is not necessarily true regarding the English-based law enforcement system. In fact, a good case can be made that the English system in Nigeria breeds and encourages more of the negative characteristics identified by the Survey Reaction Participant. After all, English law dominates the Nigerian environment, yet official prejudices and miscarriages of justice – especially in law enforcement, courts, and prisons – are rife.

However, the following are the two main superior qualities of indigenous law enforcement over English law enforcement. The first quality is the widespread view and acceptance of the indigenous system as "owned" by the citizens and thus deserving of their faith and support. This sense of ownership fuels the citizens' drive and commitment to ensure that the indigenous system succeeds. The second quality is the general belief within the various Nigerian cultures that God (Earth, Supernatural, etc.) sees all, hears all, and knows all, and will accurately identify and reward or punish each person for actions and omissions, even if government systems and other human authorities fail to do so. For the English system on the other hand, the focus is on proof based on verified evidence. Thus, a person found "not guilty" in the English system is not responsible and cannot be punished. Constructive vigilantism, being a key aspect of the indigenous system, can be a useful component of social control in the postcolony.

Therefore, vigilantism can be a strategic means of law enforcement and social control. It can produce positive results beginning at the grassroots level. Consequently, vigilantism should be redefined and promoted in Nigeria as a healthy venture that allows the members of each community to partner with the Local, State, and Federal law enforcement agencies for improved social control. As has been pointed out in this book, relevant and useful information from community members is vital for preventing and solving crimes. Often, local community vigilante group members have the vital information that the official police need. Furthermore, community vigilante members are frequently the first line of defense for their community. Thus, before the official law enforcement personnel arrive at the scene of a crime or attempted crime, community vigilante members are usually present on the scene to manage the situation. And vigilante group members are usually able to identify useful lead sources to solve crimes that the official police are otherwise unable to solve. Generally, the vigilante members are unpaid or unsalaried volunteers[14] whose main interest is to secure their community, such as through a neighborhood watch program. Indeed, on many community events and ceremonies, vigilante members spearhead efforts to maintain security and order. Also, a private person can hire the vigilante members' services for security of life or property.

---

14 However, vigilante members may receive goods, services, or other benefits rather than specific salary or monetary compensation.

As demonstrated, vigilante groups in Nigerian communities play a vital role in protecting the citizens and their properties, especially in those parts of the country where the official police are unable or unwilling to perform credible law enforcement functions. These vigilante groups, which are commonly found in all parts of Nigeria, should be recognized and encouraged to operate within the relevant laws. Such vigilante operations will reduce the citizens' dependency on the official police. Official recognition of the role of constructive vigilantism in law enforcement will empower vigilante members to perform some key police duties, such as arrest and short-term detention of a crime suspect, in the absence of the police. As soon as practicable, a person arrested by a vigilante group should be turned over to the official police for further investigation, prosecution, etc. Again, a key benefit of including vigilante groups in official law enforcement is that it allows the community members a stake and hands-on participation in securing their community.

Seven, *Partner With the Private Sector to Provide Up-to-Date Equipment for Law Enforcement*: Reconstructed law enforcement should include official and unofficial dedication to the use of the latest law enforcement technology. In this arrangement, law enforcement personnel will be properly equipped for social control. Otherwise, crime fighters will likely lose a challenge in which the criminals have an upper technological hand. Regrettably, this has been the situation in the police fight against armed robbery, in particular, in Nigeria. Often, the police are forced to use outdated or inferior guns and other weapons to try to subdue armed robbers who routinely use sophisticated machine guns and communications devices in operations. The fire power and communications advantages to the criminals are obvious. Also, modern crime fighting and social control require substantial use of scientific knowledge and process in investigation, evidence gathering, testing, management, and presentation in the criminal justice process. A police force whose members lack proper training in scientific methods and procedures will meet with very limited success in law enforcement.

Therefore, providing the police with the latest weapons, scientific expertise training, information technology, up-to-date equipment, general knowledge, etc. will strengthen the police ability to secure the society. In response to Question 22 B of Appendix A, a Survey Reaction Participant counsels as follows: "The traditional [indigenous] law enforcement agents should be reformed to work hand in hand with the police and the latter should be more equipped to enhance efficiency." The strategic importance of safety and security for all other aspects of a society's life cannot be overstated. Steps should be taken to provide for the safety and security. Consequently, the annual budgets of the Local, State, and Federal governments should routinely provide for the best crime-fighting technology possible, including funds for scientific training, purchase of weapons, communications paraphernalia, etc. However, the governments alone need not provide the funds.

To ensure that sufficient funds are available for law enforcement, the governments should make concerted efforts to co-opt private businesses, organizations, groups, and individuals to join in the efforts to properly equip, train, and otherwise support the police for more effective and efficient law enforcement. It seems logical that such private entities will join in the efforts because of the promise of increased and better security of lives and properties; it makes business sense to spend a little more to protect oneself and property. While asking private parties to assist with equipping the police, the governments must use the funds realized in the process with utmost transparency and judiciousness. Many contributors to the Nigerian Police Equipment Fund (PEF) have had bad experiences, including diversion and misuse of funds. Steps must be taken to avoid a repeat of those experiences. It is only then that private parties would invest willingly and confidently. Note however that whatever the contributions private parties make to equip the police, the governments are ultimately responsible for securing the lives and properties of the citizens. Providing such security is the basic function of government. Therefore, the governments remain accountable on the issue of the security of the citizens' lives and properties.

Eight, *Demand and Enforce High Character and Ethics Standards for Law Enforcement Personnel*: Williams (2003) reports on a Nigerian national survey in which the citizens ranked the Nigeria Police Force (NPF) as the country's most corrupt public institution. Also, in "The Federal Government and the Nigeria Police" (2007), *The Guardian* editorializes that the NPF is the "most visible symbol of corruption in Nigeria." See further Abati (2008). This common conclusion is hardly surprising. Bribery and corruption are major impediments to law enforcement in Nigeria, especially via the NPF. Often, the twin ills of bribery and corruption lead to, or provide the basis for, police brutality against innocent citizens. Tales of police bribery, corruption, and brutality are all too common (Iloegbunam, 2002; Abati, 2002; Jamiu, 2005).

In "Police Brutality in Afahakpo Enwang" (2007), about 100 NPF personnel invaded an Akwa Ibom state community while the citizens slept in the night and murdered several community members while raping others. The police also destroyed property. Allegedly, these police actions occurred because the police had illegally collected money from commercial transporters and hid the money in the bushes. But before the police could take away their illegal collections, the money went missing. Angered by their loss of the loot, the police placed the blame on the community members and decided to avenge the loss. Indeed, such occurrences are all too common. In the absence of strong corrective measures to deal with the uniformed criminals in our midst, the undesirable NPF and other law enforcement personnel operate with impunity (Amao, 2002). See also Last (2007) who reports on police "entrenched abuses" and how the police routinely execute Nigerians alleged to be "armed robbery suspects" without resort to due process.

Most of the Survey Reaction Participants involved in the research for this book hold the view that police corruption is a major problem confronting law enforcement in Nigeria. Asked to express relative confidence in effective social control between indigenous and English systems in Nigeria (Question 12 of Appendix A), a Survey Reaction Participant offers this perspective: "The Nigeria Police Force model should be ideal. But in Nigeria, the corruption in Nigeria Police is so alarming that the populace has lost complete confidence in them, and [that] renders Native-based [law enforcement] acceptable." Another Survey Reaction Participant agrees with this view, as follows: "Where the police has[sic] not lost focus through corruption, law enforcement is better done by police, otherwise native-based [systems] such as OPC [Odu'a People's Congress] and Bakassi Boys will be welcome."

The innumerable cases of police corruption in Nigeria lead to this question: How can police corruption be minimized to ensure law enforcement effectiveness and efficiency? Increasing the earnings of police officers and personnel does not appear to reduce corruption ("The Nigerian Police Force – A Friend or Enemy?" 2008). Ways to address the corruption scourge include recruiting only enlightened or educated persons with the proper character and ethics to resist the corruption temptations. Also, persons already employed in policing should be constantly reminded to demonstrate high character and ethics, with sanctions against those that fail to do so. More than in the past, the character and ethics of an applicant to a law enforcement position should weigh heavily on a decision regarding hiring such a person. Professional evaluation of a prospective employee's character and ethical standings should be built into the application and interview process. As much as possible, the evaluation should have high predictive validity. Accurate determination of a prospective employee's suitability for employment and prospects as a law enforcement official will save the police organization and the country future human and material costs that would otherwise result from such negative qualities as incompetence, bad judgment, corruption, and abuse of police powers.

Persons already employed in law enforcement should be routinely evaluated on job performance. As in the case of prospective police officers, character and ethics considerations will form major portions of the evaluations of serving officers. Character and ethics are central to law enforcement ("Between the People and the Police," 2002). Considering the importance of discretion in law enforcement, only individuals with good character, ethics, and judgment should be placed in positions to exercise law enforcement authority over the citizens. It is trite that discretion is at the heart of performing law enforcement duties. It is also pedestrian that law enforcement action or inaction can lead to the loss of a citizen's life or liberty. Therefore, prospective and serving officers found to perform below acceptable judgment, character, or ethical level in evaluations should be disciplined as necessary. Discipline for a serving officer should include suspension, dismissal, criminal prosecution, and sentence, if convicted.

Nine, *Indigenize Law Enforcement*: The NPF remains structured along the lines of colonial British policing. It is impossible to separate the NPF from colonial or neo-colonial Britain even though the contemporary officers and personnel of the NPF are Nigerians exclusively. The reality of the official police as a colonial legacy remains strong. Umaru Yar'Adua's government of Nigeria reinforced this colonial legacy when in 2007 (47 years after Nigerian independence from Britain) the Nigerian regime officially invited the British police to help to build an effective and efficient police organization for Nigeria (Idonor, 2007; "Nigeria Asks UK to Train Police," 2007; Chesa, 2007; Nwankwo, 2007). It is ironic and damning of the Nigerian postcolonial society that five decades after Nigeria severed the British imperialist cord, a Nigerian government, allegedly to build an effective and efficient police, invited Britain to Nigeria to build a Nigerian Police even though it was Britain that had entrenched and set Nigeria on the path to its present ineffective and inefficient policing.

Prior to Yar'Adua's invitation of the British police, the erstwhile Olusegun Obasanjo's government had signed an aid pact with the USA ("Nigeria, U.S. Sign Pact on Aid to Police," 2002; Oladotun, 2002). The agreement is another illustration of the wrong points of emphasis for law enforcement in Nigeria. Government policies should focus mainly on utilizing indigenous systems, strategies, and human and material resources, which are abundant. Efforts at building an effective and efficient Nigerian police in concert with Britain or the USA are likely to fail because neither Britain nor the USA has much, if any, stake in good policing in Nigeria. Such stake, along with all the expertise and knowledge needed to build an effective and efficient policing system, is located among Nigerians, not among foreigners.

Recognizing that the NPF is a colonial legacy that needs to be changed to address the security and law enforcement needs of contemporary Nigerians, "The Federal Government and the Nigeria Police" (2007) contains the following observation (at pp. 1-2):

> The Nigeria Police Force has deep roots in our colonial past. It is a force both in nomenclature, operational doctrine, culture and orientation. It was created to serve the purposes of the state, which in the colonial period, was often at variance with the desires and aspirations of the people. This institutional and cultural inheritance has not changed much, almost half a century after independence. Instead the force, as an extension of the state, has imbibed the worse attitude of the ruling elite: a rapacious and buccaneering pillaging of state resources for personal accumulation. The Nigeria Police Force has become the eternal symbol of the failure of the state to meet its prime responsibility: providing for the security and well-being of the citizenry. It is also the most visible symbol of corruption in Nigeria. The president will do well to recognise that the Nigeria Police Force requires urgent and fundamental reorganisation in its structure, orientation, operational doctrine, culture and modus operandi. The government has to re-organise the police to meet the expectations of Nigerians. The police have to be changed from a force to a people-oriented organisation: responsible to the people, run by the people and operating for the people. Nigerians want a police organisation that will provide community service functions; that will focus on primary police duties such as crime prevention, detection and investigation. They want a police institution that will protect them from the menace of armed robbers and hired assassins.

This quote accurately captures Nigerians' views of the NPF and the changes needed to improve law enforcement in the country.

Indigenous law enforcement is well positioned to provide many of the needed changes to law enforcement in Nigeria. Therefore, the country's reconstructed law enforcement should be predicated on indigenized policing. Home-grown law enforcement will identify, adopt, and utilize effective and efficient indigenous, as well as useful aspects of English and other, strategies for improved law enforcement (Okafọ, 2007). The *Bakassi Boys* model in southeast Nigeria, which has proved effective and efficient (Okafọ, 2007), among other indigenous models, deserves to be incorporated into a reconstructed system. Aura is an important component of the effectiveness and efficiency of the *Bakassi Boys* in southeast Nigeria. The widely held belief in the magical power of the *Bakassi Boys* to identify hidden offenders weighs heavily on the minds of the citizens. Many citizens interviewed in the course of the research for this book emphatically stated that the *Bakassi Boys* have the capacity to accurately identify, and have on numerous occasions accurately identified, criminal offenders for offenses committed in secrecy. Also, that the criminals have subsequently verifiably confessed to their crimes. Thus, the widespread perception, fear, and respect for this form of law enforcement are powerful. As much as is practicable within a constitutional State, the services of the *Bakassi Boys* and other similar organizations should be utilized.

The power of indigenous law enforcement processes, such as those involving the *Bakassi Boys*, is present in other African societies. This power is an important aid to effective and efficient social control. In the midst of the December 2007 disputed presidential elections in Kenya, which returned President Mwai Kibaki to office, supporters of the opposition Orange Democratic Movement (ODM), believing that the ODM won the election, staged massive protests against the presidential poll results. Some criminals took advantage of the unrest to loot property. The Kenyan police were powerless to control the situation. Thus, crime victims lacked protection. As a result, victims resorted to witchcraft, an indigenous mode of protection. Shortly after the looting, offenders voluntarily returned stolen property to the owners and to the police ("Kenyans Hand Back 'Cursed' Loot," 2008). According to one criminal who had a change of heart (p. 2): "I am fearful for my life because of the ghosts, that is why I decided to return the property." The police acknowledged the important role of witchcraft in crime control in the country. However, one senior police officer quipped (at p. 2): "Whether ghosts exist or not, our work has been made easy. I wish there were ghosts all over the country." What is undeniable is that Kenyans' belief in witchcraft has led to increased social control by encouraging criminals to return what they had stolen without official criminal justice intervention.

The Kenyan experience shows that the effectiveness and efficiency of a justice system depends partly but importantly on the perceptions of the persons whose behaviors are sought to be controlled. Citizens' positive perception of a justice system will likely encourage them to exercise greater self-control than they would in the midst of a negatively perceived system. Similarly, citizens' positive perception of a justice system will likely encourage them to abide more by the prescriptions of the system's social control regime than they would abide by the rules of a negatively perceived system. In short, negative perception will lead to reduced controls (self-control, social control, etc.). Therefore, where the citizens of a reconstructed justice system hold their indigenous system (or some element thereof) in high esteem, the indigenous system should be made a core component of the reconstructed system, to increase positive public perception.

Unfortunately, instead of fashioning proper policy and program to blend indigenous and foreign law enforcement methods, it is habitual for Nigerian governments to seek to outlaw the indigenous processes and organizations. The Olusegun Obasanjo presidency (1999-2007) initiated legislation to proscribe the ethnic-based law enforcement organizations in the country. But the government proscription effort does not address the facts that justify the existence of these organizations (Onuorah, 2002). Unfortunately, the Human Rights Watch group has fallen into the same error by advocating for the proscription of these law enforcement organizations (see "The Bakassi Boys: The Legitimization of Murder and Torture," 2002; "Government Must Disband Vigilante Groups," 2002). There is little doubt that any official law banning these indigenous law enforcement organizations will produce, at best, qualified success. The organizations can operate underground as long as the citizens need the organizations to safeguard and regulate life and property (Olarinoye, 2002).

To be sure, in spite of their usefulness for security and social control, some of the *Bakassi Boys*' law enforcement practices may contradict criminal suspects' rights and modern notions of decency. Thus, such practices will need to be modified, as necessary, for a reconstructed law and justice system. In answer to Question 12 ("Are you more confident in indigenous law enforcement or English law enforcement for effective social control?"), Appendix A, one of the Survey Reaction Participants (a senior law student) states:

> It is not a matter of this or that. Bakassi Boys today is accepted because of the failures recorded in the hands of the police. Even at that the idea of killing people in the streets is devoid of the sanctity of the human person. Enforcement of the law on the principle of "kill and you will be killed" does not augur well especially when the process of detection is shrouded in secrecy. Since the police seem to have failed, I suggest a blend of both the Native based with the English based [law enforcement styles], assuming they can both be blended.

Further, in response to Question 22 B of Appendix A, the Survey Reaction Participant states: "In the area of law enforcement there is every need to involve native law enforcement agencies especially now that the number of police is so small to effectively check crime in the country." I share the Survey Reaction Participant's sentiments, especially where the resulting mixed model emphasizes Nigeria's indigenous systems and incorporates useful elements of the English and other foreign ideas to complement the indigenous system. Also, the resulting model will bring deficient indigenous practices in line with citizens' constitutional rights.

One of the biggest obstacles to the official adoption and use of indigenous law enforcement and other indigenous social control methods in the modern State is the perception that the indigenous system is crude, backward, and belongs to a bygone era. Justified or not, this view is widely held, especially in the face of Western media onslaught that constantly reminds the "third world" citizens that they need to abandon their roots and essences and escape to a developed human condition, which the West invariably defines as living in uniformity with Western notions, interpretations, and ideals. Thus, courageous and wise citizenry and leadership are central to the indigenization of a postcolony's law enforcement and other aspects of justice – courage to rediscover and advance the indigenous ideals and wisdom to understand and properly use complementary ideas from other societies for more effective and efficient social control.

Ten, *Improve the Ratio of Police to Citizens*: Aside from corruption, remuneration, technological, and other inadequacies facing policing in Nigeria, the sheer number of the officers and personnel is grossly inadequate for effective social control of the country. In 2001, the then police commissioner of Lagos State (Nigeria) stated that the 12,000 officers and personnel under him were inadequate to effectively police the state and its 12.5 million residents. Note that 4,000 of the 12,000 were drivers, artisans, and other staff categories, while the other 8,000 were line personnel. Based on these numbers, 1 police officer in Lagos is available to about 1,042 residents. This ratio is against the 2001 United Nations (UN) advised proportion of 1 police officer to about 400 people (see "Okiro at *The Guardian*, Lists Obstacles to Police Efficiency," 2001). According to Okiro (at p. 1):

> The United Nations approved ratio of police and the citizen is a policeman to 400 persons. This UN ratio may have been obtained using a parameter based on the city of New York where the United Nations headquarters is sited. New York, being a developed city, the streets are well mapped out, houses are properly numbered, there is constant electricity supply and effective communication is available to all, including members of the police force. The Lagos City is the reverse of that scenario. In Lagos, save for may be developed areas like the Victoria Island, Ikoyi, Surulere, Isolo and a few others, enclaves like Ajegunle, Amukoko, Ajangbadi, Shibiri and others are often times haphazardly numbered and do witness perennial outages making it difficult for policemen in response to distress call to such places to trace scenes of incident swiftly.

One of the Survey Reaction Participants for this research, a Local Government Councilor, presented an even worse picture when he put the existing ratio at 1 police officer to 400,000 Nigerians. That is a daunting burden on a Nigerian police officer. Note that the UN has since revised its recommendations on proper policing ratio. Its revised ratio is 1 police officer to 100 residents ("Okiro and the Number of Policemen," 2008). That is reasonable and will likely lead to more effective and efficient law enforcement. However, Nigeria has taken no significant step to adequately address the problem of insufficient law enforcement personnel in the country years after Okiro's 2001 statement. An expansion of the grassroots base of policing in postcolonial Nigeria to involve more citizens in the effort will likely alleviate the insufficiency of personnel.

Specifically, to address the gross shortage of police officers in Nigeria, the federal government, which currently controls the NPF, should take emergency measures to increase the number of police personnel. The measures should include the hiring, training, and deployment of many more police officers throughout the country. Assuming that the size of the NPF is 377,000 police officers ("Okiro and the Number of Policemen," 2008),[15] the aim should be to triple the size of the force in the shortest time possible. This will tackle the palpable inadequacy of police officers in many parts of the country. Of course, such a task force-like increase in the NPF strength should not compromise the high quality expected of good police officers. In this era of extreme unemployment, qualified Nigerians are available to be recruited into policing if the conditions of service are good. Also, even in the process of effecting quick hiring, training, and deployment, adequate checks of the characters of prospective employees should be performed. As noted in this book, the character and ethics of officers and personnel are vital to the performance and image of policing. So far, the NPF has suffered significantly on this score. New recruits should not compound the force's problems.

It is important to mention that the recommendation for recruiting more police officers and personnel under the NPF umbrella is offered as an interim measure. It should be implemented with minimum delay while the necessary constitutional and legal negotiations for redesigning law enforcement along the lines suggested in this book take place. Simply expanding the size of the NPF, to be run as a larger version of the current NPF, will not solve the country's law enforcement problems. Control and influence over the police organizations have to be significantly extended to the different layers of government and to the citizens.

Eleven, *Redesign Police Training Curriculum*: Revamping the curriculum for police training in Nigeria will be a major law enforcement reconstruction step. The mindset of the average cop in Nigeria needs to change. After overhaul, under the new curriculum, police personnel should be taught to view and relate to citizens civilly and courteously, to serve the country by serving the citizen, and to carry out all police duties lawfully and honorably. The likelihood of achieving these ideals depends greatly on the police orientation – the methods and processes for recruiting, training, supervising, assessing, and re-training police personnel. Ferreira's (2002) observations on these issues are instructive:

---

15 The report that IGP Okiro does not know the number of police officers and personnel in the NPF is highly embarrassing, to say the least. Of course, this exemplifies the stunning incompetence in the NPF.

... we need to redesign the Nigeria Police training curriculum. The psychology of the colonial anti-people police whereby the people were seen in the minds of policemen as unruly gangs of anti-government rioters, should by now, be confined to the dustbin of colonial history, which by our historical claim, ended some forty-two years ago.[16] We remember that our military politicians re-colonised our people until very recently. The present government has a duty to discard the colonial police mentality into the graveyard of the past. The new Nigerian policeman must, during training, be thoroughly immersed in psychology to enable him respond, even on his own, intelligently to unexpected human situations. His psyche must be such that he must continuously remember that correction of the lawless citizen back into the line of order in society is his objective and not thoughtless decimation of the lawless citizen. Fifthly, the police training colleges should routinely accept only recruits and trainees that have been psychologically screened. If[sic] does no good to our society for those who are required to prevent and control crime to be no different from the criminals. A structured psychological assessment must aim at recruiting emotionally stable and psychologically balanced personnel to become officers and men of the Nigeria Police. Of course, even after enlistment and training, annual psychological re-assessment should be an important part of routine police personnel management. Those who have acquired emotional instability or psychological disruption should be routinely weeded out of the police.

Ferreira's (2002) prescriptions, if implemented, will go a long way to properly prepare and position NPF training recruits and graduates to perform their assignments within the Nigerian constitution and laws. To ensure this, the new training curriculum will strongly emphasize the need for police officers to always function within the ambit of the law, using ethics and good judgment. Police officers and personnel who violate the constitution or other law will be disciplined as appropriate in each circumstance, including criminal prosecution and the imposition of criminal sanction.

Chapter Summary and Conclusion

What are the important procedural and substantive elements of a reconstructed Nigerian law and justice system, with particular reference to law making and law enforcement? What are the most effective and efficient ways to enforce such laws? How can the country's indigenous and foreign systems work together to achieve greater social control? These questions capture some of the major challenges facing law making and law enforcement in contemporary Nigeria. This chapter has attempted to respond to the questions. In essence, efforts at reconstructing law and justice will include repositioning credible, effective, and efficient traditions,

---

16 As of the year of the cited source – 2002.

customs, and indigenous laws (customary law) as the foundation of the modern State laws. Also, credible, effective, and efficient indigenous methods of law enforcement will have to be maintained and routinely used even in the modern State. However, indigenous laws and enforcement procedures that have fallen out of step with modern standards will be modified. But in transforming indigenous laws and procedures, "modernism" should not be used as an excuse to destroy or emasculate an otherwise viable indigenous law or a process for its enforcement. Perhaps most importantly, sincere, committed, and patriotic political leadership is required to effect the substantial changes necessary in the current postcolonial laws and the modes of enforcing them.

References

Abati, R. (2002, July 7) "Our Policemen Have Gone Mad Again" in *The Guardian*, http://www.ngrguardiannews.com/editorial_opinion/article1; Internet.

Abati, R. (2005, April 30) "Ehindero's Police" in *The Guardian*, http://www.guardiannewsngr.com/editorial_opinion/article02; Internet.

Abati, R. (2008, January 11) "Much Ado About Police Reform" in *The Guardian*, http://www.guardiannewsngr.com/editorial_opinion/article02//indexn2_html?pdate=11010...; Internet.

Abudu v. Eguakun (2003, July 11) Nigerian Supreme Court Case Number 77/1996. See Guardian Law Report at http://www.ngrguardiannews.com/law/article04; Internet.

Akiri, C. (2004, June 21) "Translating the Constitution" in *The Guardian* (Nigeria).

Amao, O. (2002, November 18) "The Problem With the Police" in *The Guardian*, http://www.ngrguardiannews.com/editorial_opinion/article4; Internet. "Arms for the Civil Defence Corps?" (2008, January 6) in *The Guardian* (Nigeria).

Baah, R. A. (2000) *Human Rights in Africa: The Conflict of Implementation*. New York, New York, USA: University Press of America. "Between the People and the Police" (2002, December 20) in *The Guardian*, http://www.ngrguardiannews.com/editorial_opinion/article1; Internet.

Boda, M. (1999, February 25) "Building Credibility Without a Constitution" in *CNN* online, http://www.cnn.com/SPECIALS/1999/nigerian.elections/stories/boda.essay/; Internet.

Braithwaite, J. (2005) *Crime, Shame and Reintegration*. New York, USA: Cambridge University Press.

Brown, S. E., Esbensen, F.-A., and Geis, G. (1991) *Criminology: Explaining Crime and Its Context*. Cincinnati, Ohio, USA: Anderson Publishing.

Chesa, C. (2007, November 27) "Yar'Adua Seeks Britain's Assistance for Police" in Daily Independent, http://odili.net/news/source/2007/nov/27/701.html; Internet.

Constitution of the Federal Republic of Nigeria 1999.

Cunneen, C. (2002) "Restorative Justice and the Politics of Decolonization" in E. G. M. Weitekamp, and , H.-J Kerner., eds. *Restorative Justice: Theoretical Foundations*, Portland, Oregon, USA: Willan Publishing, pp. 32-49.

Enahoro, A. (2002) "The National Question: Towards a New Constitutional Order," a guest lecture at the Yoruba Tennis Club, Onikan, Lagos, July 2, 2002. See http://www.waado.org/NigerDelta/Essays/Politics/NationalQuestion-Enahoro.html; Internet.

Ferreira, A. (2002, July 7, p. 3) "New Orientation for the Police" in *The Guardian*, http://www.ngrguardiannews.com/editorial_opinion/article3; Internet.

Ganagana, M. (2007, September 5) "Nigeria Among Safest Countries in the World, Says Okiro" in *Daily Sun*, http://www.sunnewsonline.com/webpages/news/national/2007/sept/05/national-05-09-2007-...; Internet.

"Government Must Disband Vigilante Groups" (2002, May 21) *Human Rights Watch*, wysiwyg://25/http://allafrica.com/stories/printable/200205210001.html; Internet.

Hart, V. (2003, July) "Democratic Constitution Making" in *United States Institute of Peace Special Report* 107. Report is available Online at http://www.usip.org/pubs/specialreports/sr107.html; Internet.

Hirschi, T. (1969) *Causes of Delinquency*. Berkeley, California, USA: University of California Press.

Idonor, D. (2007, November 27) "Britain to Reorganise Nigeria Police" in *Daily Champion*, http://odili.net/news/source/2007/nov/27/804.html; Internet.

Iloegbunam, C. (2002, June 25) "The Police Farce" in *Vanguard*, http://www.vanguardngr.com/news/articles/2002/June/25062002/c4250602.htm; Internet.

Jamiu, H. (2005, May 10) "Encounter with the Police" in *The Guardian*, http://www.guardiannewsngr.com/editorial_opinion/article04; Internet.

"Kenyans Hand Back 'Cursed' Loot" (2008, January 8) in *BBC NEWS* online, http://news.bbc.co.uk/1/hi/world/africa/7176673.stm; Internet.

Kolajo, A. A. (2000) *Customary Law in Nigeria Through the Cases*. Spectrum Books.

Lanier, M. M. and Henry, S. (1998) *Essential Criminology*. Boulder, Colorado, USA: Westview Press.

Last, A. (2007, November 18) "Inquiry Call Over Nigeria Deaths" in *BBC NEWS* online, http://news.bbc.co.uk/1/hi/world/africa/7100741.stm; Internet.

"Legislator Wants Constitution in Nigerian Languages" (2000, February 24) in *The Guardian*, http://www.ngrguardiannews.com/news2/nn777402.html; Internet.

Madunagu, E. (2002, December 5) "The Nigerian State and Its Laws" in *The Guardian*, http://www.ngrguardiannews.com/editorial_opinion/article4; Internet.

"Nigeria: Government Misleads World About Death Penalty Record" (2007, December 17) *Amnesty International*, http://www.amnesty.org/en/for-media/

press-releases/nigeria-government-misleads-world-about-death-penalty-record-20071217; Internet.
"Nigeria, U.S. Sign Pact on Aid to Police" (2002, August 19) in *The Guardian*, http://www.ngrguardiannews.com/news/article6; Internet.
"Nigeria Asks UK to Train Police" (2007, November 27) in *BBC NEWS* online, http://news.bbc.co.uk/1/hi/world/Africa/7114493.stm; Internet.
"Nigeria Confirms State Executions" in *BBC NEWS* online, http://news.bbc.co.uk/1/hi/world/africa/7148720.stm; Internet.
Nigeria Security and Civil Defence Corps Act, 2003.
"Nigeria Upgrades Main Local Languages" (2007, April 13) in *Afrol News*, http://www.afrol.com/articles/12070; Internet.
Nwankwo, C. (2007, November 27) "Insecurity: Yar'Adua Invites Britain to Assist Police" in *Punch*, http://odili.net/news/source/2007/nov/27/420.html; Internet.
Nzimiro, I. (1972) *Studies in Ibo Political Systems: Chieftaincy and Politics in Four Niger States*. Berkeley, California, USA: University of California Press.
Ogbu, A. (2004, November 8) "Obasanjo Seeks Mandatory 10-Year Review of Laws" in *ThisDay News*, http://www.thisdayonline.com/news/20040812news05.html; Internet.
Okafọ, N. (2003b) "Religious Labels and Conduct Norms in Government" in *NigeriaWorld* (March 13). See http://nigeriaworld.com/articles/2003/mar/132.html; Internet.
Okafọ, N. (2005, March 1) "Foundations of Ọkija Justice" in *NigeriaWorld*, http://nigeriaworld.com/articles/2005/mar/033.html; Internet.
Okafọ, N. (2007) "Law Enforcement in Postcolonial Africa: Interfacing Indigenous and English Policing in Nigeria" in *International Police Executive Symposium (IPES) Working Paper Series*, Number 7, May 2007, pp. 1-24.
Okafọ, N. (2008) "Understanding the Historical Challenges of Reconciling Nigerian and English Laws for Modern Nigeria" in *Africa & Beyond*, January-March, pp. 59-61.
Okereafọezeke [a.k.a. Okafọ], N. (1996) *The Relationship Between Informal and Formal Strategies of Social Control: An Analysis of the Contemporary Methods of Dispute Processing Among the Igbos of Nigeria*. UMI Number 9638581. Ann Arbor, Michigan, USA: University Microfilms.
Okereafọezeke [a.k.a. Okafọ], N. (2000) "Repugnancy Test (Policy) and the Impact of Colonially Imposed Laws on the Growth of Nigeria's Native Justice Systems" in *The Journal of African Policy Studies*, Volume 6, Number 1, pp. 55-74.
Okereafọezeke [a.k.a. Okafọ], N. (2002) *Law and Justice in Post-British Nigeria: Conflicts and Interactions Between Native and Foreign Systems of Social Control in Igbo*. Westport, Connecticut, USA: Greenwood Press.
Okereafọezeke [a.k.a. Okafọ], N. (2003) "Human Rights in Africa: The Conflict of Implementation, by Richard Amoako Baah" (book review) in *Africa Today*, Volume 50, Number 1 (Spring/Summer), pp. 120-122.

Okereke, Godpower (1995) "Police Officers' Perceptions of the Nigeria Police Force: Its Effects on the Social Organization of Policing" in *Journal of Criminal Justice*, Vol. 23, No. 3, pp. 277-285.

"Okiro and the Number of Policemen" (2008, November 4) in *The Guardian*, http://www.ngrguardiannews.com/editorial_opinion/article01//indexn2_html?pdate=04110...; Internet.

"Okiro at *The Guardian*, Lists Obstacles to Police Efficiency" (2001, April 13) in *The Guardian*, http://www.ngrguardiannews.com/news2/nn818305.html; Internet.

Okocha, O. C. J. (2003, December 23) "Only National Conference Can Make a New Constitution for Nigeria" in *The Guardian* (Nigeria).

Okoli, A. (2007, December 18) "Lawyer Chides Discrimination Against Women" in *Vanguard*, http://www.vanguardngr.com/index.php?option=com_content&task=view&id=3208&Itemid=45; Internet.

Oladotun, R. (2002, December 20) "US Denies Imposing Police System on Nigeria" in *ThisDay News*, http://www.thisdayonline.com/news/20021220news08.html; Internet.

Olarinoye, G. (2002, June 5) "Centre for Constitutional Governance Condemns Bill on Ethnic Militia" in *Vanguard*, wysiwyg://19/http://www.vanguardngr...les/2002/June/05062002/w1050602.htm; Internet.

Onuorah, M. (2002, October 5) "Obasanjo Explains Clampdown on Bakassi Boys" in *The Guardian*, http://www.ngrguardiannews.com/news/article6; Internet.

Oyekanmi, R. (1999, August 19) "Nigerian Languages Can Aid Development, Says Bamgbose" in *The Guardian*, http://www.ngrguardiannews.com/features/ft758509.htm; Internet.

"Police Brutality in Afahakpo Enwang" (2007, October 10) in *The Guardian*, http://www.guardiannewsngr.com/editorial_opinion/article01; Internet.

"Re-inventing the Nigeria Police" (2005, June 3) in *The Guardian*, http://www.guardiannewsngr.com/editorial_opinion/article01; Internet.

Soyinka, W. (2000, March 3) "Constitution and Continuity" in *The Guardian*, http://www.ngrguardiannews.com/politics/pp778201.html; Internet.

"The Bakassi Boys: The Legitimization of Murder and Torture" (2002, May) *Human Rights Watch*, Volume 14, Number 5 (A).

"The Federal Government and the Nigeria Police" (2007, June 11) in *The Guardian*, http://www.guardiannewsngr.com/editorial_opinion/article01; Internet.

"The Nigerian Police Force – A Friend or Enemy?" (2008, February 1) in *Sahara Reporters*, http://www.saharareporters.com/www/report/detail/?id=504; Internet.

"The Panel on Police Reform" (2008, January 21) in *The Guardian*, http://www.guardiannewsngr.com/editorial_opinion/article01//; Internet.

"UN Calls for Halt to Executions" (2007, December 18), *Amnesty International*, http://www.amnesty.org/en/news-and-updates/news/un-calls-halt-executions-20071218; Internet.

Usigbe, L. and Salem, T. (2008, January 12) "Reps Clash Over Guns for Civil Corps" in *Vanguard*, http://www.vanguardngr.com/index.php?option=com; Internet.

Van Ness, D. (2002) "The Shape of Things to Come: A Framework for Thinking About a Restorative Justice System" in E. G. M. Weitekamp and H.-J. Kerner, eds. *Restorative Justice: Theoretical Foundations*. Portland, Oregon, USA: Willan Publishing, pp. 1-20.

Williams, A. (2003, November 30) "Report Rank Police, Nigeria's Most Corrupt Public Institution" in *The Guardian*, http://www.guardiannewsngr.com/news/article05; Internet.

Chapter 7
Model Law and Justice: Adjudication and Corrections

Chapter Introduction

The following are the two broad components of this chapter on the ingredients of a reconstructed postcolonial law and justice system: Case Processing and Adjudication; Corrections and Other Post-trial Actions. The subtopics cover two of the four relevant subject matters and the applicable agencies of law and justice, such as those of Nigeria. Chapter 6 addressed the other two subject matters: Rule and Law Making; Rule and Law Enforcement.

Case Processing and Adjudication

Official case processing and adjudication (that is, hearing and deciding grievances, conflicts, and disputes in government courts and tribunals) in contemporary Nigeria are mainly English system-based. Thus, the postcolonial Nigerian judicial system lacks many crucial elements of reconstructed law and justice. This section of this book focuses on strengthening the argument that credible, effective, and efficient case processing and adjudication components of a reconstructed law and justice system should be predicated mainly on an indigenous-based, rather than foreign-based, judiciary. This means that the structure, process, and other key elements of the postcolonial judiciary will be redesigned and redefined to reflect the country's indigenous foundation. At present, the fundamentally important indigenous ingredients of justice processing and adjudication are absent in Nigeria's official judiciary. The enormous advantages of reconstructing the country's judicial institution and process to reflect the indigenous character are identified and discussed in this section.

A survey of contemporary Nigerian law and justice system identifies the following key issues as requiring the identified actions as parts of an effort to redesign the process for hearing and judging cases in the country.

One, *Entrench the Idea of Law as the People's Statement of Their History*: It should be beyond argument that a people's laws should reflect in their core the citizens' history, experiences, knowledge, and expectations. This means that every law that a court or other judicial body is called upon to apply and decide will derive its meaning, objective, and goal from the citizens. However, in the appropriate circumstances, judges will consider outside influences – immediate neighbors as well as farther removed peoples – additionally, as and to the extent necessary, from case to case. A law interpreted and applied consistent with this construing model is more likely to provide meaningful answers to the citizens' needs. In the absence of proper focus on the indigenous laws and systems, it is easy for citizens to feel alienated in their homeland. Unfortunately, the Nigerian postcolonial law and justice system largely compels the average citizen to be alienated, in Nigeria. This is because of the prominence of English law in Nigeria – both in terms of specific English-based provisions and the unduly high regard many Nigerian law makers and judges accord English interpretations in the application of Nigerian laws.

In answer to Question 9 of Appendix A ("Which system of laws do you prefer: the customary law of your ethnic group or English law, and why?"), a Survey Reaction Participant states: "I prefer the customary law of my ethnic group [because] the English law is strange to me." Based on scientific research and other available information, it is safe to conclude that the English legal system is strange to most Nigerians. Being thus strange, it is unreasonable to expect contemporary Nigerian law makers and court judges (all of whom are native Nigerians) to comfortably, insightfully, and properly interpret and apply foreign, English-based laws to Nigerian circumstances. The law makers and judges are (or should be) naturally equipped to espouse their indigenous legal principles and life philosophies. Therefore, the correct position is that Nigerian law makers and judges are predisposed, and owe it as a duty, to rely mainly on local (Nigerian) legal principles, philosophies, and standards to make policies and determine cases. It is however disappointing that many contemporary Nigerian law makers and judges, on a variety of issues, prefer English interpretations to the indigenous Nigerian analyses.

In addition to the observations regarding Nigerian law makers and judges, the current system that relies too heavily on foreign (English) ideas has effects on Nigerian parties to a case. The effects are easy to see. They include parties' discomfort and lack of satisfaction with, as well as rejection of, English-based decisions. Instances abound of cases that went through the lengthy official judicial process, through all layers of the official court system, with a "final" decision issued at the end after many years of litigations and appeals. Notwithstanding, dissatisfied parties simply resume their disputing because they are unhappy with the judgment. At that point, such a dissatisfied party shifts the disputing process from the arena of the "official" to the ground of the "unofficial" law and justice. Regardless of the sphere of law and justice in which a disputing process occurs or is resumed, the process breeds discontent and uproar among the citizens (disputants, witnesses, relations, acquaintances, community members, etc.). Therefore, a reconstructed law and justice system should include every reasonable effort to ensure that a credible, effective, efficient, and generally accepted case processing and adjudication process is put in place and used to manage citizens' grievances, conflicts, and disputes.

In the final analysis, it is unreasonable to expect Nigerian parties to a case to fully understand and accept verdicts predicated on foreign rationales and expectations. It is thus necessary to reconstruct Nigerian law and justice to capture, explain, and advertise the rich historical bases for the various traditions, customs, and laws, along with the judicial decisions resulting from them. Such historical exposition will demonstrate marked differences between Nigerian (indigenous) law and English law. Contrasting Nigerian (indigenous) law and English law will show that in most situations the divergent historical experiences of the Nigerian and the English peoples, respectively, disqualify English laws from being applied to Nigerians.

Two, *Create an Indigenous-Based and Progressive Court Model*: Restructuring the present court system in Nigeria is one of the most critical steps towards indigenized, effective, and efficient case processing and justice in the country. What is needed is a court structure that reasonably and effectively synthesizes credible aspects of indigenous and foreign judicial systems and processes. The existing court structure in Nigeria reflects at best an extremely measured attempt to synthesize indigenous Nigerian and English systems. The result is that the system is more dual than truly blended. The existing court structure, which has three components (see Figure 7.1 – Federal Court Structure, Figure 7.2 – Northern States Court Structure, and Figure 7.3 – Southern States Court Structure) does not sufficiently synthesize the indigenous Nigerian and English case processing and adjudication models.

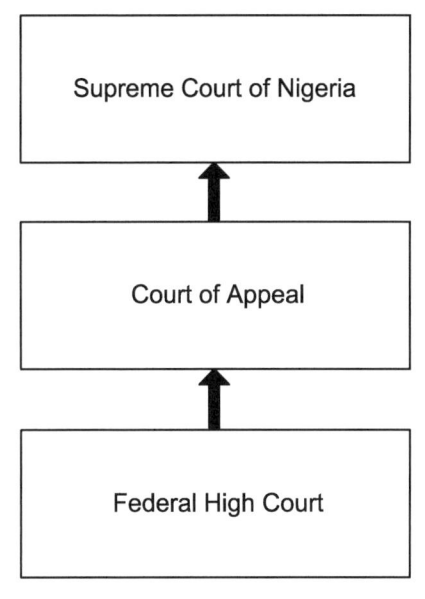

Figure 7.1 Federal Court Structure

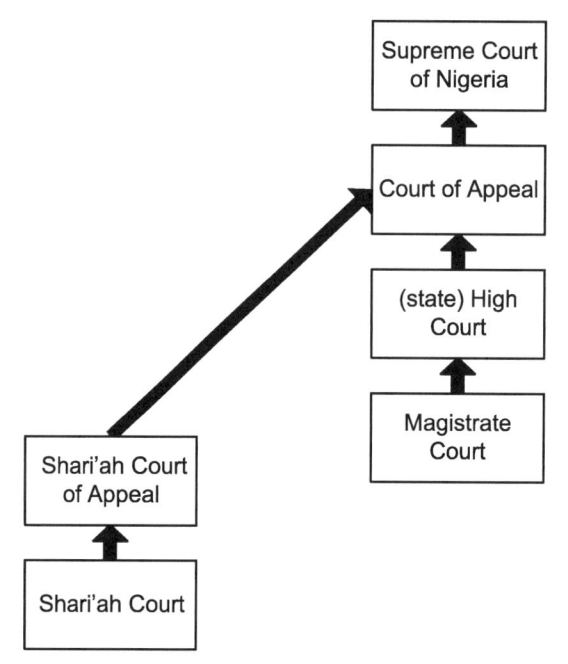

170 Reconstructing Law and Justice in a Postcolony

Figure 7.2 Northern States Court Structure

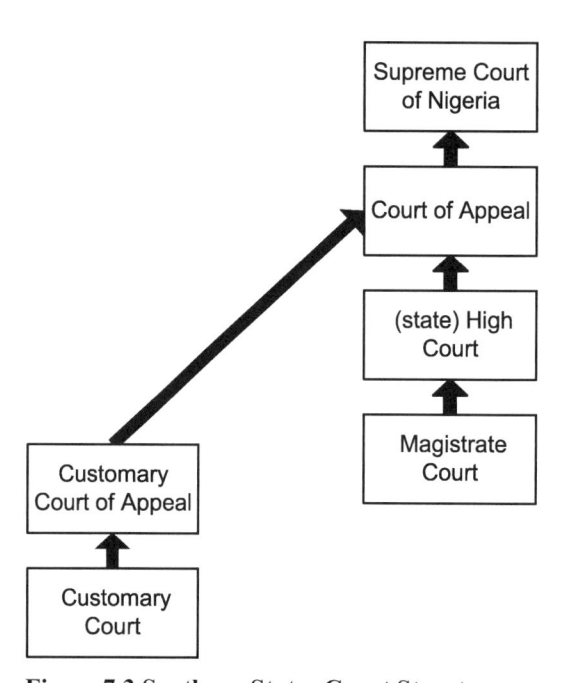

Figure 7.3 Southern States Court Structure

In the present system, grievances, conflicts, and disputes rooted in traditions, customs, and native laws (customary law) are heard in the "Customary Court" (southern states), and the "*Shari'ah* Court" and such other religious- and indigenous-based official courts (northern states). Note that, unlike the southern states' "Customary Court," the north's "*Shari'ah* Court" is entirely or at least substantially based on a religion (Islam). This religious foundation is incompatible with the theme of this book. This is an important point and will be addressed in greater detail later in this chapter. In the meantime, in the current system, appeals from the Customary Court and the *Shari'ah* Court go to appellate courts on indigenous/religious matters, such as the Customary Court of Appeal and the *Shari'ah* Court of Appeal, respectively. In some instances, customary law-based cases are appealed to the Supreme Court. On the other hand, statute-based and English common law-based cases are taken to the Magistrate Court, state and Federal High Courts, Court of Appeal, and the Supreme Court.

The hierarchical arrangement shows a mixture of dual and blended institutions and processes, with the system being more dual than blended. The English-based system operates significantly separately from the customary system, with the former dominating the latter. In some circumstances, however, aspects of both systems are managed together, even if they are not unified. The result of the unevenness in the Nigerian judicial institutions and processes is a case processing and adjudication configuration that confuses the average citizen. A confusing court structure takes away from the judicial system's credibility before the citizens and thus unnecessarily complicates the justice system's ability to provide effective and efficient social control. Therefore, the following additional steps are necessary to sufficiently synthesize the indigenous and foreign case processing and adjudication institutions and processes in Nigeria. The steps will help to avoid many of the pitfalls of the current judicial system and create an ideal environment for more effective and efficient management of cases in the country.

A key step concerns the structure and jurisdiction of each court, in the state judicial system and in the federal judicial system. The structural arrangements and jurisdictions of the courts should be made more citizen-friendly, particularly at the state level. "More citizen-friendly" characteristics include greater citizen access to the courts (more court divisions), less confused court structure, reduced mystification surrounding the judicial system and its processes, and improved ability of average citizens who prefer to do so to initiate and conduct their cases in the judicial system with minimal professional legal assistance. On structure and jurisdiction issues in the federal court system, matters litigated in these courts are generally statutory. Thus, as long as our law making idiosyncrasies are changed to reflect the home-grown principles and philosophies advocated in this book, the processing and adjudication of issues in federal courts can conveniently be carried out in a manner consistent with the theme of this book (indigenization of law and justice). Relying on home-grown principles and philosophies to try and decide cases will result in judicial decisions that align more accurately with Nigerians' general understanding and expectation.

Whereas federal courts hear and decide mostly statutory matters, it is a different story for the state courts. These courts entertain and adjudicate mostly issues arising from traditions, customs, and native laws. Other issues are based on statutes and the English common law principles of general application. It is therefore in these state courts that more fundamental changes of focus and emphasis are required to bring the official court system and process in the country in line with long established indigenous institutions, practices, and contemporary expectations.

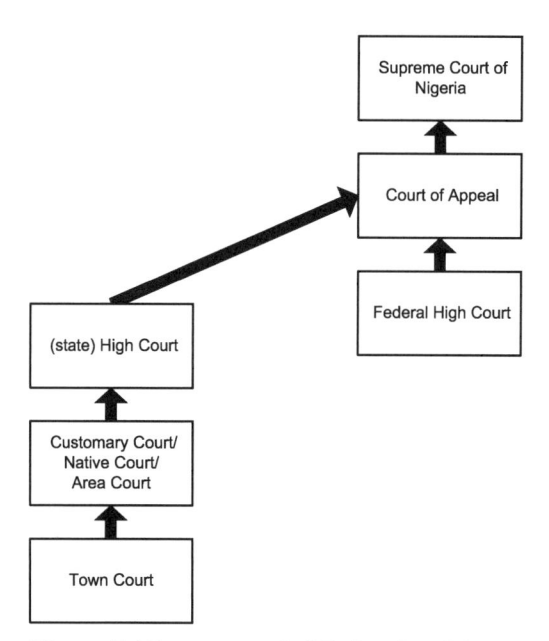

Figure 7.4 Recommended Federal and States Court Structure

Figure 7.4 represents the court structure recommended for each state and the federation, respectively, in a reconstructed Nigerian law and justice system. In the proposed arrangement, the reconstructed court structure for a state will be founded on indigenous institutions as modified by contemporary circumstances. Generally, Nigerian communities understand, support, and follow their indigenous institutions and processes in regulating relationships. To achieve indigenization, the court process for litigating an issue will be grounded in the traditions, customs, and native laws (customary law) applicable in each jurisdiction. This means that the customary law of a small, insular town may differ from that of a big, cosmopolitan town or city. For convenience, this small or big town/city is called "Town" for the purposes of describing the recommended judicial process. The determination, interpretation, and application of a Town's traditions, customs, and indigenous laws will to be based on evidence, which will consider the applicable official law, such as a local, state, or federal statute, as well as the historical and prevailing norms of the Town. A Town Court will have jurisdiction at this judicial level. Depending on the population of a Town, it may need more than one Town Court to try cases. A case tried at the Town Court level will be appealable, at least in theory, ultimately to the Supreme Court of Nigeria (SCN). Of course, negotiated exceptions will have to be made so that questions such as those on interpretations of the constitution, disputes between states, disagreements between a state and the federal government, etc. can be litigated in the apex court (SCN) or the Court of Appeal.

Figure 7.4 thoughtfully retains what is good about the existing court structure in Nigeria, while recommending important changes to improve the system. Figure 7.4 seeks to synthesize and streamline the dual indigenous and English-based court processes. This will simplify the process and make the court system and process friendlier to the average citizen (non-lawyer). The following comments on each of the courts recommended in Figure 7.4 will help to clarify the advocated remodeling.

Federal Court System – The three main federal courts in the current system are the Federal High Court, Court of Appeal, and the Supreme Court of Nigeria (SCN), from the lowest to the highest. These courts are retained in the system recommended for the federation in Figure 7.4. As in the present system, the Federal High Court in the recommended court structure (Figure 7.4) will hear and decide federal matters, except that its subject matter jurisdiction will be expanded to all cases on federal laws, policies, and programs.[1] To accommodate the added subject matter jurisdictional responsibilities, more divisions of the Federal High Court will be created. A combination of population and land distance will be used to determine the number of the court divisions to be made available in a state. More densely populated parts of the country will have more court divisions, especially where long distances separate one court division from another. Therefore, the availability of transportation means and other relevant conditions applicable to each population may be considered for this purpose. However, as many of these divisions as necessary will be created. The objective will be to open up the court system and make it more accessible to the citizens.[2]

Regarding appointment as a judge, to qualify for appointment as a Federal High Court judge in the new system, a lawyer must pass a "customary law

---

1 Again, to be sure, negotiated exceptions will have to be made so that questions such as those on constitutional interpretation, disputes between states, disagreements between a state and the federal government, can be litigated in the first instance in the apex court (the Supreme Court) or the Court of Appeal.

2 This should not be construed as argument for, nor is it intended to support, a more litigious society. Proposing mechanics for a more open and accessible court system is not the same thing as encouraging citizens to sue more. Rather, the procedure is designed to produce more relevant, rational, and acceptable justice.

knowledge" test. This test is explained in the following paragraphs along with the qualifications for appointments to the Court of Appeal and the SCN. The Court of Appeal will continue to hear appeals from the Federal High Court, as is currently the situation. Further appeals will proceed to the SCN, as is presently the situation. I will return to the qualifications of persons to be appointed as Court of Appeal and SCN justices, respectively, shortly.

State Court System – Figure 7.4 includes a hierarchical representation of the five courts recommended for case processing in a Nigerian state court system. Figure 7.4 is a modified version of Figure 1.1 in Question 23 of Appendix A. After carefully considering the structure previously anticipated in Question 23 of Appendix A, I was convinced that a revised Nigerian state court system should begin with a Town Court, rather than an "Extended Family Court." An "Extended Family Court" would be too intimate and too informal for an official government to run. Establishing such a court throughout the country would be an unnecessarily cumbersome and the cost of running them would be prohibitive. Also, leaving out the "Extended Family Court" from the state court system ensures that the family and the extended family units will continue to provide vital opportunities for unofficial (non-governmental), informal case processing. Consistent with the need to preserve the unofficial, informal process, the "Traditional Ruler's Cabinet" (see Figure 1.1 in Question 23 of Appendix A) is not a part of Figure 7.4. Note further that Figure 7.4 excludes the three judges previously projected for a High Court in Figure 1.1, Question 23 of Appendix A. Careful consideration of the issues reveals that constituting three judges for each High Court room will be wasteful. It may even delay proceedings needlessly due to the multiple umpires (judges) that would have to be involved in the process.

However, even the Town Court will not, nor should it, remove the essential need for community institutions, such as a town's or community's traditional ruler and the cabinet (customary or native institutions), to hear and resolve grievances, conflicts, and disputes unofficially and mainly informally. These customary institutions make invaluable contributions to social control in Nigerian communities (Okereafoezeke, 1996; 2002), and they should be retained even in a reconstructed law and justice system. Consider the following additional argument in support of retaining the family and the extended family as unofficial, informal social control agencies. Huge financial, material, and human resource expenses would be required to make the family and extended family units into official government agencies. Also, it seems that such a move would have the counter effect of imposing unneeded regulatory and oversight burdens on the government as well as the family and the extended family, which are natural, grassroots level, traditional institutions for managing relationships informally. This argument to leave the family and extended family institutions out of the official judicial structure extends to the *shari'ah* system and the *Shari'ah* Court (religious system and religious court).

As mentioned, the present (official) *Shari'ah* Court in northern Nigeria is based on the Muslim religion, thus excluding non-Muslims from its processes.

Consequently, and consistent with the theme of this book, it seems more practical to create a new (official) court for the North as part of law and justice reconstruction. The new court, to be known as "Native Court," "Area Court," or by any other name, will hear and determine grievances, conflicts, and disputes from all citizens regardless of religion. The court will process cases in much the same way as the South's Customary Court. This means that the new court will not be based on any religion nor will it apply religious law. As recommended in this book, case processing based exclusively on religion should be left to informal, non-governmental groups to be used for managing civil grievances, conflicts, and disputes. In any case, the reconstructed Customary Court and Native Court will have criminal jurisdiction only to the extent allowed by the constitution.

The issue of the place of the *shari'ah* and other religion-based legal systems and laws in a reconstructed law and justice system is discussed further as issue/step number six of this section ("Case Processing and Adjudication") of this chapter. The issue/step number six is captioned "*Stipulate and Enforce Constitutional, Rather than Religious, Framework for Courts and Case Processing*".

The new court structure recommended in Figure 7.4 is based on a consideration of many relevant factors. As indicated, the new structure will allow a case to be initiated in the Town Court (the lowest court in a state system) and appealed hierarchically through the SCN, which is the court of last resort. Also, the idea of appealing a case from a Town Court through the SCN is merely theoretical for an overwhelming majority of cases. By far, most cases will be settled without reaching the SCN. Moreover, the recommended law and justice reconstruction should include the following policy change to more reasonably manage the SCN docket. For cases based on customary law, state statutes, policies, and conducts (other than those involving interpretations of the Constitution), and federal statutes, policies, and conducts (other than those involving interpretations of the Constitution), the SCN should be empowered by the constitution or other law to decide whether or not to hear an appeal sought to be brought before it. This recommendation is novel for Nigeria. At present, the SCN hears virtually every case brought before it. The recommended policy change will resemble the "rule of four" in the USA. The "rule of four" allows the US Supreme Court (that country's court of last resort) to poll its nine justices to decide whether or not the court should hear an appeal brought before it. If four or more of the nine justices vote "yes," the court will hear the appeal; otherwise, the court declines hearing without going into the merits or substance of the case. This rule allows the US Supreme Court to concentrate on cases with potentially wide constitutional significance for the country.

The SCN should be given power such as the US "rule of four," to hear and determine only cases that in the opinion of the SCN have constitutional or other significance. However, the exact stipulation as to how the court will decide whether or not to hear a case brought before it can differ from the US model. The stipulation will probably be different considering Nigeria's circumstances. For example, one important factor that should be considered in specifying whether the justices believe that a case before it should be heard and decided is the number of the justices that make up the SCN *vis-à-vis* the number for the US Supreme Court. Because the SCN is made up of more justices [potentially 21 justices – Section 230 (2) (b) of the Nigerian Constitution 1999] than the US Supreme Court (9 justices), it seems necessary to require the consent of more SCN justices for a case to be heard and decided by the court. Also, unlike the US "rule of four," the SCN may be legally required to hear and determine every appeal against a judgment based exclusively or substantially on interpretation of a provision of the constitution. This requirement will aid Nigeria's constitutional growth and development. The SCN has a critical role to play in explaining, clarifying, and ensuring the application and enforcement of the constitution. At this stage of the country's constitutional and legal development, the authority and final voice of the SCN is essential to iron out and purify fundamental constitutional and legal principles.

As indicated, a policy that empowers the SCN to use a USA-type "rule of four" on such issues as described in this book will allow the court to concentrate on issues of constitutional consequence for Nigerians, rather than remain bogged down by unmanageable caseload. Justice Alfa Belgore, who later served as Nigeria's Chief Justice, supports this view. Referring to the impracticality of the present policy that requires the SCN to hear virtually every case brought before it, he expressed his position on this issue as follows (Ologbondiyan and Ogbu, 2004, at p. 1):

> The Supreme Court should concern itself purely with Constitutional issues and general issues of law. Not when you start a case in Wuse [a Nigerian community] Magistrate court, you go to High Court, from there to Appeal Court and to the Supreme Court over a stall in a market. If that is not done, and you labour the justices at the Supreme Court with such cases, they will be overburdened and fall one by one. The youngest of all the Justices of the Supreme Court is 60 years.

In short, the SCN is not the appropriate venue for litigating minor, private grievances, conflicts, and disputes. The highly learned justices' wisdom should be used more efficiently, to properly direct the constitutional and legal growth of the country and its institutions.

As mentioned by Justice Belgore, the ages of the justices of the SCN are relevant to issues of law and justice reconstruction. There is no doubt that a justice should be physically healthy enough to carry out the functions of the office. Relative youth *may* be a plus in this connection. But, it is important to note that youth and physical strength do not necessarily correlate. There are many older persons who are physically stronger than their younger counterparts. Therefore, considering the enormous experiences and skills that justices have acquired over the years, it is reasonable for the country to ensure that the society continues to benefit from the justices' intellectual assets beyond the present compulsory retirement age. At present, a justice of the SCN who attains 70 years retires mandatorily. It may be time to further examine this termination age and, possibly, raise it to 75-80 years. Generally, a 75-80-year person can be very productive to the extent of functioning effectively as a justice. However, the power to impeach and remove from office an unproductive justice or a justice that abuses his/her authority or powers should be retained and used whenever necessary.

As demonstrated, the twin issues of the SCN caseload and the justices' retirement age should be re-examined as aspects of law and justice reconstruction.

However, the following observation further supports the recommendation to institute a USA-type "rule of four" policy for the SCN. A case that has, for instance, been decided at the Town Court level, appealed to the Customary Court, appealed further to the High Court, and may be to the Court of Appeal, should be concluded without involving the SCN (see generally Figure 7.4). Even in those circumstances where a case is initiated in the first instance before the High Court, if the case is further appealed to the Court of Appeal, that should be enough to dispose of the matter unless the SCN sees an important reason to get involved to ensure justice.

In short, the SCN should be empowered to choose the appeals it will hear based on three considerations: (1) the constitutional importance of a case – interpretation of the constitution; (2) the impact of a case on the relationship between the federation and a state government or between state governments; (3) to correct substantial injustice by a lower court. Any one or a combination of the three grounds will justify the SCN accepting to hear an appeal brought before it. This policy will undoubtedly lessen the number of cases to which the SCN has to attend. The policy will also allow the SCN to live up to its critical role of ensuring that Nigerian courts have clear and correct constitutional and legal principles to guide the courts in rendering just decisions. A policy similar to the US "rule of four" will apply to cases initiated in a Nigerian state court system as well those initiated in the federal system. However, there is greater justification for limiting the appeals of cases from a state court system to the SCN because there are many appellate rungs for cases emanating from a state system. Moreover, limiting appeals from state courts to the SCN and the other federal courts will strengthen and promote federalism, which Nigeria professes, provided that state courts protect citizens' rights. Further, limiting appeals from state courts to federal courts will highlight and emphasize the important concept of *community justice processing*.

The idea of community justice processing partly inspired the court structure presented in Figure 7.4. The idea will be particularly well represented in Figure 7.4's Town Court, as well as the Customary Court (southern Nigeria) or Native Court, Area Court, etc. (northern Nigeria), and the High Court. The community justice processing philosophy will ensure that case processing is grounded in relevant statutes, traditions, customs, and native laws, along with the relevant communities' notions of justice in each case. By means of the new Town Court, Customary Court or Native Court, Area Court, etc., and High Court, justice processing will be closer and more meaningful to the average community member. Thus, a community member will have closer proximity to the courts to be able to participate directly (as fact witness, expert witness, party, or other community stakeholder) or indirectly as a member of the larger society, in the management of cases. The cases will have to be processed and decided in ways that are consistent with the relevant laws, traditions, customs, and native laws, and community practices.

A Nigerian judicial reform panel had proposed a court similar to the Town Court recommended in Figure 7.4. The Justice Kayode Eso panel on judicial reform had recommended the establishment of "Village Courts" for minor disputes. The National Judicial Council (NJC) rejected the Eso panel's recommendation arguing that the existing Customary and Area Courts try cases at the village level [see "National Judicial Council (NJC) on Justice Kayode Eso Report," 2002]. The rejection by the NJC is erroneous and unfortunate. The Eso panel's "Village Courts" would have brought the judicial process closer to the citizens. The "Village Courts" would have been able to provide justice that is more efficient (less costly) and more effective (decisions that are more acceptable to parties thus increasing case resolutions).

Note however that the "Village Courts" recommended by the Eso panel would be more localized (restricted to the village level as the geographical jurisdiction) than the Town Court recommended in Figure 7.4. Also, the Eso panel's "Village Courts," as proposed by the panel, would have been limited to trying civil cases. On the contrary, I recommend that the Town Court in Figure 7.4 be given jurisdiction over criminal as well as civil matters, throughout each town or city. The Town Court in Figure 7.4 will be authorized and defined as the court of first instance for most civil and criminal disputes in the country. The court's proximity to the citizens and its grassroots qualities will endear it to the citizens of each town or city. Thus, its decisions are more likely to be accepted by disputing parties. It is reasonable, then, to hypothesize that an overwhelming majority of the court's decisions will be accepted by the parties and not appealed further.

The terms and conditions for appointment as a judge or justice have to be specified as a part of the proposed law and justice reconstruction. To be appointed as a judge or justice of any of the courts in Figure 7.4 [Town Court judge, Customary Court or Native Court (or Area Court, etc.) judge, state High Court judge, Federal High Court judge, Court of Appeal justice, or justice of the SCN], a person must: (1) have graduated from the Nigerian Law School, (2) be at least Well Knowledgeable in the Traditions, Customs, and Native Laws (Customary Law/Native Law) Applicable in the Jurisdiction of the Court to which appointment will be made, and (3) have passed a Customary/Native Law Knowledge Test. All three conditions will apply to all judicial positions. However, there is a need to explain the specifics of the application of each condition to each court. Obviously, the conditions do not apply in the same way to all positions. As explained below, in the proposed model, the conditions are tougher and more restrictive for a higher judicial position than for a lower judicial rank, especially on the issue of post-Law School experience.

Condition (1) needs elaboration. For the Town Court level, even a fresh Law School graduate may be appointed if he/she satisfies conditions (2) and (3). A Town Court judge does not need extensive post-Law School experience to succeed on the job. Moreover, it would be extremely difficult, if not impossible, to find enough experienced lawyers willing to accept positions as Town Court judges. A prospective Customary Court or Native Court (or Area Court, etc.) judge will need a minimum of three years post-Law School qualification in addition to conditions (2) and (3). For a state High Court or Federal High Court judge, a minimum of ten years post-Law School graduation is necessary to ensure that the appointee has derived substantial experience to manage cases at the High Court level. A Court of Appeal justice must have graduated from the Law School at least 15 years prior to appointment. The same 15 years post-graduation will apply to a prospective appointee to the SCN. Thus, the main distinguishing factor in making judicial appointments in a reconstructed court system will be the number of years that have elapsed since a prospective appointee's Law School graduation.

On the other hand, every appointee to the office of judge or justice of any court in a reconstructed law and justice system must have satisfied conditions (2) and (3), namely: "well knowledgeable in the traditions, customs, and native laws (customary law/native law) applicable in the jurisdiction of the court" and "passed a customary law knowledge test," respectively. Requiring every judge or justice in the country to be well knowledgeable in customary law and to pass the customary law knowledge test will ensure that customary law-based issues are not watered down, minimized, or ignored at trial or on appeal by judges who do not understand customary law. The specific requirements for verifying an appointee's customary law knowledge and success in the customary law knowledge test will vary depending on the jurisdiction of the prospective appointee's position. Definitions of the concepts are provided as follows.

"Well knowledgeable in the traditions, customs, and native laws (customary law/native law) applicable in the jurisdiction of the court" refers to reasonable comprehension of the customary law/native law applicable to a jurisdiction so as to be able to hear and decide cases arising from the jurisdiction by properly applying the relevant customary laws/native laws. This level of knowledge may be established by documented evidence of previous research works, publications on customary law, customary law cases tried as a lawyer, or customary law cases heard and decided as a lower level judge (such as when a Town Court judge is sought to be appointed as a Customary Court, Native Court, or Area Court judge), or a combination of such documented evidence. In any case, the appointing authority must be reasonably satisfied that the appointee has sufficient knowledge to appropriately hear and determine cases in the prospective court by applying the relevant customary law/native law provisions and principles.

"Customary law knowledge test" is required to further verify the customary law credentials of a prospective appointee to the office of judge or justice. The test will contain a mixture of questions, all on the relevant customary laws, to determine an appointee's level of knowledge of the substantive and procedural customary laws/ native laws applicable in the relevant jurisdiction. The test may be standardized and made uniform within each state since judges (Town Court, Customary Court, Native Court, or Area Court, and High Court judges inclusive) may be transferred from one state court jurisdiction to another. For appointees to the Court of Appeal and the SCN, the appointing authority should ensure that the test is sufficiently universal to identify the differences and similarities among customary law/native law provisions, principles, and systems throughout the country. This will be necessary to ensure that these appellate courts are properly grounded to hear and determine cases from all parts of the country. Since the customary law/native law knowledge of appointees to the Court of Appeal and the SCN has to cover wider geographical jurisdictions, this will likely dilute the appointees' indigenous law expertise level. Fortunately, this will not matter much because these are appellate courts, which do not have to investigate, establish, and apply customary laws from scratch. An appellate court uses a lower court's findings and application as reference points.

To be sure, the jurisdiction of all the courts proposed in Figure 7.4, including the Customary Court and Native Court (Area Court, etc.), will cover criminal as well as civil cases. Note that the "Customary Court" in the South and the "Native Court" (or "Area Court," etc.) in the North will have to operate within the Nigerian constitution. This means that *criminal shari'ah* will not apply as presently designed and promoted by the 12 northern *shari'ah* states of Nigeria. Nonetheless, in the recommended model, the new Native Court or Area Court will take over the jurisdiction of the present *Shari'ah* Court. Also, according to Figure 7.4, the jurisdiction of the present Customary Court of Appeal (South) and the *Shari'ah* Court of Appeal (North), respectively, will be fused into the applicable new state High Court. This makes sense to avoid duplication and waste. The Customary Court of Appeal or *Shari'ah* Court of Appeal was created to hear appeals from the relevant Customary Court, or *Shari'ah* Court or Area Court, as the case may be. A reconstructed state High Court, such as is proposed in this book (Figure 7.4), will be positioned to more effectively and efficiently perform the functions of the present Customary Court of Appeal or *Shari'ah* Court of Appeal, respectively. Generally, for all the courts in the redesigned system, by appropriate law, the jurisdiction of a court may be delimited where necessary and as determined by a representative legislature.

The necessary combination of the three identified criteria for appointment as judge or justice, namely: formal Law School education, documented knowledge of the applicable traditions, customs, and native laws, and passing the customary law/native law knowledge test will arm a judge of the reconstructed High Court well to hear and decide cases brought before the court, both in the first instance and on appeal. Therefore, the current Magistrate Court will be unnecessary in the proposed court system. The modified layers of courts will be sufficient to handle cases that the Magistrate Court currently manages. For the small to medium-sized town, a Town Court will suffice. However, for each state, it will be necessary to create additional divisions of each of the Customary Court, Native Court (or Area Court, etc.), and High Court. More divisions of the Court of Appeal will also be necessary throughout the country. This will decongest the courts and minimize delay in trials.

Finally, Figure 7.4 appreciates the crucial role of a court or tribunal of first instance in a society's judicial processing. A court or tribunal of first instance is the beginning judicial avenue for cases in a society. The court is the basis of the society's judicial process. It is critical to get this level right because everything that happens at the top of the court system (the appellate courts) depends on the quality of the proceedings at the first level. In recognition of this, in September 2007, Babatunde Fashola, the governor of Lagos State, set up a 12-member committee to review the administration of justice at the Magistrate and Customary courts levels in the state. Among other charges, the committee was to recommend means to improve access to the first level of justice and suggest modifications to increase public confidence in the first level and advance law and order. These charges to the Lagos state reform committee, specifically the twin issues of access to court and public confidence in the court, are noble. In line with this, the Town Court recommended in Figure 7.4 of this book will improve citizen access to justice. Establishing the court will reduce the intimidation suffered by parties, especially the uneducated, poor persons. The court will thus increase the citizens' confidence in the court system and help to promote law and order in the country.

Three, *Institute and Maintain Continuous Training of Judicial Officers on Customary Law*: Every officer of the court (judge, prosecutor, defense attorney, etc.) as well as judicial observer should appreciate the importance of continuous, on-the-job training. This is essential to keep abreast of developments and changes in the substantive and procedural laws. Continuous, on-the-job training is even more critical regarding customary laws because of the historical neglect these indigenous laws have suffered in colonial and postcolonial Nigeria. Therefore, a reconstructed Nigerian law and justice system has to make room for, and mandate, all judges, justices, and prosecutors (all of whom are government employees) to successfully complete designated trainings, workshops, lectures, etc. on customary laws periodically. The continuous, on-the-job training will equip public as well as private judicial officers to properly evaluate and apply relevant customary laws in ways that are consistent with the other laws and the citizens' aspirations.

In the proposed continuous, on-the-job training plan, participation and completion will be verified by both the organizing authority and an independent test to gauge the extent to which a participant understands the issues addressed in each event. Judges, justices, and prosecutors, being government employees, can easily be required to comply with the continuous training and test. Although they work privately, legal practitioners will be strongly encouraged to complete the same trainings, workshops, lectures, etc. as judges, justices, and prosecutors will do. It is very likely that the private practitioners will comply because even a private practicing lawyer who fails to do so may compromise his or her case before a judge who has benefited from the trainings, workshops, etc., particularly where the prosecutor has also derived greater knowledge of the relevant customary law issues.

Four, *Make Traditions, Customs, and Native Laws Prominent in Law Departments and Law School Curricula*: Among other reasons, this is important to better prepare future judges and justices, as well as solicitors and advocates, to perform their duties before the reconstructed courts. Even a new Law School graduate should be well knowledgeable in customary law. At present, customary law is taught as an afterthought, rather than as the foundation of law and justice in Nigeria. Under the proposed arrangement, the curricula for law training will be redesigned in such a way as to ensure that substantive and procedural customary law takes its rightful place as the foundation of social control in the country. Customary law principles and philosophies relevant to issues at hand will be actively explored and offered (through teaching, research, and publications) for addressing those issues. The new model will justify and mandate judges and justices, presiding over cases, to ask lawyers important questions about the customary laws relevant to the cases argued by the lawyers. Answers to such questions will likely, and should, help to determine the court's decision in each case. For lawyers, judges, and justices, knowing, understanding, and properly applying relevant customary law principles and philosophies to cases will no longer be a matter of choice, but of necessity.

Five, *Provide for Emergency and Continued Funding of Research on Customary Laws*: The very limited availability of funds for research on indigenous issues and systems in Nigeria highlights the long neglect of this all-important sector of the society. Conscientious people who would research, publish, and help to develop the indigenous systems have been marginalized for long – in the colonial as well as postcolonial eras. Rather, much greater attention and funds have been devoted to developing the foreign English-style system. This trend has to be reversed as a part of law and justice reconstruction. Consistent with the theme of this book, Local, State, and Federal government funders, as well as private persons and organizations, owe it to invest substantially in developing the indigenous systems through increased research money. The Local, State, and Federal governments, in particular, ought to take all necessary steps to encourage researchers and authors to do and produce more work on the country's customary laws. This will help greatly to educate the citizens on the provisions, workings, and possibilities of these laws. As much as possible, efforts should be made to rectify the neglect of the past and avoid continuing the same fundamental error. Local, State, and Federal government annual budgets should include specific allocations for research and development of the customary law systems and processes. Surely, these governments have the resources for this very important aspect of the country's national life, if only the government leaders have the will to pursue this course of action.

Six, *Stipulate and Enforce Constitutional, Rather than Religious, Framework for Courts and Case Processing*: The point here is that a reconstructed judicial process should be spared the drawbacks that religion mania inflicts on its population. In recognition of the wide influence of various religions on every society, the object is not to rid the judicial process of all religious influences. That would be impossible to attain. Religion and belief generally have some influence on virtually every human behavior, including case processing. However, the issue is whether, especially as regards social control pertaining to criminal conduct, a religion or specific religions should found and control the process. It seems that it would be highly undesirable and counterproductive for a religion to prescribe the behavior standards and criminal punishments for all the members of a society. Attempting to use a religion in this manner would be highly offensive to those citizens who profess different religions or hold different beliefs. Effort in a reconstructed law and justice system to impose a religion to control the citizens will alienate and emasculate those citizens that do not share the controlling religious belief. Over time, the excluded citizens will likely react negatively to the imposition; some of their reactions will likely be criminal. Thus, the society will become less stable and weaker. The multiplicity of religious beliefs and groupings makes nonsense of any attempt to impose one religion as an instrument for coercively regulating all the members of a diverse society.

Further, such imposition will vitiate the "community justice processing" concept, which has been explained in this book as a conscious, meaningful involvement of citizens at the grassroots, along with uses of statutes, traditions, customs, and indigenous laws, to manage cases. The desirable community-based justice process must be distinguished from the undesirable religion-based justice process. The former is founded on compromises among the citizens of a community who, although they hold multiple religious persuasions, understand that harmonious coexistence inevitably requires the citizens to accord equality to all religions. On the other hand, the religion-based justice process recognizes one, and only one, religion as the true source of citizens' rights, duties, and the mechanisms for their application and enforcement. Therefore, a free and peaceful citizenry in a stable, strong, and progressive society have to be able to civilly articulate their general rules of conduct beyond those of their respective religions. The best and most efficient evidence of this expression is a modern State constitution, which contains social contractual terms written by the citizens either directly or indirectly through their elected representatives.

By the contractual terms expressed in the form of a constitution, coercive rules – especially the criminal variety – will be limited to the principles and issues on which the members of a society generally, through their free deliberations and votes or the votes of their elected representatives, agree. These must be enshrined in the citizens' constitution. The constitution will identify and define the guidelines for coexistence, the sanctions for breaches, and the limits of those sanctions. Every citizen is to be bound by those provisions. Thus, it seems beyond question that the *criminal shari'ah* in some of Nigeria's northern states violates the *Constitution of the Federal Republic of Nigeria, 1999* (Nigerian Constitution 1999) (sections 260-264 and 277; Akhaine, 2000; see also Nwabuikwu, 2002). In Akhaine (2000), Mohammed Bello, a former Chief Justice of Nigeria, affirmed that a Nigerian constitution is superior to Islamic law.[3] Therefore, this form of *shari'ah* has no place in a reconstructed law and justice system. It amounts to imposing the

---

3 It is appropriate to point out that Bello is a Muslim. Yet, he did not hesitate to subject Islamic law to the Nigerian constitution, as it should be.

principles of one religion on citizens who profess many, many religions and non-religions in a constitutional state.

In some cases, *criminal shari'ah* protagonists and enforcers have, in the name of Islamic law, arrogated to themselves the right to pronounce other citizens guilty and impose the death penalty, all without resorting to a law court (Soyinka, 2002; Usigbe and Ozoemena, 2002). Thus, *criminal shari'ah* threatens the unity and freedoms of Nigerians ("Shame in Zamfara," 2000; Abati, 2000). To avoid this situation in the first place, section 10 of the Nigerian Constitution 1999 was written. The section expressly forbids the adoption of a religion as a State (or part thereof) religion. The section 10 provision should be fully enforced and retained in a reconstructed law and justice system. Recognizing that some aspects of the *shari'ah* contradict modern State principles, Smock (2005) accurately expresses the proper philosophical outlook of *shari'ah* in a modern society, as follows (at pp. 1 and 3):

> In northern Nigeria, shari'ah needs to be both modernized and made compatible with universal human rights, pluralism, and democracy while remaining genuinely Islamic [p. 1]. The challenge facing modern Muslim societies is how to reapply the principles of shari'ah in social, economic, and political contexts that are markedly different from those that existed during its original development [p. 3].

The *shari'ah* and other religious doctrines will have to adapt to the modern State's prescriptions for coexistence, unity, rights protections, and modernity, not the other way around. Therefore, the *criminal shari'ah* policy in northern Nigeria, as presently constituted, does not meet Smock's (2005) challenges.

A wise solution to the *shari'ah* law dispute in Nigeria, and disputes surrounding other religious legal systems, is to constitutionally allow religious leaders and their members to create and use the principles of their respective religions to manage *civil* (or personal) disputes among those of their flock who voluntarily decide to manage their cases by their religious principles. This policy will allow and encourage religious groups to participate actively in managing cases among their members, with the proviso that those cases are limited to civil, rather than criminal, matters. Thus, if adopted, the new system will distinguish between civil and criminal disputes under the umbrella of the country's constitution, similar to the present setup. By way of definitions, civil disputes are disputes between private persons or groups, which disputes do not involve allegations of offenses against the criminal laws of the country or part thereof. The country's constitution and other laws define such disputes as *civil*, rather than *criminal*. Whereas the new system will allow religious groups and private persons to manage civil cases among consenting parties, criminal cases (disputes involving accusations of violations of State-defined crimes) can only be tried in State (official) courts.

A religion in a diverse society cannot be a credible State coercive instrument of social control in a reconstructed law and justice system. This is especially so regarding criminal cases, which threaten the accused person's life or other liberty. In such a situation, it is important that the majority of the citizens regard the applicable criminal law and procedure as just and fair to all, not just to members of a certain religion. A criminal law based on one of many religions in a country is unlikely to be so highly regarded by the majority of the citizens, especially those citizens of a different religion. Even in civil cases, no person in a reconstructed law and justice system can be compelled to have a dispute managed by a religious judicial process. No Nigerian community is monolithic. A community's members are differentiated on religion, ethnicity, culture, tradition, etc. On religion, even in the twelve so-called "core Northern" states or "*shari'ah* states" of Nigeria, where the *criminal shari'ah* has been so strongly promoted (Bauchi, Borno, Gombe, Jigawa, Kaduna, Kano, Katsina, Kebbi, Niger, Sokoto, Yobe, and Zamfara), there are indigenous African animists (practitioners of the indigenous African religions), who preceded Christians and Muslims. Therefore, all the citizens deserve reasonable accommodation in a reconstructed law and justice system. The best way to achieve such accommodation is to make necessary compromises among the different religions and non-religions.

This compromise will avoid forcing citizens to choose between allegiance to their culture and allegiance to the State. Rowan Williams, the Archbishop of Canterbury, fearing "the stark alternatives of cultural loyalty or state loyalty" ("Sharia Law in UK is 'Unavoidable'," 2008, p.1), suggested that the United Kingdom should adopt some aspects of the civil *shari'ah* law to allow Muslims to manage some of their civil cases within Islam. His suggestion seems reasonable, especially because it is consistent with what the UK has already done by allowing the setting-up of Jewish religious courts (Jewish Beth Din), which operate in the UK (see also "Williams Under Fire in Sharia Row," 2008). However, even if the UK State adopts civil *shari'ah*, no religious judicial system in a reconstructed law and justice system ought to be allowed to determine (criminal) guilt or lack thereof. Stated differently, a religious court should not try criminal cases because of the extreme nature of criminal sanctions. The State has overwhelming interest and duty to protect its citizens. As such, the State's court alone should try and determine allegations of crimes. This principle applies even if a religious leader argues that a citizen prefers to be judged by a religious process. Thus, no *criminal shari'ah*, for instance, will be allowed in a reconstructed law and justice system. Rather, the *shari'ah* system of case management will be used unofficially (non-governmentally) and mainly informally to handle civil cases, just as many other unofficial social control processes are used. This form and extent of use is similar to what obtains in the family unit, extended family, village, etc.

The following point further strengthens the argument and conclusion against using a particular religious system to try and determine criminal matters. Regrettably, in Nigeria, and perhaps in many other parts of the world, politicians, religious leaders, and other advocates of *criminal shari'ah* and other criminal justice systems based on various religions, do so mainly for political, material, and other selfish, rather than Godly, interests. For these influential apostles of religious law, it is an effective means of mobilizing a trusting and ill-informed citizenry to advance the authority figures' beliefs and interests (Okafọ, 2003b). Regarding the *criminal shari'ah* in Nigeria, such leaders devise, disguise, and apply the *shari'ah* principles to the unwary citizens who generally do not question God's orders. I often wonder: What if the leaders' interpretations, applications, and enforcements, as personified by the *criminal shari'ah*, were applied to the leaders and their behaviors? Would the leaders accept their fates with the same enthusiasm they have used to visit the *criminal shari'ah* on other Nigerians? Highly unlikely. As one commentator suggested, a good test of the leaders' commitment to the *shari'ah* system and the faith they pontificate is to apply the harsh *criminal shari'ah* process and penalties in judging the leaders and their corrupt behaviors ("Islamic Law Should be Applied to Corrupt Politicians," 2002; see also Obijiofor, 2002).

Seven, *Use Indigenous Languages for Case Processing*: A key policy change that will advance the proposed reconstructed law and justice system concerns the means of communication in case processing. At present and since colonization, most Nigerian courts use the English language to do business because it is the country's "official language." The argument is that the English language is Nigeria's *lingua franca* and so should be used to transact every official business, including law and justice matters. However, this practice is detrimental to the course of justice for two main reasons. One, it is practically difficult, if not impossible, for most Nigerians to adequately express themselves (that is, fully understand and accurately convey their views) in English, including the broken or pidgin variety. Two, because of the official promotion of the English language and the consequent relegation of the indigenous languages, the average Nigerian is intimidated and thus incapable or unwilling to assert himself or herself in an indigenous language. A party to a case in Nigeria's adversary court process who does not or cannot strongly argue his/her case in English is highly disadvantaged. The result is a justice system that intimidates many citizens into shying away from presenting their cases in the strongest terms possible because of the citizens' absent or limited ability in the official English language.

The use of the English language to intimidate many Nigerians is widespread. As mentioned, it affects those citizens with little or no ability to speak English. But this form of intimidation is extended to well-educated Nigerians as well. Even where it is obvious that a citizen has the ability to communicate well in the English language but chooses to communicate in his language, the intimidation persists. Lartey (2007) reports that in one instance, a Master's in Business Administration degree holding Nigerian who, admittedly spoke English fluently, decided to testify before an Elections Petitions Tribunal in his language (Yoruba), rather than in the English language. The panel of judges struggled to understand the witness, even though an "interpreter" (p. 1) was provided.[4] At one point, a judge of the

---

4 More accurately, the language aide to the tribunal in Lartey (2007) is a "translator" rather than an "interpreter." A translator is a person who relays communicated information from one language to another, such as from Yoruba to English and *vice versa* in Lartey

panel fumed: "Perhaps it will help us if this man with a Masters degree speaks in English" (p. 2). The witness was thus compelled to testify in English. It seems that the judges were frustrated and lost patience with the witness because he chose to speak to them in a language (Yoruba) other than *the judges'* language – "the language of the law" (English). This is embarrassing, unfortunate, and regrettable, but not surprising. As I have pointed out in this book, there is a broadly held view among lawyers (practitioners, judges, etc.) that the law is exclusive. One of the ways to maintain the exclusivity is to use the foreign English language to do the business of law and justice. It does not matter that this is happening in a country where the overwhelming majority of the citizens do not communicate in English or do not do so fluently. By using the foreign English language in law and justice matters, most citizens will not understand the law sufficiently to challenge it.

This unfortunate line of reasoning that disadvantages most citizens is consistent with many elite Nigerians' view of the role of English culture in Nigeria. After I graduated from Law School, I practiced law briefly before proceeding to graduate school. On one occasion during the law practice, I was discussing with a lawyer colleague about Nigeria's leadership and developmental problems. My colleague, who had obtained a degree in the USA before studying law in Nigeria, expressed the view that Nigeria should teach and pursue a developmental policy that traces what the Western world does. In particular, according to him, for Nigeria to develop the country should use the English language as the exclusive means of communication. He stated: "English is the language of technology." At the time, I felt uncomfortable with his view, but I did not challenge him strongly. I should have. Years later, my colleague's statement reminds me that many educated Nigerians too readily label English and other Western ideas as superior to ours or other ideas they do not understand. I wonder what my colleague thinks about the French, Germans, Russians, Chinese, Japanese, etc., who have developed technologically and otherwise with languages other than English.

The citizen in Lartey (2007) should be celebrated, not vilified. He should not be made uncomfortable in any way. At any rate, the language issue negatively impacts the course of justice in Nigeria. Official and unofficial attitudinal and policy changes are needed to reposition the indigenous languages for more effective and efficient justice. A constitutional provision or other law is necessary to save and strengthen Nigerian languages (Okoro, 2003; "Are Indigenous Languages Dead?" 2006; Edike, 2006). Every Nigerian language should have at least the same status as English (Ohiri-Aniche, 2006; Elumoye, 2007). Judges, law practitioners, and other courtroom workgroup members (Neubauer, 2007) have to discard their negative attitudes to the indigenous languages. In a reconstructed law and justice system, judges and justices will be required to hear and determine cases in the indigenous languages of the parties, unless a party wishes to do so in English. A party that wishes to present a case in an indigenous language will be encouraged

---

(2007). Unlike an interpreter, a translator does not delve into the detailed and specialized meanings of the terms used in communication.

to do so. At a minimum, translators will be routinely used. There is no shortage of Nigerians who can serve as translators, even if on part-time basis. The new system will take necessary steps to avoid judicial intimidation of parties and witnesses such as occurred in Lartey (2007). Also, each judicial decision will be published in the relevant indigenous language as well as in English (Okereafoezeke, 1996; Okereafoezeke, 2002).

Eight, *Revolutionize Judicial Recording System*: Recording case proceedings in Nigerian courts is tedious. It is painful for the judge who has to write in long hands, the lawyers, and the other court officials involved in a trial, who have to work at the judge's pace. Inevitably, the judge's pace is frustratingly slow, thus lengthening judicial proceedings. The manual method of recording proceedings causes hardships for the parties and the country in general because of the resulting delays in completing a case. But, the courtroom participants have no choice but to wait for the judge to proceed at his or her rate. Also, it is not too difficult to understand the health hazard this method of recording could impose on the court officials, especially the judge. A judge may have to retire earlier from the Bench to preserve some health. In this age of the computer, the State and the court system can and should make room for computerized recording of proceedings. This will undoubtedly improve the working conditions of the judge and the other court officials. It will also deliver a more efficient judicial process by allowing the lawyers and other participants to quickly present their issues to the court. Moreover, quick dispensation of cases engenders parties' confidence in the justice system.

Nine, *Appoint, Maintain, and Retain Judges with Sound Legal, as Well as Moral, Principles*: Judges that lack strong moral precepts are capable of destroying a legal system, even if those judges are expert lawyers. An immoral judge can ruin even a perfectly designed justice system. Thus, legality and morality are required of all judges in particular in a reconstructed law and justice system. As the report of the Justice Kayode Eso panel on judicial reform shows, there is no dearth of corrupt judges in Nigeria. Other law and justice commentators (example Onagoruwa, 2002a; 2002b) have chronicled the idiosyncrasies of the unscrupulous judicial arbiters of citizens' fates. Often, the dishonest judges' brazenness is stunning. As an example, an ex-governor and his alleged co-conspirator and lover, fearing criminal charges for stealing state money, money laundering, and other forms of corruption, went to a Federal High Court and obtained an injunction against the Economic and Financial Crimes Commission (EFCC), which is the investigative and prosecuting arm of the federal government for such crimes. The court prohibited EFCC from arresting or prosecuting the ex-governor and his partner/lover.

Ordinarily, a scrupulous court, having carefully considered the facts, may issue such an order to protect a citizen's legitimate right from abuse, as the Federal High Court did in the case of the EFCC versus the ex-governor and his lover. However, the judge in this case was a sister to the ex-governor's lover. Even entry-level law students and all persons of basic decency know and understand that a person cannot in fairness be a judge in his or her own cause, including the causes of blood relatives, friends, and associates. Can the judge in the case under review claim ignorance of this fundamental principle of judging and justice? It is not difficult to surmise that the inexplicably stupendously rich ex-governor and the hangers-on around him must have passed some of their stolen wealth to this immoral judge. Otherwise, the judge would not take such a risk.

Persons of immoral character really have no business on the bench. Writing on the tenets expected of justices of the SCN, Eghagha (2002, p. 1) states: "Certainly, we cannot associate these honourable men with anything except justice, fair play, truth, honesty, firmness, a strong aversion to corruption and tribalism." Without doubt, these virtues are expected of all judges, in all the courts in the state and federal jurisdictions. A reconstructed law and justice system will hold corrupt judges, such as the Federal High Court judge referenced in the preceding paragraphs, to their conducts. They will be accountable to the citizens who suffer as a result of judicial corruption. Opening up the judicial system for more citizen participation will discourage potentially corrupt judges from implementing their nefarious schemes. Also, strong judicial ethics monitoring, by reputable and transparent citizens, will eliminate most corrupt behaviors on the bench. These steps will help to ensure the credibility of the courts and the larger justice system.

Ten, *Advertise and Emphasize the Importance of Oath and Affirmation:*[5] Citizens' belief in the ability and efficacy of a court in particular, and a justice system in general, to identify and punish a person that lies to the court is strategically important to the survival, effectiveness, and efficiency of the system. Lawyers and non-lawyers in Nigeria understand that whether or not a party to a case is identified as having lied to the court depends on whether or not objective, verifiable evidence is presented to prove that the accused has lied. Otherwise, a person who lies but is not proved to have done so will escape legal liability. The system's reliance on objective proof of a "lie" to the court seems to encourage persons to withhold the truth so long as the system does not prove it. The widespread lack of genuineness with which oaths and affirmations are regarded in judicial proceedings and many public transactions in Nigeria prompted a chief judge to advise all citizens to regard oath and affirmation with seriousness, rather than as a mere formality ("Plateau CJ Advises on Oath Taking," 1999).

Truth-telling should be understood as an act that rises over and above the statements of the law. It is not sufficient to merely comply with the legal requirements. Therefore, to encourage parties and their witnesses to tell the truth to the court, it is important in a reconstructed law and justice system for the court (judge), lawyers, and other court officials to stress to the parties that statements and other representations to the court must pass an invariably higher truth test. The higher truth test should appeal to the need for parties and witnesses to accurately represent events based on each party's or witness's belief in a Supreme Being or other supernatural, or belief in the supremacy of the land, etc. By this, parties and witnesses will be discouraged from construing a statement as "true" simply

---

5   Aspects of Oath and Affirmation were discussed in Chapter 6.

because it meets the threshold of what is legally permissible, which invariably is a narrow and self-serving legal truth standard. The reconstructed law and justice system will appeal to each party's or witness's true belief to encourage the person to tell the truth in the system.

Every Nigerian community has historically held a set of beliefs to guide its members in their dealings with others. To this end, the use of indigenous deities to swear in parties and witnesses in courts should be encouraged. The reemphasis of this belief will serve to remind the citizens that each person will inescapably be held directly or indirectly (through offspring, relatives, etc.) responsible for falsely taking an oath or affirmation to secure or preserve an undeserved advantage. Research shows that indigenous control processes, including the belief and truth-telling components, are more compelling on the behavior of Nigerian Igbos, for example, than foreign controls (Oli, 1994). Oli's (1994) study of Traditional versus Christianized Igbos on the relative compelling ability of each group's beliefs on behavior, led Oli (1994) to this observation and conclusion:

> The fear of spirits is gradually replaced by belief in expiation of sins, and an increased resort to devious means for achieving greatness. Control by tradition is replaced by police control. The English legal system notion that one is presumed innocent until detected and proven guilty, replaces fear of the omnipresence of spirits, admission of guilt and certainty of punishment (at p. 26).

> Information tends to support the original hypothesis that traditional Igbo social control systems are more compelling [than Christian social control systems] on behavior (at p. 29).

Therefore, it is necessary in a reconstructed law and justice system to establish and implement a credible and balanced process that observes and enforces the right of the accused to be "innocent until proved guilty" and at the same time encourages parties and witnesses to tell the truth, the whole truth, and nothing but the truth. A continuation of the present English-based oath or affirmation model fails the credibility test. The model, being foreign, has little significance for average Nigerians. The model deviates from the citizens' daily experiences. In view of this and as stated, the proper mechanism for extracting the truth from each party or witness is greater emphasis on the citizen's belief and the generally accepted consequences of failure to be truthful. The reconstructed law and justice system will strongly emphasize to each party or witness the tenets of his/her faith or other belief and the consequences of violating the faith or belief. Such consequences may be highlighted by, for instance, invocation of a party's deity and the related activities. In the final analysis, it seems that a wider and official support for the use of the indigenous processes for accessing the truth will compel a party or witness to be truthful.

Eleven, *Encourage Responsible Judicial Activism*: To earn and preserve their common reference as "the last hope of the common man," Nigerian courts in a reconstructed law and justice system must always responsibly evaluate, interpret, and apply all laws (indigenous-based and English-styled) for the singular purpose of achieving justice. To this end, laws, policies, programs, and other actions that breach or threaten citizens' economic, social, political, or human rights should be struck down as unjust and thus unlawful. Law does not exist in a vacuum. Rather, law – good law – reflects its society and the citizens' needs and wishes, not the preferences of a few privileged and well-connected persons:

> Good law (that is, firm, fair, predictable and yet reasonably flexible, generally accepted, progressive law) evolves or is made for the general population or a substantial portion thereof, not a specific individual or special interest. Good law comes into being to prevent or correct a social, not private, problem (Okafọ, 2007).

Therefore, to be good, law should be crafted to address the general interests of the citizens. Bad law cannot satisfactorily address the citizens' overall concerns. And "law," as popularly understood, is a public phenomenon. At all times, the judge, court, and other justice officials should seek the goodness quality in law for the public's good. It follows that the judge, court, and other justice officials should find the goodness in every law and deploy the law to solve society's problems. Finding the goodness that is, or should be, in law may require creativity on the part of the judge and other justice officials. When in doubt, the officials should prefer the interpretation of the law that ameliorates the general citizens' concerns, even when such meaning of the law is not obvious.

Chukwudifu Oputa, former justice of the SCN, while urging SCN justices and the country's other judges to follow judicial activism in decisions, states as follows (Uchegbu and Nwogu, 2003, at p. 2):

> Laws should never be an end ... but merely a means to an end, a means and instrument of safeguarding our people from arbitrariness and from oppressive actions by government and its functionaries or by powerful conglomerate. Our judges should mould and interpret our laws to produce justice. They should realize that majestic generalities in our constitution and the laws have a content and a significance which vary from age to age.

Thus, judicial activism in a reconstructed law and justice system will embody three main ideas/characteristics, as follows: (a) justice as the end or purpose of every law; (b) flexible judicial procedure to attain justice; (c) courageous judge, lawyer, and other court and judicial officials to search for, find, and use the necessary path to achieve justice in every circumstance. Additionally, judges, lawyers, and other officers of the judicial process must have social conscience and be willing to make personal, material, and other sacrifices to further justice (Fagbohungbe, 2003).

As long as this judicial activism is practiced with the rational focus and credible foundation to ensure justice, most Nigerians will support it. At the building stages of the USA, the US Supreme Court, led by Chief Justice John Marshall, courageously assumed the power to judicially review acts of the Legislative and Executive branches of the government to determine their compliance with the US constitution (*Marbury v. Madison*, 1803). Non-compliance with the constitution led to a judicial declaration of unconstitutionality. Although the US constitution did not expressly confer "judicial review" power on the US Supreme Court, Marshall's court took up the responsibility. More than two centuries later – because of the 1803 judicial activism – the power of judicial review is entrenched as a means of checking government powers in the USA. And, the power is not, nor should it be, limited to the US Supreme Court. Such judicial activism in Nigeria will help to build and strengthen a reconstructed law and justice system that responds to the needs of the generality of the citizens.

Twelve, *Expand and Enforce the Power of Private Prosecution*: The power to approach a Nigerian court with accusation of crime against another person is vital to justice. This is because the court is a passive institution. It does not initiate a case, but must wait for a case to be brought before it. Otherwise, the judicial process will not apply. Criminal prosecution in Nigeria is largely a government business. The federal and state Attorneys-General and designated police personnel are the main prosecutors. With leave, a private person may prosecute an accused criminal. Even then, the applicable Attorney-General (A-G) may constitutionally discontinue the prosecution of any criminal case, whether prosecuted by the A-G or someone else, by entering *nole prosequi* (literally, "I will not prosecute"). Since the government of the day controls the A-G and the police, the government can, and often does, shield its members and friends who commit crimes. This was the situation when in November 2004 political opponents of the then Governor Chris Ngige of Anambra State swooped on the state in a wave of criminal venture. They entered the state, particularly the capital city of Awka and the commercial city of Onitsha, in about forty-three vehicles, and burned and destroyed government properties, including the Government House (the seat of government), the legislators' residential quarters, and two state-owned broadcasting stations. No person was arrested or prosecuted for the crimes which cost Anambra State billions of naira (Onwubiko, 2004). It is an open secret that the criminals and their sponsors were then-President Olusegun Obasanjo's friends and associates, hence the refusal by the police and the A-G to arrest and prosecute.

The Anambra State experience and the murder of Dele Giwa, then Editor-in-Chief of *Newswatch* magazine, illustrate the importance of private prosecution. According to Chief Gani Fawehinmi (Giwa's attorney), Giwa's murder by parcel bomb on October 19, 1986 pointed to the leaders of the then military junta of General Ibrahim Babangida, if not Babangida himself. Fawehinmi's efforts to privately prosecute Babangida and his associates were frustrated by the refusal to grant leave for private prosecution. Expanded private prosecution authority in a reconstructed law and justice system would enable Fawehinmi and Anambra taxpayers to prosecute the alleged criminals. In such instances where those charged with investigating and/or prosecuting crimes refuse or fail to carry out their duties, an expanded private prosecution authority would entitle any citizen with *locus standi* (strong, verified interest) in the matter to prosecute. There is no doubt that in the two cases discussed here, the five communities that lost properties in the criminal destruction in Anambra State and Fawehinmi in the Giwa murder, respectively, have strong and verified interests in the respective cases. They will thus be able to prosecute in a reconstructed judicial process. Such expanded and enforced private prosecution authority will force government prosecutors and law enforcement officials to be more accountable.

Corrections and Other Post-trial Actions

The issues in this section of this chapter concern the proper forms and methods of society's reactions to persons convicted of crimes in a reconstructed law and justice system. On this, it is necessary to appreciate that many indigenous Nigerian societies, like other Africans, often differentiate between the criminal and the crime. This means that the society understands that, even though a person's conduct is bad, the person may be recoverable or capable of rehabilitation and not necessarily bad. The adage, "Do not throw away the baby with the bathtub" is instructive here. Therefore, indigenous Nigerian communities have a variety of corrective measures to crimes, such as offender correction and rehabilitation, compensation and indemnification of the victim, remorse and forgiveness, and punishments and other sanctions. A measure is applied as response to a crime depending on the best fit for the circumstances. The largely homogenous indigenous community has a strong interest in carrying along all, or at least most, of its members. Everyone's contribution is needed to build and sustain a strong, secure, and progressive community.

The changes to the Nigerian community as a result of colonization and migration have made the society heterogeneous, such that even the pre-colonial societal norms that were settled and generally accepted are subject to increased challenge from within and outside each community. However, despite the marked differences between the pre-colonial and postcolonial Nigerian societies, there are many aspects of the indigenous modes of offender corrections and management that can be used for great benefit in modern social control in the country, and thus should be retained. On the other hand, there are many aspects of convict disposal and management under English law in Nigeria that should be discarded for ineffectiveness and/or inefficiency. The objective in this connection should be to build a credible criminal justice system capable of proper offender management for the greatest good of Nigeria.

Thus, in a reconstructed Nigerian criminal justice system, the following issues concerning offender corrections and other post-trial actions, along with recommended redresses, need to be tackled for more effective and efficient social control.

One, *Ensure Humane and Proper Prison Conditions for Rehabilitation*: The deplorable state of the Nigerian prisons and jails must be corrected as part of any reform effort in a reconstructed law and justice system. Many reports have been published on the unacceptable living conditions in prisons (see "The Condition of Our Prisons," 2002; Sanni, 2007; Ajayi, 2007; "The Prison Riot in Ibadan," 2007; Agande, 2007; Taiwo, 2007). The messy, desperate conditions to which inmates are subjected in Nigerian jails and prisons include gross overcrowding, lack of hygienic conditions, absence of reform opportunities such as through skills training, insufficient food, and excessive and illegal pretrial detention. In some instances, inmates are detained pending trial ("awaiting trial detainees" or ATDs) for upwards of ten years without being charged to court. Many do not know the crimes for which they are detained. Others are detained for much longer than they would have served in prison had they been tried, convicted, and sentenced to the maximum prison term. Yet others have been jailed for so long that their accusers have forgotten about them (see "The Condition of Our Prisons," 2002). Pretrial detention appears to be most responsible for the congestion in Nigerian prisons. "The Prison Riot in Ibadan" (2007), while examining the 2007 riot in Ibadan prison, points out that more than sixty-seven percent (67%) of the inmates in the country's 227 prisons are pretrial detainees (ATDs). This is unconscionable, say nothing of illegal.

However, the congestion resulting from the overload of ATDs combines with other factors to present the prevailing subhuman conditions in Nigerian prisons. Any wonder that inmates frequently riot to protest their conditions? Between 2002 and 2007, there were prison riots in many prisons, including Okene, Kogi State (2002), Makurdi, Benue State (2002), and Ibadan, Oyo State (2007). "The Prison Riot in Ibadan" (2007) illustrates this problem, the related difficulties, and possible solutions, as follows (at p. 3):

> The truth is that congestion, coupled with inadequate funds for prisons service and conceivable human failings, have combined to violate the original concept of the prison as a reformatory centre. The Nigerian prison system dehumanises whoever passes through it; its managers are often sadistic; the facilities are antiquated. This development has put a question mark on the country's system of justice administration, besides worsening the country's human rights image in the international community. To resolve this, whatever efforts that may be made to improve the prison system must be complemented by similar reforms in the Police, the courts and government. The Police for instance can eschew the habit of arbitrary arrest and detention, often on flimsy and untenable excuses. The courts must find a way to accelerate criminal trial, while government should build more prisons and rehabilitation centres. The option of parole and suspended sentence should be considered as is the case in other countries.

"The Condition of Our Prisons" (2002) further recommends that the federal government should build a "'model prison' that would serve as a benchmark for the revamping of the many neglected prisons dotted all around the country" (at p. 2). The "model prison" idea may be useful. If it is implemented along with my recommendations in this chapter for prison reform and offender management, the steps would show that the federal government is leading the states and the local governments by example, on this issue.

Two, *Establish and Maintain a Standing Committee on Prison Monitoring*: Many publications document the numerous existing illegal, inhumane, and unfair prison conditions in Nigeria, some of which are described in the preceding two paragraphs. Many other writings record these situations as well (see as examples Agande, 2004; "Caring for the Nation's Prisoners," 2005; "Nigeria to Free Half its Inmates," 2006; Oretade, 2006). The documented circumstances make it necessary to routinely oversee the jail and prison conditions and the overall state of the inmates throughout Nigeria. The numerous forms of illegal, excessive, unfair, and inhumane conditions that the chief judge of Abia state found when in 2003 he and other judges and magistrates visited Umuahia (Abia state capital) prison make this recommendation necessary. Their findings include: an inmate was in prison for felling his mother's orange tree; some inmates were imprisoned without warrant or with expired or unsigned warrants; many inmates were in prison for offenses not known under Nigerian criminal laws (Njoku, 2003). According to the chief judge, "The news saddens *us* more than it normally should. This is because given the environment in this country, it could just be the tip of the iceberg" (at p. 1).[6] See also Ige (2002) in which the Anambra state chief judge decried prison congestion.

Considering the seriousness of the prison conditions and their threats to justice in Nigeria, I recommend the formation of Prison Monitoring Committees (PMCs) at the Federal, State, and Local government levels. The committee will consist of, among other members, representatives of the Nigerian Bar Association (NBA) at each government level. The NBA at the national level, the state chapter of the NBA, or the applicable local chapter of the NBA, as the case may be, will be represented on the relevant PMC. Other members of the PMCs will be representatives of the Ministry of Justice (state or federal ministry, depending on whether a jail or prison is state- or federal-owned), representatives of registered civil rights organizations, and representatives of the relevant federal, state, or local government, as the case may be, to be nominated by the applicable national legislature, state legislature, or local legislature. The diverse membership of the PMCs will ensure input from many public and private stakeholders in prisons and corrections. It will also reduce the likelihood that an agency or group will dominate the process.

The monitoring committee will be charged with the responsibility to routinely and with minimum publicity visit the jails and prisons within its jurisdiction. The committee will review inmates' records and report to the judge with jurisdiction over each area on what the committee found. Where it finds illegal, unjust, or unfair detention and/or living conditions for inmates, the committee may recommend

---

6 Italics are in the original source.

to a judge with jurisdiction to order the release, with or without condition, of a deserving inmate. Unless strong and clear evidence contradicting the committee's recommendation is presented to a judge with jurisdiction within a reasonable time, a deserving inmate will be released, with or without condition. Although some chief judges from time to time visit prisons and release some unlawfully incarcerated persons (Ige, 2002), the PMC recommended here (a standing, rather than *ad hoc*, endeavor) will formalize the policy and require the committee members to account for their activities, which presently is lacking. Already, the Plateau State's Criminal Justice Committee pays periodic visits to prisons to assess conditions (see "Magistrates to Write Exams Before Promotion – CJ," 2009). This should be encouraged and extended to all the other states, with the modifications recommended in this book.

In the PMC model recommended in this book, a detainee who disagrees with a PMC's decision not to recommend release may appeal to a judge with jurisdiction over the matter. Therefore, the PMC recommended here does not take away from, but adds to, the existing constitutional guarantees to challenge unlawful detention. The unique advantage of the PMC is its capacity to speed up the remediation of illegal, unfair, and unjustified detentions. This is because the committee is specifically charged with the responsibility to routinely identify, report, and help to correct such errors.

Three, *Emphasize Corrections in Offender Management*: Nigeria's official criminal justice system is overly punitive. The system views a convict as well as his/her crime as bad and the convict as deserving of punishment. This official attitude appears to be at variance with the general customary expectations and preferences of the citizens. Often, the punishment imposed by the official criminal justice system does not fit the crime because the punishment goes beyond what is needed to redress the offense. On the other hand, indigenous forms of offender management are more reflective of the citizens' views of proper societal reactions to crimes. However, every crime is a transgression of a general societal norm. The focus of societal reaction thereto should be on encouraging and extracting compliance with the norms, rather than on inflicting pain and suffering on transgressors and alienating them from the rest of society. Consistent with the British colonial criminal justice policy in Nigeria, contemporary criminal laws in Nigeria remain primarily tailored to punish. Harsh sentences are commonly directed and imposed because the applicable criminal laws were enacted either by colonial Britain or in line with the British colonial philosophy of punitive sanctions (Okereafọezeke, 1996; 2002).

A new philosophy and model of responses to crimes is necessary for a reconstructed Nigerian criminal justice system. The new version will contain a mixture of indigenous and foreign approaches, depending on the effectiveness and efficiency of each measure. Indigenous courts and tribunals in Nigerian communities have for long (pre colonization) managed a range of offenses – minor, major, and all others between them. Erstwhile colonial and present postcolonial official policies limit the powers and authority of these indigenous courts. The result is that official laws have assigned only very limited powers over minor crimes to these indigenous courts. However, consistent with the recommendation in this book (see Figure 7.4), the indigenous and English courts and processes should be synthesized. If this is done, traditions, customs, indigenous laws (customary law), and practices as well as English-style laws will have to be equally considered for offender management depending on the needs in each case. With this, various forms of reactions to crimes will become available to the courts, including reprimand, fine, probation, suspended sentence, parole, work release, community service, responsible adult supervision, and restitution. These offender management options will be established and used in the new system. No longer will the system rely on purely punitive sanctions, such as jail and imprisonment, and the death penalty. Note that these offender management tools will be further expanded for juvenile convicts because of their greater chance of being reformed over adult offenders.

Reprimand, fine, suspended sentence, probation, parole, work release, community service, restitution, and responsible adult supervision, or some combination of the options seems to be a viable way to reduce the current overindulgence in punishment in the criminal justice system. All the options appear reasonably well understood except for "community service" and "responsible adult supervision." These two options are therefore explained as follows. The proposed "community service" will place a convict (typically a simple offender, misdemeanant, or nonviolent felon, as well as a violent felon deemed capable of community reform) in the charge of an official (governmental) or unofficial (non-governmental) community institution, agency, organization, or other authority. The aim will be to mold the convict's behavior by supervising him/her through specified tasks stipulated in the judgment and sentence. The supervising authority will, periodically and especially at the end of the prescribed term, report the convict's progress to the court or to the Corrections office with jurisdiction, as the court may direct.

"Responsible adult supervision," a more privatized form of community service, deserves some explanation. By this, a convict will be handed over to a responsible adult family member or other responsible community member with the will and capacity to correct the offender. The responsible person will be charged with the task of helping the offender to change his/her behavior. The judge will give the responsible person a reasonable period of time to guide, supervise, monitor, and periodically account to the court or the Corrections office with jurisdiction, as the court may direct, on the offender's progress. Either "community service" or "responsible adult supervision" may be used where appropriate, depending on the seriousness of each offense. For instance, less serious crimes may be subjected to "responsible adult supervision," while the "community service" option is used to manage more serious crimes. To different degrees, both forms of offender management will involve average citizens in society's Corrections activities and thus allow the citizens to own the efforts and results. These should translate to improved social control.

Considering the differences in their life experiences and years of behavior formation, a juvenile offender is presumed to be more likely to be reformed than an adult offender. Notwithstanding, both categories of offenders should be considered for reform in a reconstructed law and justice system. Therefore the "community service" and "responsible adult supervision" ideas should definitely be implemented for suitable juvenile offenders and such other adult offenders as are deserving of the management methods. In the proposed model, if at the end of the imposed supervision term or at an earlier time (depending on the offender's progress) the court or the Corrections, depending on the sentencing court's directive, determines that the offender is sufficiently reformed, he/she will be discharged from the system. Otherwise, the sanction may be revised upward, that is made more punitive. There is no rational excuse for not enacting and implementing the "community service" and "responsible adult supervision" policies in Nigeria considering the country's grievous error of needlessly imprisoning minor, first-time, non-violent offenders.

The recommended citizen-centered corrections philosophy, evidenced by "community service" and "responsible adult supervision," will return primary responsibility for offender management and corrections to the community, rather than the official government. Major (more serious) criminals tend to begin their criminal enterprises with minor (less serious) crimes. In time, the minor criminal learns the ropes and ventures into major or more serious crimes. Thus, if the community successfully intervenes after a minor or even first major crime is committed and helps to change an offender's behavior for the better, the larger society will be saved the problems of more serious crimes in the future. Whatever the mode of society's response to a crime, the objective should always be to create a more ordered, just, and peaceful society. Often, punishment does not advance this objective. In such circumstances, less exclusionary, more dignifying, but firm societal reactions are needed. Indigenous responses to crimes are better suited for these situations. Judges in state and federal courts ought to freely apply and utilize these options within a reconstructed law and justice system.

The following observations are necessary to further clarify this recommendation Three, *Emphasize Corrections in Offender Management*. Even before co-opting the indigenous corrections models as proposed, the current prisons system in Nigeria can be modified for increased corrections and offender reform by taking the following clear, rational steps, in no particular order.

Step one, decentralize the country's prisons system. If Nigeria takes this step, rather than the federal government controlling the prison system for the entire country (population estimated at 140 million), each of the thirty-six states will control inmates within its jurisdiction who are serving prison terms for state crimes. Every state will further devolve responsibility for minor offenders to each of its local government authorities, according to geographical jurisdiction over the place where each crime was committed. Local Government control will allow for greater community input to offender management.

Step two, change the name "Prisons System" to "Corrections System." This may appear superficial but it can symbolize much more than a nominal tag. Added to the implementation of the other steps recommended in this book, the name change will serve as a strong reminder to the inmates and other citizens that the goal of the system has shifted to the reform, rather than punishment, of the offender.

Step three, reduce punishment and increase corrections in the system. This will require administrators and top officials of the new "Corrections System" to emphasize incarceration and punishment less and heighten emphasis on behavior control, monitoring, and corrections. When top "Corrections System" officials preach the change in focus, lower level line and staff personnel in the system will follow the lead. At present, it seems that all that the prisons personnel understand and care about is inmate suppression and punishment. Little or no regard is given to the future of the inmate or society. For example, what changes is incarceration instilling in the inmate to ensure that he/she contributes positively to the society after release from prison? There is no evidence that prisons personnel make significant efforts to address this central question. The lack of corrections-oriented training for prisons personnel explains this lack of focus.

Thus, even within the context of the current "Prisons System," the country's offender management policy, training, and activities ought to be focused on corrections. In response to Questions 22 (d) and 13, Appendix A, a Survey Reaction Participant, a Local Government Councilor at the time of the research, correctly observes:

> Casting a culprit in prison and abandoning him there to rot does not help the individual. Prisons should be places of correction – where an inmate regrets the offense he has committed and through education and counseling, changes his perspective in life. He learns a self-sustaining trade while in prison ... [Corrections] gives one the opportunity to make amends and later come back to the society to contribute his quota for growth and development.

At present, the English-style offender management model dominates Nigeria. The punishment focus of the present Prisons System is not sustainable. Training and retraining of the new Corrections personnel with a view to transforming their professional minds are highly desirable. Philosophical and methods changes are necessary to increase the utility of the system. However, while some changes can be made within the existing Prisons System, more meaningful and far-reaching reconstruction of the country's responses to criminals and crimes requires deliberate policy and effort to allow indigenous models to participate as no less than equals in offender management.

Four, *Incorporate Mixed, Graduated Responses to Crimes*: Mixed, graduated responses to crimes are essential to corrections in a reconstructed law and justice system. It is safe to state that most criminals are neither violent nor particularly dangerous to society. And, consistent with the indigenous Nigerian belief that most offenders are good people and can be reformed, practical steps are necessary within a reconstructed system to allow such reforms to take place. Thus, it is neither necessary nor sustainable to impose highly punitive sanctions for minor, first-time, or even nonviolent major offenses. More correction-minded societal responses make more sense. The courts should be empowered to impose an appropriate penalty, depending on such factors as the seriousness of each crime as well as whether or not the offender has recidivated, from such options as the following (not necessarily in this order): reprimand, suspended sentence, fine, responsible adult supervision, community service, restitution, probation, work release, parole, or some combination of the options. For a first time offender, for example, the court in a reconstructed law and justice system should initially impose the lowest sanction except where aggravating circumstances, such as excessive violence, necessitate stronger punishment. On the other hand, a repeat offender should receive stronger sanction.

Of the nine offender management options identified in the preceding paragraph, reprimand (warning) is perhaps the least punitive sanction. A simple offender or misdemeanant may be issued with an official warning and directed to avoid committing any crime, perhaps within a specified period of time. Again, this will be made even more readily available where the convict is a juvenile. Imposing such a low-level sanction will allow the criminal justice system to: (a) give the offender a second chance to change his/her behavior for the better; (b) take a firmer stand in the future by imposing a stronger sanction on the offender if he/she recidivates. Note that the graduated responses will include indigenous as well as English-based sanctions options, as appropriate. Mixed, graduated responses to crimes and criminals may include a new policy allowing jails and prisons to hold more dangerous inmates in custody while also supervising other offenders under various other supervision programs outside the prisons and jails. The jailing model in Indian Country, USA, supports this policy recommendation (Minton, 2002). The dual role for jails and prisons will demonstrate to the public as well as to the officials of these custodial facilities that their responsibilities are not limited to warehousing convicts, but should emphasize the positive transformation of offenders. However, if the dual functions will overwhelm the prisons and jails, they should continue to manage incarcerated offenders while a different department of the new Corrections System should be charged with the responsibility to supervise the free offenders.

To be sure, in the interim period before the more challenging aspects of the recommendations in this book are implemented, it seems that one of the easiest steps that can be taken to improve the quality of the Nigerian criminal justice system is to create and use probation and parole options for offender management. Probation is a popular offender supervision method in the USA, for example. In this approach, a convict, instead of serving a prison or jail term, is subjected to supervision by a court-appointed criminal justice official for a specified time period. In that period, the convict is expected to abide by the conditions specified by the court, otherwise the probation is subject to revocation and the convict sent to prison. At the time of a probation sentence, the supervision replaces the prison term that would have been imposed. Generally, probation is used mainly in misdemeanor cases or those involving young or first time offenders. In appropriate circumstances (such as where the crime at issue is nonviolent or an offender is not regarded as a further threat to the victim or the community), probation is applied to adult convicts. So, probation decisions are made on the basis of evidence and the court's discretion.

On the other hand, parole is a conditional release from prison before the convict has served the prescribed prison term in full. Thus, the prisoner pledges to fulfill specified conditions and generally be of good behavior so as to be released from prison earlier than previously specified by the sentencing judge. Common conditions for parole include that the prisoner should find and maintain employment through the remainder of the initially imposed prison term, should report periodically to the nearest police station, and should not commit another crime in that period. If adopted, both probation and parole can be effective means of avoiding or reducing prison congestion in Nigeria, even in the context of the present criminal justice system. The federal and state legislatures should enact laws empowering judges to use probation and parole options, as appropriate, to dispose of deserving convicts. The federal legislature appears to recognize the lacuna created by the absence of probation and parole options in the country's criminal justice system, hence their effort towards establishing a parole system for the country (see Daniel, 2008). This initiative should be adopted as a criminal justice policy at the federal and state levels without undue delay. The present trend of incarcerating major as well as minor offenders has to be reversed. The trend is unsustainable. It is too expensive for the country to continue. It does little justice to minor offenders by excessively punishing them. It dehumanizes many convicts as a result of the special "ex-con" label placed on them by the incarceration. It compromises the futures of too many citizens (such as convicts' dependents and other relatives) needlessly.

Note that, although a probation and parole system styled after the USA approach will substantially decongest Nigerian prisons and jails and improve justice, the USA style does not replace the "community service" and "responsible adult supervision" models recommended in this book for Nigeria. Even with probation and parole sentencing options in Nigeria, the need for the "community service" and "responsible adult supervision" offender management options will remain because of the unique qualities of the latter two options. However, in the short term, probation and parole will serve a useful purpose for Nigeria. In the longer term, the recommended "community service" and "responsible adult supervision" options should be established to better position the Nigerian criminal justice system. If implemented, the options will incorporate non-governmental rehabilitation efforts involving community social control systems, processes, and responsible individuals in the management of convicts. Also, the options will extend beyond minor crimes or misdemeanors to include major crimes or felonies. The options will be rooted in the indigenous philosophy that favors efforts to rehabilitate all offenders in the belief that all (or most) citizens are capable of modifying their behaviors to accord with society's standards.

Five, *Ensure Faster Application of Sanction or Other Correction*: One of the major drawbacks of the English-style criminal justice system in Nigeria is that there is substantial time lag between crime and punishment for the crime, assuming that the offender is identified, tried, and convicted. The maxim, "Justice delayed is justice denied" holds that the victim of a crime expects redress within a reasonable time from the commission of the crime. After this period, any sanction for the crime loses some of the necessary impact to assuage the victim's suffering. One of the attractions of the *Bakassi Boys* justice model in southeast Nigeria and other indigenous enforcement systems is that they are widely regarded as quicker than the English model. Incorporating a modified *Bakassi Boys* method into a reconstructed law and justice system in Nigeria will speed up the sanctions and corrections process. Of course, it is important to ensure high quality justice while pursuing quick justice.

However, beyond the elements of the *Bakassi Boys* that may or may not be incorporated into a reconstructed system, the time period between the commission of a crime and the sanctioning or correction of the offender needs to be shortened. Strategies for accomplishing this include the incorporation and uses of many indigenous methods for managing offenders. These indigenous methods are already in place and widely used and need not be invented. Replicas of the *Bakassi Boys* model can be found throughout the country and should be co-opted and used, with necessary modifications. In general, the indigenous methods rely greatly on the citizens, working together in mainly unofficial (nongovernmental) capacities. Fellow citizens act as checks on one another to eliminate or minimize abuses and other forms of corruption. Other strategies for shortening the time between crime and sanction include hiring and training or retraining of more "Corrections," rather than "Prisons," personnel. Accordingly, the mindset of the employees in a reconstructed law and justice system will need to be changed to emphasize offender reform rather than offender punishment. For avoidance of doubt, serious punishment will remain an option, but only after a reasonable determination that reform or correction is inappropriate and minor sanction or punishment is ruled out. Whatever the form of a society's reaction to crime in a reconstructed law and justice system, increased speed of application is essential.

Six, *Outlaw Capital Punishment*: Worldwide, the death penalty is one of the most controversial issues in criminal justice. The controversy is wasteful and avoidable. Thankfully, this form of punishment is in desuetude. Progressive European countries, Canada, and other reform-minded nations have enacted policies consistent with this reasoning. These countries have taken steps to eliminate the death penalty from their criminal justice systems. Does this mean that in these countries persons found guilty of first degree murder and other similar egregious crimes deserving of the stiffest societal reaction are treated with kid gloves? No. Rather it means that other tough but less controversial forms of punishment are imposed. Unfortunately, Nigeria uses death to punish some crimes, including murder. What is more, the country's procedures for implementing this punishment are questionable. The human rights group Amnesty International, in 2007, accused Nigeria of secretly executing some convicts (Ojiabor, Soniyi, and Adeyemi, 2008).

Even a "developed" country can have an inferior criminal justice system. A study of the USA illustrates the fundamental errors in its system, including the continued use of the death penalty as well as the insidious incarceration and subjection of the US population, especially the racial minorities, to criminal sanctions. These occur in a country that touts itself as the world's beacon of freedom, rights protection, and human advancement. The US criminal justice system in which the federal system and the systems of about 37 of the 50 states use the death penalty is, for that fact alone, one of the most punitive and thus backward systems in the world. This is so especially when this fact is viewed together with the country's rate of imprisonment (number of persons in jails and prisons per one hundred). The US imprisonment rate, which shows that the country imprisons more citizens than any other country ("1 in 100 Americans Behind Bars, Report Finds," 2008) evidences the punitive mindset that supports the death penalty in the country. Notwithstanding its capital punishment and overall harsh criminal justice system, crime flourishes in the USA. Nigeria, in reconstructing its law and justice system, must avoid this. Rather, "socioeconomic and political policies that help to prevent crimes and enhance the correction of offenders – instead of the current preoccupation with repressive policing and cruel and unusual punishments within [Nigerian] prisons" ought to be adopted (Alemika, 1993, at p. 1).

A reconstructed Nigerian law and justice system will do well to abrogate capital punishment throughout the country for four main reasons. First, capital punishment is too expensive to implement. Even when compared to the longest prison term (life imprisonment), capital punishment remains far more expensive. A death penalty process involves the following stages/issues: trial, numerous appeals, long wait for execution, and chance of conviction or sentence error resulting in unjustified killing. The financial, material, and human costs are immense. Second, capital punishment arouses high emotions and needless eruptions of sentiments among the citizens, for and against the penalty. Third, this form of punishment is barbaric. It is unsettling for a 21st Century State to calculatedly ritualize, stage, and publicize the deliberate ending of the life of one its own or other human being. It should not make a difference that the criminal is one of the worst behaved in the population. Fourth, Nigerian officials responsible for executing death row inmates have demonstrated unwillingness or reluctance to do so. For a variety of reasons (religious, moral, philosophical, social, political, etc.), these officials (president at the federal level and governors in the states) have essentially refused to sign the necessary death warrants for executions to take place. Thus, many condemned persons are on death row for years, sometimes for decades, after sentences.

Neither the Constitution nor other law specifies a deadline for a sentence of death to be carried out. To compound matters further, there is a dearth of persons willing to work in the criminal justice system as hangmen. Even in the country's austere and high unemployment period, far fewer hangmen than needed are willing to accept the employment. The result is that the number of condemned persons on death row, accumulated over the years, now stands at well over seven hundred ("Amnesty Int'l: 736 Persons on Death Row in Nigeria," 2008). *The Guardian* editorializes this and related issues as follows:

> Over the years, successive heads of state and state governors have shown extreme reluctance and aversion to signing death warrants, either for moral or metaphysical constraints, with the result that we now have about 725 condemned prisoners, including 11 women, on death row; some of them for several years. The failure to execute the condemned criminals is also ascribed to the dearth of hangmen. A strange excuse, this! The trend in some industrialised nations has been to first stop executing prisoners and then to substitute long terms of imprisonment for death as the most severe of all criminal penalties. The United States (U.S.) is a notable exception to this trend ("Death-row Prisoners and the Government," 2009, p. 2).

What then is the point of retaining a legal mandate to impose capital sentences that responsible officials, probably in reaction to the views of the generality of Nigerians, refuse to enforce? However, the form of *dramatization of evil* (Tannenbaum, 1938) that inheres in the death penalty process should be avoided because there is a more effective and efficient way of managing this class of criminals.

The notorious debate over capital punishment is an avoidable friction for a postcolony. It is avoidable because there is at least one other procedure (offered below) for handling capital criminals that does not bog down a society in endless class or other sectional pontificating and espousals of moral superiority and pretenses of toughness against criminals and crimes. However, objection to capital punishment is not limited to the needless heat generated by the extreme punishment. An equally strong, if not stronger, objection to capital punishment lies in the unevenness of its application, imposition, and execution. In Nigeria, for example, capital punishment, like other forms of punishment, is invoked by the prosecutor (the State), which decides whether or not to seek death as punishment on conviction. A decision to ask for the death of the accused on conviction is communicated to the court at the point of charging the accused. On conviction, the judge and/or jury decides whether or not to impose capital punishment. A person convicted and sentenced to death is executed by the prisons/corrections department, as scheduled.

The phases of implementing capital punishment show the important role of discretion in the process. Discretion is essential and desirable in the justice system. Discretion should be encouraged provided that it is used responsibly and fairly. It is difficult to accept an argument that capital punishment is used fairly in Nigeria, or the USA, or any other country for that matter. Available evidence contradicts such argument. I know of no country in which rich and poor persons accused of capital crimes have an equal chance of receiving the death penalty. Invariably, the poor have a greater chance of being punished with death than the rich or well-to-do. In short, the accused person's socioeconomic status (education, occupation, wealth, income, place of residence, fame, etc.) hugely influence death penalty decisions. The more of the socioeconomic status variables an offender has, the less likely he/she is to be sentenced to death. Thus, the following characteristics, among others, define a death row inmate: poor, uneducated, and largely unknown beyond his[7] family and friends. It is commonly said, and with good reason, that no rich person is on death row, the gravity of the person's crime notwithstanding. By means of their financial resources, connections, and avenues for influence, the rich always have options to plead down their crimes and the sanctions.

Also, capital punishment is objectionable because of its irreversibility. Every human activity, including judging cases and imposing criminal sanctions, contains errors of omission and commission. As a result, safeguards should be in place to identify and correct mistakes. The finality of death negates the possibility of correcting or reversing capital punishment, once it is executed. Numerous cases in Nigeria and the USA, as examples, show that criminal trial, conviction, sentence, and appeals are not sufficient to avoid errors in criminal justice processes, including capital punishment. However long it takes to manage a capital case from trial to appeals, there is always room for errors of omission and/or commission. Police and prosecutors have been known to fabricate evidence to convict an innocent person. If he is lucky, the non-capital convict spends years in prison before being declared "innocent" and released. Similarly, a capital sentence recipient who spends decades on death row before his innocence is shown is fortunate. However, where he is executed before being found innocent, he can no longer be redeemed alive. It is grossly unfair and immoral to execute a person for a crime he did not commit. To avoid this most unfortunate situation in the future, the following modified form of life in prison should be adopted. Key elements of this recommendation are that the convict remains alive (lest he be exonerated in the future) and contributes positively to the society, as explained below.

Capital punishment should be abrogated in a Nigerian reconstructed law and justice system and replaced with the following policy. A person convicted of a capital crime (crime currently punishable by death) will be sentenced to life in prison with hard labor without the possibility of release before natural death. This means that a person so sentenced (and convicts in this category should be few relative to the overall prison population) cannot be reviewed for possible parole. Also, "hard labor" means that the convict will be required to work in a productive capacity. The prison personnel will assign the convict to a suitable profession, job, or trade, according to competence, qualification, and availability. The convict will work for at least six days per week, twelve hours per day. In short, the convict will become a worker for the State, with the State owing the convict nothing more than what is necessary for reasonable health and sustenance. This will ensure that

---

7 Overwhelmingly, death row inmates are male. Therefore, gender seems to be a relevant variable for predicting the likelihood of receiving a death sentence.

the convict produces what he/she consumes, what the criminal justice system and the rest of society need to pay for the convict's custody and maintenance, as well as compensation for the capital crime victim's surviving close relatives. Thus, a percentage of the convict's products and proceeds will go to pay for his/her imprisonment. The balance will be paid to the surviving close relatives of the capital crime victim, such as spouse, children, parents, siblings, etc.

"Armed robbery" is a major source of death row inmates in Nigeria. As a result of the recommended policy change, it is essential to redefine this crime as follows. Capital punishment will no longer be a sentencing option for armed robbery. Armed robbery resulting in death will attract life in prison with hard labor without the possibility of release from prison before natural death. As explained in the preceding paragraph, the sentence will do away with a parole possibility; also the convict will be imprisoned with hard labor. Where the victim of an armed robbery suffers grievous injury, such as permanent incapacitation, a convicted armed robber will be sentenced to a maximum life imprisonment without the possibility of release from prison before natural death, depending on the aggravating versus mitigating circumstances of each case. Less injury to the victim will attract a reduced number of years in prison. Taking another's property with force or threat thereof but without physical or significant psychological injury to the victim will result in even fewer years in prison.

In short, the different "armed robbery" scenarios demonstrate the possible grades of punishments to be imposed on armed robbery convicts according to the death or extent of the injury that the offender inflicts on the victim. It seems retrogressive to continue with the present system that sentences every armed robber to death even where neither death nor significant injury is inflicted. At present, the focus of criminal law penalties for armed robbery is too much on loss of property. The focus should be shifted to death or injury to the victim as a result of the offender's conduct. Thus, where neither death nor grievous injury is inflicted, capital punishment should not be imposed.

The following advantages will accrue from the implementation of the policy recommended above. (a) The policy will humanize the reconstructed law and justice system by doing away with capital punishment, which is State-sanctioned killing. (b) It will remove the needless confrontations between individuals and groups in society over capital punishment. (c) It will severely deal with persons who have committed the worst crimes in society, while minimizing the drama surrounding capital punishment. (d) The system will leave room for error correction by releasing a deserving convict where evidence subsequently shows that the conviction and/or death sentence should be overturned. The irreversibility of an enforced death sentence makes this advantage particularly attractive. No monetary compensation from the State suffices for a deliberate State killing of an innocent person. The very nature of a criminal justice system as an imperfect human arrangement means that it includes built-in errors. In essence, death penalty ignores these errors. When the criminal justice system sentences a convict to death and executes the offender, the system erroneously suggests that it has attained perfection. The system in effect claims that there is no mistake (and none will be discovered in the future) to rectify. Numerous cases of erroneous executions in the USA, Nigeria, and other countries prove otherwise. The recommended alternative to capital punishment will remove the irremediable injustice stemming from a mistaken execution.

Seven, *Promote the Use of Unofficial Sanctions*: Official enforcement of a sanction requires the objectivity and verifiability of both the sanction and its mode of implementation. Due to objectivity and verifiability concerns about their elements, several indigenous-based sanctions and enforcement methods may not be suitable as *formal procedures* in an official justice system. However, the indigenous-based sanctions and enforcement methods may be used as *informal procedures* in an official justice system. Among the Igbos, for example, the objective and verifiable enforcement unease may work against such measures as *igba ekpe* (shaming by publicly parading and taunting offender) and ostracism (community or other group members isolating, shunning, and excluding offender from the group) (Okereafoezeke, 1996; 2002). Despite the questions about the suitability of including these sanctions in the official criminal justice system, their capacities for offender management are reasonably secured. They have been shown to contribute to effective social control (Okereafoezeke, 1996; 2002). In answering Question 13, Appendix A, a Survey Reaction Participant (a final year Law student) observes that ostracism is "the excommunication system in which no member communicates in any way either social[ly] or otherwise with an offender. No marriage alliance or even collection of fine from him is allowed. A[sic] knowledge that a given action would jeopardize one's relation with others in the society will always restrain such actions."

Considering their collective capacity to continue to contribute to effective social control, unofficial offender management methods, such as shaming, that do not violate the constitution should be maintained with Local and State government encouragement and support, without making these methods parts of the official criminal justice system. These self-help offender management methods should remain unofficial (non-governmental), but the relevant Local and State governments should encourage and support communities and their agencies to use these forms of shaming, for example, to respond to crimes. Appropriate "government encouragement and support" in this connection involves relevant government agencies explaining to community groups that they are free to use the forms of offender management provided that the procedures do not violate the constitution or other law. Also, the government can contribute financially to a community program or other effort to use these offender management options.

Chapter Summary and Conclusion

In Nigeria, case processing and adjudication, as well as the agency responsible for the activities (courts), suffer serious deficiencies. Similarly, corrections and other post-processing measures, together with the relevant criminal justice organization (prisons), are flawed. This chapter has articulated the most serious obstacles to effective and efficient justice in the country regarding the two areas of the criminal justice process. Altogether, 12 case processing and adjudication issues along with seven post-conviction problems were identified and explained, and solutions to the problems were proffered. At the risk of appearing reductionistic, three of the problems relating to case processing stand out. These are: (a) the need to indigenize the sources and interpretations of Nigerian criminal laws; (b) the need to restructure the court system and formalize and broaden the role of the indigenous courts and judging processes; and (c) the importance of using indigenous languages in court proceedings. Regarding post-conviction problems and solutions, the following are the dominant issues. Issue One is the proper role of indigenous strategies for offender corrections (at present these are either insufficiently used or ignored). Issue Two is the need to dedicatedly monitor Nigerian jails and prisons, by means of a Prison Monitoring Committee (PMC) at each of the Federal, State, and Local government levels. The PMC will ensure that citizens are not detained unlawfully or unfairly. If the recommendations in this chapter are implemented in a reconstructed law and justice system, the quality of justice will rise and the system will become more effective and efficient.

References

"1 in 100 Americans Behind Bars, Report Finds" (2008, February 28) *Associated Press*, http://www.msnbc.msn.com/id/23392251; Internet.

Abati, R. (2000, March 31) "Children of the Sharia" in *The Guardian*, http://www.ngrguardiannews.com/editorial2/en781005.html; Internet.

Agande, B. (2004, April 29) "Nigerian Prisons Worse than Nazi Camps – Idahosa" in *Vanguard*, http://www.vanguardngr.com/articles/2002/cover/f429042004.html; Internet.

Agande, B. (2007, October 11) "FG Raises Prison Inmates' Feeding Allowance", *Vanguard*, http://www.vanguardngr.com/articles/2002/cover/october07/11102007/f511102007.html; Internet.

Ajayi, O. (2007, September 21) "13 Killed in Ibadan Jail Break" in *Vanguard*, http://www.vanguardngr.com/articles/2002/headline/f112092007.html; Internet.

Akhaine, S. (2000, February 11) "Bello, Ex-Chief Justice, Faults Sharia's Adoption" in *The Guardian*, http://www.ngrguardiannews.com/news2/nn776113.htm; Internet.

Alemika, E. E. O. (1993) "Trends and Conditions of Imprisonment in Nigeria", *International Journal of Offender Therapy and Comparative Criminology*, 37(2), pp. 147-162.

"Amnesty Int'l: 736 Persons on Death Row in Nigeria" (2008) in *ThisDay*, http://www.thisdayonline.com/nview.php?id=125922; Internet.

"Are Indigenous Languages Dead?" (2006, January 5) in *BBC NEWS* online, http://news.bbc.co.uk/1/hi/world/africa/4536450.stm; Internet.

"Caring for the Nation's Prisoners" (2005, August 5) in *Vanguard*, http://www.vanguardngr.com/articles/2002/editorial/ed05082005.html; Internet.

Constitution of the Federal Republic of Nigeria, 1999.

Daniel, A. (2008, June 19) "Senate Considers Parole System Over Prison Congestion" in *The Guardian*, http://www.guardiannewsngr.com/news/article02//indexn2_html?pdate=190608&ptitle=Se...; Internet.

"Death-row Prisoners and the Government" (2009) in *The Guardian*, http://www.ngrguardiannews.com/editorial_opinion/article01//indexn2_html?pdate=12010...; Internet.

Edike, T. (2006, November 20) "Igbo Language May be Extinct in 20 Years" in *Vanguard*, http://www.odili.net/news/source/2006/nov/20/315.html; Internet.

Eghagha, H. (2002, July 30) "Judging the Supreme Court" in *The Guardian*, http://www.ngrguardiannews.com/editorial_opinion/article4; Internet.

Elumoye, D. (2007, November 28) "Lagos Assembly May Adopt Yoruba as Official Language" in *ThisDay*, http://www.thisdayonline.com/nview.php?id=96451; Internet.

Fagbohungbe, T. (2003, December 23) "Wanted: Lawyers with Social Conscience" in *The Guardian* (Nigeria).

Ige, I.-Ol. (2002, June 24) "Anambra CJ Decries Prison Congestion" in *Vanguard*, http://www.vanguardngr.com/news/articles/2002/June/24062002/Se3240602.htm; Internet.

"Islamic Law Should be Applied to Corrupt Politicians" (2002, August 25) in *Sunday Times*, http://allafrica.com/stories/printable/200208250031.html; Internet.

Lartey, O. (2007, October 30) "Ekiti: Masters Degree Holder Testifies in Yoruba" in *Punch*, http://odili.net/news/source/2007/oct/30/435.html; Internet.

"Magistrates to Write Exams Before Promotion – CJ" (2009, April 10) in *ThisDay*, http://www.thisdayonline.com/nview.php?id=140491; Internet.

Marbury v. Madison, 1803 5 U.S. 137.

Minton, T. D. (2002, May) "Jails in Indian Country" in *Bureau of Justice Statistics Bulletin*, US Department of Justice.

"National Judicial Council (NJC) on Justice Kayode Eso Report" (2002, October 22) in *The Guardian*, http://www.ngrguardiannews.com/law/article1; Internet.

Neubauer, D. (2007) *America's Courts and the Criminal Justice System*. Wadsworth Publishing.

"Nigeria to Free Half its Inmates" (2006, January 5) in *BBC NEWS* online, http://news.bbc.co.uk/1/hi/world/africa/4583282.stm; Internet.

Njoku, J. (2003, June 10) "See What a CJ Found" in *Vanguard*, http://odili.net/news/source/2003/jun/10/74.html; Internet.

Nwabuikwu, P. (2002, December 4) "Before We All Become Fanatics …" in *The Guardian*, http://www.ngrguardiannews.com/editorial_opinion/article3; Internet.

Obijiofor, L. (2002, August 30) "One Nation, Two Laws" in *The Guardian*, http://www.ngrguardiannews.com/editorial_opinion/article04; Internet.

Ohiri-Aniche, C. (2006, February 10) "A Constitution to Save Nigerian Languages" in *The Guardian*, http://www.guardiannewsngr.com/editorial_opinion/article03; Internet.

Ojiabor, O., Soniyi, T., and Adeyemi, K. (2008, January 14) "Prisons Service Defends Execution of Convicts" in *Punch*, http://odili.net/news/source/2008/jan/14/430.html; Internet.

Okafọ, N. (2003b) "Religious Labels and Conduct Norms in Government" in *NigeriaWorld* (March 13). See http://nigeriaworld.com/articles/2003/mar/132.html; Internet.

Okafọ, N. (2007) "Rule of Law, Political Leadership, and Nobel Peace Prize: Analysis of the Obasanjo Presidency 1999-2007" in *NigeriaWorld* (January 12). See http://nigeriaworld.com/articles/2007/jan/122.html; Internet. See also "Analysis of the OBJ's Presidency" in *SaharaReporters* at http://www.saharareporters.com/da001.php?daid=204; Internet. See further "Analysis of the OBJ's Presidency" in *Daily Triumph* at http://www.triumphnewspapers.com/archive/DT19012007/ana19107.html; Internet. http://www.triumphnewspapers.com/archive/DT22012007/any22107.html#; Internet.

Okereafọezeke [a.k.a. Okafọ], N. (1996) *The Relationship Between Informal and Formal Strategies of Social Control: An Analysis of the Contemporary Methods of Dispute Processing Among the Igbos of Nigeria*. UMI Number 9638581. Ann Arbor, Michigan, USA: University Microfilms.

Okereafọezeke [a.k.a. Okafọ], N. (2002) *Law and Justice in Post-British Nigeria: Conflicts and Interactions Between Native and Foreign Systems of Social Control in Igbo*. Westport, Connecticut, USA: Greenwood Press.

Okoro, T. (2003, December 31) "Imminent Death of Igbo Language" in *Daily Champion* (Nigeria).

Oli, S. I. (1994) "A Dichotomization: Crime and Criminality Among Traditional and Christianized Igbo", in A. T. Sulton, ed. *African-American Perspectives on: Crime Causation, Criminal Justice Administration and Crime Prevention*. Englewood, Colorado, USA: Sulton Books.

Ologbondiyan, K. and Ogbu, A. (2004, January 19) "Constitution Review: Reduce Number of Supreme Court Justices – Belgore" in *ThisDay*, http://www.thisdayonline.com/news/20040120news05.html; Internet.

Onagoruwa, O. (2002a, October 8) "The Exit of Immoral Judges" in *The Guardian*, http://www.ngrguardiannews.com/editorial_opinion/article03; Internet.

Onagoruwa, O. (2002b, October 9) "The Exit of Immoral Judges (2)" in *The Guardian*, http://www.ngrguardiannews.com/editorial_opinion/article04; Internet.

Onwubiko, E. (2004, December 10) "Anambra Councils Seek to Compel Trial of Arsonists" in *The Guardian*, http://www.guardiannewsngr.com/news/article02; Internet.

Oretade, F. (2006, February 17) "Govt Plans Halfway Home for Prison Inmates" in *The Guardian*, http://www.guardiannewsngr.com/news/article03; Internet.

"Plateau CJ Advises on Oath Taking" (1999, August 3) in *Post Express*, http://www.postexpresswired.com/postexpr...; Internet.

Sanni, T. (2007, September 13) "Failed Jailbreak: Panel of Inquiry Instituted" in *ThisDay*, http://www.thisdayonline.com/nview.php?id=89188; Internet.

"Shame in Zamfara" (2000, March 31) in *The Guardian*, http://www.ngrguardiannews.com/editorial2/en781001.html; Internet.

"Sharia Law in UK is 'Unavoidable'" (2008, February 7) in *BBC NEWS* online, http://news.bbc.co.uk/1/hi/uk/7232661.stm; Internet.

Smock, D. (2005, September) "Applying Islamic Principles in the Twenty-first Century" in *United States Institute of Peace*, Special Report 150.

Soyinka, W. (2002, November 27) "Aliyu Shinkafi's Fatwamania" in *Nigeriaworld*, http://odili.net/news/source/2002/nov/27/123.html; Internet.

Taiwo, J. (2007, October 11) "Prisons Reform: FEC Approves N200 Daily Per Inmate" in http://www.thisdayonline.com/nview.php?id=91961; Internet.

Tannenbaum, F. (1938) *Crime and the Community*. Boston, Massachusetts, USA: Ginn.

"The Condition of Our Prisons" (2002, October 2) in *The Guardian*, http://www.ngrguardiannews.com/editorial_opinion/article1; Internet.

"The Prison Riot in Ibadan" (2007, September 21) in *The Guardian*, http://www.guardiannewsngr.com/editorial_opinion/article01; Internet.

Uchegbu, A. and Nwogu, M. (2003, August 29) "At NBA Conference: Oputa Canvasses Equitable Justice" in *Daily Champion*, http://www.champion-newspapers.com/news/teasers/article_4; Internet.

Usigbe, L. and Ozoemena, C. (2002, November 27) "Federal Govt Voids Fatwa Against ThisDay Reporter" in *AllAfrica.com*, http://allafrica.com/stories/printable/200211270097.html; Internet.

"Williams Under Fire in Sharia Row" (2008, February 8) in *BBC NEWS* online, http://news.bbc.co.uk/1/hi/uk_politics/7233335.stm; Internet.

PART 4
For a Fresh Philosophy of Justice

Introduction to Part 4

Part 4 of this book, consisting of Chapter 8 and Summary and Conclusion, offers considered ideas, explanations, and rationalizations for a new outlook on law and justice in a postcolony. Chapter 8 focuses on the shared responsibility of building and sustaining a more effective and efficient law, justice, and social control system. The author identifies the various roles of official (governmental) and unofficial (non-governmental) persons, groups, and institutions in a postcolony in the quest for renewed law and justice. One of the sad realities of postcolonial life is that the citizens of a postcolony often fear and/or distrust their (official) government and its agents. As a consequence, these citizens do not want to be involved with the government in law and justice matters, among other issues. To a large extent, this situation remains in Nigeria.

The average Nigerian regards a government policy, program, or other effort as belonging to "them" rather than "us". The sense of common ownership, which is a prerequisite for the success of a public enterprise, is markedly absent or diminished. This extends to situations where the citizens are employed, for pay, to achieve a public purpose. In such a situation, these citizens are merely interested in fulfilling the minimum obligations to receive their remunerations. They have little or no interest in achieving the goal of the policy, program, or effort. No wonder then that the Igbo (Nigeria) refer to civil and other public service jobs, which developed from British colonization, as "ọrụ oyibo" ("white man's job"). The idea is that these jobs belong to "them," not "us", and we will not do anything beyond what we must to earn a living! A reconstructed law and justice system has the potential to address this underlying citizens' fear of, and/or cynicism towards, the postcolonial State. Therefore, reconstructing law and justice in a postcolony implicates the need to re-orientate the citizens generally. By this, the citizens will be exhorted to demonstrate greater patriotism by contributing more positively to the country's development.

The Summary and Conclusion portion of this book emphasizes reduced criminalization (decriminalization) and increased role of civil response for suitable offenses. As shown throughout this book, for Nigeria, excessive criminalization and punishment are antithetical to indigenous systems and beliefs. The country's present high criminalization results from, and is a legacy of, British colonial rule over Nigeria. Civil, rather than criminal, responses to crimes should be encouraged whenever appropriate.

Chapter 8
Sharing the Responsibility of Law and Justice Renewal

Chapter Introduction

The central issue in this chapter is responsibility distribution in a postcolony regarding the reconstruction and sustenance of law and justice in the society. There is little doubt that to be successful, a law and justice system must utilize and expand positive roles for individuals, groups, and organizations in public as well as private sectors. Recognition of this fact is relatively easy. The greater challenge is in demarcating the proper roles of the stakeholders and fashioning a system to encourage them to contribute their utmost to the overall society's goal of high quality justice through an effective and efficient process. This chapter identifies explicit ways in which specific persons, bodies, and groups in official government and unofficial sectors, such universities and other educational institutions, professional organizations, such as the Nigerian Bar Association, town and community groups, can contribute to improved justice in a reconstructed law and justice system.

Elements of Shared Responsibility for Justice

The official (governmental) and unofficial (non-governmental) sectors of a postcolony bear joint responsibility to reconstruct and develop the society's law and justice. However, the nature and degrees of relative responsibility vary among the federal, state, and local governments and their agencies, public institutions and organizations, private institutions and organizations, community groups and institutions and leaderships, private groups, individuals, etc. To facilitate law and justice reconstruction in a postcolony, each of the categories of institutions/persons should have specific roles consistent with its capacity, including finance, geographical and subject matter influence, expertise, and organizational mission and expectation. It seems inescapable that the official governments will bear responsibility for tying together all the efforts by all the stakeholders – public and private – towards a reconstructed law and justice system. Invariably, the official governments and their agencies are at least responsible for formalizing (through constitution making, legislation, etc.) the process for implementing a reconstructed system. This is necessary because the backing of State enforcement powers is crucial to encourage the citizens to comply with a law and justice system. In the Nigerian example, the Federal Government, being the country's most powerful and influential official government, bears the greatest amount of the responsibility in this regard.

Overseeing law and justice reconstruction efforts in Nigeria necessarily includes understanding the principles and operations of the country's indigenous systems. Thus, the personnel of the official governments in Nigeria, led by the Federal Government, have to understand the country's customary laws. That is the only way that they could effectively help to educate the citizens on the indigenous systems and processes. However, unfortunately, the reality is that the different levels of government (Local, State, and Federal) and their officials are themselves alienated from their respective indigenous laws and systems. Many of the officials, who would be expected to lead the effort to educate their citizens on the legal obligations expected of the citizens, do not sufficiently understand the applicable indigenous rules, laws, norms, and other standards of conduct. In many instances, these officials tend to understand and demonstrate preference for the English system over Nigeria's indigenous systems. No one can teach that which he/she does not understand. Therefore, it is imperative that steps be taken to encourage and expect government officials, particularly those charged with disseminating information and educating the public on reconstructed law and justice principles, to learn those principles for themselves. Then, the officials will be better positioned to utilize government avenues to strengthen understanding and appreciation of the principles by sharing the indigenous systems' knowledge as a part of educating all the citizens.

A study of the Nigerian justice system and the general society identifies the following topics and groups as vital components and stakeholders in efforts towards effective and efficient social control in a reconstructed law and justice system. On each of the identified subjects, in no particular order, the following actions are recommended as parts of law and justice reconstruction.

First, *Institute and Maintain Citizen Education through Mass Mobilization*: Mass education of Nigerians will be required for the law and justice reconstruction recommendation in this book to be fruitfully implemented. Citizen cooperation is vital. An avenue to explain and inculcate the necessary changes to the existing system cannot be overemphasized. From 1987 through 1993, Nigeria experienced a form of mass mobilization, albeit for a broader purpose than law and justice reform. The General Ibrahim Babangida regime (1985-1993) instituted the Mass Mobilization for Self Reliance, Social Justice, and Economic Recovery (MAMSER). As a political orientation, MAMSER's key goals included nurturing a foundation for the regime's transition to civilian rule program by educating the citizens about politics and the political process, increasing participation in political debates and elections, and helping to restore the citizens' pride in, and dependence on, Nigerian goods and services. Had MAMSER survived the Babangida regime, its expressed focus on indigenous goods and services would have been a basis for educating Nigerians about the elements of a reconstructed law and justice system. Unfortunately, like most programs and policies in the country, it died with the regime that authored it.

Knowledge of traditions, customs, and indigenous laws often flows from having and maintaining working and social relationships with community elders and other custodians of traditions, customs, and laws, such as traditional rulers and chiefs. Such knowledge also derives from other forms of participation in community ceremonies, functions, and events. However, the diverse nature of the Nigerian postcolonial State makes it difficult for a citizen that resides outside his/her indigenous community to keep up with evolving traditions, customs, and laws in the indigenous home. And, it is erroneous to assume that customary law can continue to inhere and be ingrained in us in the modern State without informal and formal socialization efforts. Therefore, the cosmopolitan character of present-day communities necessitates formal arrangements to educate the citizens about applicable traditions, customs, and laws. Moreover, the long-standing undeserved advantages that colonial Britain arrogated to English law, which successive postcolonial Nigerian regimes have sustained, justify official government intervention on behalf of the indigenous systems.

Thus, a MAMSER-like program will be needed to mobilize Nigerians on law and justice renewal. An organization, perhaps to be called the Citizen Mass Mobilization Committee on Law and Justice Awareness (CMMCLJA), which could be shortened to Citizens for Law and Justice, should be charged with leading the national effort in this regard. Citizens for Law and Justice will be necessary to re-orientate Nigerians to indigenous-based, homegrown law, justice, and social control. The requisite mobilization will derive from joint public and private efforts. The respective efforts of private and public agencies and groups will be coordinated to maximize the quality of law and justice. To this end, a Citizens for Law and Justice committee will be formed at the federal, state, and local government levels. The committee at each level will mobilize and educate the citizens on the fundamental elements of law and justice and the citizens' roles for more effective and efficient social control. The education of the citizens will include explanation of the provisions of the constitution and other fundamental aspects of justice. The committee at each government level will lead the efforts to educate the citizens in its geographic jurisdictional.

At the federal level, the Citizens for Law and Justice committee will consist of representatives from each of the following institutions and groups: two representatives of the federal executive branch of government, two representatives of the federal legislative branch, two representatives of the federal judicial branch, two representatives of each federal university/college of tertiary education, two representatives of the Nigerian Bar Association (NBA), two representatives of the Nigeria Police Force (NPF), and two representatives of each state government. Each state committee will be made up of: two representatives of the state executive branch of government, two representatives of the state legislative branch, two representatives of the state judicial branch, two representatives of each state university/college of tertiary education, two representatives of the state chapter of the NBA, two representatives of the state command of the NPF, and two representatives of each local government. A local committee will have the following members: two representatives of the local executive branch of government, two representatives of the local legislative branch, two representatives of the state Magistracy, two representatives of the state Customary Court/Native Court/Area Court, two representatives of each autonomous community in the state, two representatives of the local chapter of the NBA, and two representatives of the local NPF.

As the preceding paragraph shows, the Citizens for Law and Justice committee will be large. This is deliberate. All the recommended committee members will represent vital constituencies to publicize and educate the citizens about law and justice reconstruction. The committee members at each of the local, state, and federal government levels will help to bring law and justice nearer to the people. So far, Nigerian postcolonial law and justice are mainly isolated and removed from the citizens. The average citizen does not understand the justice system or its logic. There is a disconnect between the citizen and the system that is supposed to give him/her justice. This committee will ameliorate the present unsustainable situation. The committee can achieve its task by public education through federal, state, and private radio and television networks, bulletins, direct mailings to the citizens, town-criers, face-to-face town hall-format meetings, conferences with community leaders, traditional rulers, and influential leaders. The various media will transmit to the citizens the goals, objectives, mechanics, procedures, expectations, and benefits of citizen mobilization and increased participation in law and justice. All the relevant media messages will be transmitted through the indigenous languages as well as the English language. Such steps will likely increase citizen participation and result in higher quality of law and justice in the society.

The Citizens for Law and Justice committee's work will cover dissemination of information about every aspect of indigenous and other laws, pointing out the good and the bad ingredients. Thus, the committee will be able to continue such ongoing government campaigns as those against female genital mutilation and oppressive widowhood practices, which are rooted mainly in traditions, customs, and indigenous laws. However, enlightenment efforts for law and justice reconstruction must be designed, understood, and implemented as a part of the society's overall efforts for increased literacy. An increased literacy program is essential in Nigeria, as in most postcolonies, to reduce, if not extinguish, the inability to read or write in the country. Therefore, to advance the course of law and justice reconstruction, "the official governments should first of all eradicate illiteracy and advance education [generally] so that the policies and programs will be meaningful to the people. You do not talk about indigenizing law and justice when about 60% of the populace are illiterate" [Survey Reaction Participant, a final year law student, in response to Question 14 – "Should the official governments (Local, State, and Federal) formulate and pursue policies and programs to indigenize law and justice in Nigeria, why or why not?" – Appendix A]. Although the Respondent is correct on the crucial role of literacy in law and justice reconstruction, other aspects of the renewal for a postcolony, such as court redesign, law enforcement restructuring, etc., can go on at the same time as improvements are made in the general literacy rate. Increased literacy will help the citizens to better appreciate the laws that apply to them, thus increasing the laws' effectiveness and efficiency. Increased literacy will also afford the citizens greater ability and resources to identify and take proper steps to enforce their rights against the government and other offending parties.

Recognition of the role of the governments in educating the citizens on their traditions, customs, and laws does not endorse official take-over and changing of indigenous systems. Government involvement cannot be a basis for officials to subsume their preferences as indigenous principles and practices. Such a thing could happen if either: (a) the responsible government officials are unwilling to work hard to identify, verify, and help advance customary laws, or (b) the officials believe that their knowledge of the existing customary laws and/or ideas for future improvements are superior to that of the general citizenry. In either case, this line of reasoning is dangerous as it seeks to impose customary law from the top whereas customary law should develop from the grassroots of society (Snyder, 1982; Shaidi, 1992; Okereafoezeke, 1996; 2002). At the grassroots level, individuals learn the dos and don'ts from their forebears, contemporaries, and the indigenous system, not from an imposed external body. Imposed indigenous law or system within a country is not significantly better than imposed foreign law or system. To advance justice, law, and social control, both forms of imposition must be avoided.

Second, *Ensure True Law Reform*: The functions and contributions of the Nigerian Law Reform Commission (NLRC) to law and justice reconstruction in the country are questionable, at best. True law reform should aim at redesigning the law and justice system to do the best justice for and to the citizens. "Best justice" can be defined as justice that is most relevant, fairest, most perceptually and scrupulously sound, logical, and historically defensible but contemporarily useful for the citizens. The law of a society should reflect the spirit of the people. The law should evince the people's belief system, mores, and other dos and don'ts. This is the surest way to ensure citizen compliance with the law. It is difficult to see where or how the NLRC has performed to these expectations. As one Survey Reaction Participant (a final year law student) put it in response to Question 15, Appendix A, "The Commission has not satisfactorily carried out its responsibility of reforming the country's laws to make them relevant. The courts have continued to adhere strictly to precedents developed in foreign lands even when those precedents do not conform with the Nigerian lifestyle and situation." Another Survey Reaction Participant (a distinguished lawyer – Senior Advocate of Nigeria) responded in part to Question 15, Appendix A, thus: "Indeed many Nigerians are not even aware of the existence of [the NLRC]. Citizens of the country should be [sensitized] about the existence and functions of the Commission and invited to get involved in law reforms."

So far, the work of the NLRC appears to be limited to slight alterations to peripheral legal statements and principles. Even where such statements and principles were derived from Europe, usually England, the NLRC typically glosses over the matter of reform by tinkering with the edges of the law or principle while preserving the basically alien legal idea. According to a Survey Reaction Participant, in response to Question 15, "I would not say [that] the Nigerian Law Reform Commission has satisfactorily carried [out] its responsibility of reforming the country's laws. The Commission is reforming existing English laws and has nothing to do with native laws." That is not reform enough. The following changes, among others, are necessary for the NLRC to contribute more meaningfully to law and justice reconstruction. The NLRC "reform" authority and power should be re-couched as "reconstruction" authority and power. The new authority and power will allow the commission to truly redesign the law and justice system for Nigerians by ridding the country, at the federal as well as state and local levels, of foreign principles and logics that are at variance with contemporary Nigeria. To achieve this, law and justice reconstruction-minded Nigerians should be put in NLRC positions to work towards this goal.

Also, reconstruction efforts should include a diversification of the NLRC membership, authority, power, jurisdiction, as well as other resources. Accordingly, the NLRC will be organized at the federal, state, and local government levels, respectively. The activities of the three administrative levels will be coordinated to avoid or minimize law and justice changes that conflict. However, the NLRC at the federal level will concentrate on scrutinizing federal laws for needed changes, consistent with the indigenization theme of this book, to create a better atmosphere for effective and efficient law and justice. Similarly, each state and local government NLRC will be concerned with the evaluation of the applicable laws within its jurisdiction for necessary corrective steps. A national director will be appointed for the NLRC at the federal level. Each state NLRC will be headed by a deputy director, while an assistant director will head each local NLRC. The respective federal, state, and local NLRC will be required to meet periodically, in addition to other constant and ongoing coordination and sharing of law and justice reform information and ideas.

The (national) director of the NLRC will report ideas and recommendations for reforms at the federal level to the government through the minister of justice.[1] At the state level, the deputy director will report to the state commissioner for justice, while the assistant director at the local level will channel ideas and recommendations for reforms to the local government executive councilor in charge of justice (or to the chairman of the council in the absence of such a councilor). The recipient of a change idea or recommendation (the minister of justice at the federal level, or the commissioner for justice at the state level, or the local government executive councilor in charge of justice or the council chairman at the local level) must forward same to the relevant legislature, except that the recipient may add his/her opinion on the issue under consideration. The legislature will consider the opinion along with the NLRC recommendation for law/justice change. The NLRC change

---

1 At present, the Nigerian Attorney-General is also the Minister of Justice. As part of the recommendations for law and justice reconstruction, an argument is made later in this chapter for these two offices to be separated.

ideas and recommendations, together with the opinion, will be considered as a legislative proposal. This will be done periodically, as necessary.

However, as previously stated, changes to traditions, customs, and indigenous laws (customary law) should begin at the most intimate, community level. This is the level at which individuals interact with one another and consensually create or modify regulating principles and rules to guide their behaviors. Customary law should not be imposed (Snyder, 1982; Shaidi, 1992; Okereafọezeke, 1996; 2000; 2002), neither should changes thereto. Therefore, established and known kinship groups, rather than individuals in a community, will form the bedrock of proper law creation and reform. In Nigeria, as in much of Africa, the kinship groups are identifiable as follows, in order of progression from the smallest and most intimate: family, extended family, village, town, and towns group. These kinship groups are largely informal, unofficial clusters. The formal, official groups are the local government, the state, and the federation. Law and justice reform by the new NLRC, for instance, will rely on ideas from both official and unofficial groups and institutions. This procedure will accommodate and reflect the periodic changes that communities make to their traditions, customs, and laws to keep up with societal evolution. For instance, Okereafọezeke (1996, pp. 290-297; 2002, pp. 209-218) shows examples of legislative enactments by Ajallị, an Igbo (Nigeria) town. The written documents represent contemporary unofficial (non-governmental) efforts to document customary law from the grassroots community level, rather than from the top, official (governmental) level.

Third, *Separate Minister (Commissioner) of Justice from Attorney-General*: The government head of the law and justice department in the federal government of Nigeria is called the "Attorney-General and Minister of Justice." The counterpart in a state is known as the "Attorney-General and Commissioner for Justice." By definition, an attorney-general (A-G) is the chief advocate of the government's case. In every instance, the A-G, who is a lawyer, is also a politician appointed to the A-G position by the ruling authority. He or she is expected to be, and is, biased in favor of the ruling group, even in the conduct of cases. Therefore, it is unreasonable to expect the A-G to, at the same time, be both partisan and non-partisan in the pursuit of justice. Unlike the "Attorney-General," the "Minister of (or Commissioner for) Justice" is *conceived* as the most prominent member of a government responsible for advancing the citizens' rights and ensuring the attainment and maintenance of a reasonable balance between the rights and duties of the citizens and those of the State. Thus, in theory, if need be, this Minister or Commissioner should have little reservation going against the interests of the government or its members to ensure the promotion of the rights of the general citizenry. However, often times, the expectation differs from the functioning. The combination of "Attorney-General" and "Minister of (or Commissioner for) Justice" highlights the divide between the expectations and realities of the combined positions. The activities of the many Nigerians who have held both positions at the same time demonstrate that it is highly unlikely that any one person can fulfill the expectations of the two offices simultaneously. The inherent chasm between the work of the "Attorney-General" and that of the "Minister of (or Commissioner for) Justice" will likely remain a feature of the two offices. Thus, where the two positions are combined in the same individual, it will not be long before the intrinsic contradiction is highlighted.

Consequently, reconstructing law and justice in a postcolony requires a clear separation between the office, authority, and power of an A-G, on the one hand, and those of a Justice Minister (or Commissioner), on the other hand. While they must cooperate with each other to succeed, the emphasis areas of an A-G and a Justice Minister (or Commissioner) are fundamentally different. As described in the preceding paragraph, the A-G should argue the government's cases, while the Justice Minister (or Commissioner) should lead the efforts to (re)build a better justice system. The Justice Minister (or Commissioner) should be responsible for coordinating all the activities towards law and justice reconstruction at the federal or state level, as the case may be. I recognize that the recommended separation of the A-G from the Minister (or Commissioner) has the tendency to increase the number of government portfolios. Such growth of government would be unacceptable in a country such as Nigeria where there are already far too many government departments and portfolios due to irresponsible and wasteful duplication of offices. Such gratuitous duplication, in turn, leads to gross ineffectiveness and inefficiency.

However, it will be unnecessary to create another government portfolio on account of the recommendation to separate the A-G from the Justice Minister (or Commissioner). Instead, the proper functions of the A-G (as defined in this chapter) should be subsumed under the present "Solicitor-General" of the federation or state, as the case may be, to form a new "Solicitor and Advocate-General (SA-G)." The new SA-G will become the government's chief legal adviser and chief advocate, much of which the present Solicitor-General does. The new SA-G will be a career civil servant in the Justice Ministry – he/she will normally be the most senior official in the Ministry. Note that the new Minister of Justice will head the Justice Ministry. Upon appointment and acceptance as SA-G, an appointee's service will be withdrawn from the Justice Ministry and transferred to the Presidency (at the federal level) or Governor's office (at the state level), to avoid conflict with the Justice Minister (or Commissioner). The new Justice Minister (or Commissioner) will be a politician, preferably lawyer-politician, appointed to implement the government's ideas to improve law and justice. Both the SA-G and the Justice Minister (or Commissioner) will serve during the term of the government that appointed them. The recommended model seems to be a reasonable solution to the present misnomer called "Attorney-General and Minister of (or Commissioner for) Justice." The model vastly improves the present set-up.

Fourth, *Establish Interdisciplinary Approach to Legal Education*: The future of law and justice in Nigeria will be better served by a more interdisciplinary approach to teaching, learning, researching, and practicing law. An interdisciplinary style will mean that law departments and the Nigerian Law School will require their students to successfully complete more non-law classes, seminars, workshops, research, and other activities in addition to purely law course requirements.

This new technique of training lawyers will include directing law students to take classes offered in other departments, and more. In addition to directing law students to take classes in other departments, law departments (and the Law School) will hire and retain several qualified social science-based lecturers within the law departments. This will increase direct contacts between the law students and other social scientists. It will also encourage all the lecturers (lawyers, social scientists, etc.) to cooperate in research projects on law, public policy, and other related issues. This new model for training lawyers is useful because law and justice issues go far beyond pure statements of laws. Nigerian law departments, in their teaching and learning, should equally emphasize legal provisions and the applications of these provisions to society.

Thus, the law departments (and the Law School) should diversify their teaching curricula, research, publications, and personnel to better understand and help to improve the effects of law on society. As examples, the following subjects deserve close study by law students to ensure that they are placed in good positions to address the related law and justice issues that confront lawyers. The subjects are: Informal Social Control versus Formal Law; Ethics versus Law; Law and Justice Reform; Justice and Law Across Cultures; Legal Pluralism; Scientific Research Methodology and Practice; Strategic Planning for Justice; Restorative Justice; Comparative Law and Justice; Comparative Criminology and Legal Theory; Justice Administration; Theoretical Explanations of Crime and Deviance; Race, Ethnicity, Crime, and Criminal Justice; Criminal Justice Policy, Analysis, and Assessment; and Informal Correctional Strategies and Offender Management Models. Legal education in the USA, for example, has benefited tremendously from this interdisciplinary formula. Thus, it is quite common and expected that criminologists, sociologists, political scientists, psychologists, etc. are hired to lecture in law departments in the USA. The identified subjects should be made parts of each Nigerian law department's curriculum to produce more rounded lawyers that would appropriately deal with law and justice issues in society.

Fifth, *Retain Competent and Experienced Professors and Lecturers by Raising the Retirement Age*: Earlier in this book, I pointed out the need to extend the age of compulsory retirement for justices of the SCN – and there is no reason that such extension should not be considered for other judges and justices. Note that at present the compulsory retirement age for a SCN justice is 70 years. However, for a university lecturer, the compulsory retirement age is 65 years. Over the decades, this strange policy has resulted in losses of great national talents and resources by way of brain drain to other countries. Two examples, it seems to me, will drive home the absurdity of the policy. Respectively, Professors Chinua Achebe and Wole Soyinka retired from the University of Nigeria and University of Ife (now Obafemi Awolowo University). Years after retiring, each of the renowned professors continues to teach, research, publish, mentor, and supervise younger researchers. Unfortunately, the professors now do these worthy activities in foreign lands, especially the USA. The professors are able to do these things in the USA because in that country the retirement age, at least for university lecturers, is not mandatory. Thus, a US professor may retire at say age 65 or continue to work many years beyond that age. Of course, he/she must remain productive (verified by annual evaluation of accomplishments mainly in the areas of teaching, research, professional development, and service).

The US model for retaining experienced and competent university professors and lecturers should be adopted in Nigeria to stop the losses of the valuable services of academics who continue to be productive. Similar to my earlier recommendation to raise the mandatory retirement age for justices, the mandatory retirement age for all university academics should be extended – to 75 years.[2] A 75 year-old professor or lecturer can function effectively in the performance of his/her job. To be sure, however, such an academic may be terminated for cause, such as where there is evidence based on evaluation performance that the professor or lecturer has not met the expected professional standard. The proposed retirement age of 75 years will allow a qualified professor or lecturer to work beyond that age. However, a person who wishes to teach beyond age 75 would be engaged to so, on a part-time basis, if the university authority determines that the person would continue to be productive. Changing the mandatory retirement age to 75 will positively impact legal education in Nigeria. The upside of retaining competent and experienced professors and lecturers is that law students will gain from the academics' substantial drives and experiences. It is reasonable to expect that only highly committed professionals will continue to teach, research, publish, and serve in a university up to age 75. Nigeria should be willing to take advantage of the services of those who are so driven and who perform so highly.

Chapter Summary and Conclusion

The responsibility for law and justice reconstruction in a postcolony belongs to all the members (corporate and individual) of the society. No one person or group can carry out the assignment without contributions from the others. This chapter has identified and explained the most vital areas in which constituent segments of a society, such as Nigeria, can make meaningful contributions towards law and justice renewal. In the final analysis, what is required is to achieve reasonable balances between the public and private sectors of society as well as among the different institutions, groups, organizations, and individuals. In Nigeria, the path to law reconstruction for more effective and efficient justice brings to the fore the following four broad issues and the solutions thereto, in no particular order of importance.

---

2 Saanu (2009) recommends raising the retirement age to 70 years. Although that would be better than the current policy, it does not sufficiently address the present situation in which highly qualified, capable, experienced, and productive professors and other lecturers are forced to retire long before they stop performing as expected.

First, an aggressive literacy program is necessary to help educate the citizens generally. Specifically, a citizen mass mobilization program is important, perhaps as a constituent part of the general literacy program, to sensitize the citizens on their human, constitutional, and other rights, as well as their duties and obligations in society. The mass mobilization program may be spearheaded by a new agency to be called the Citizen Mass Mobilization Committee on Law and Justice Awareness (CMMCLJA, or Citizens for Law and Justice for short). The program will consist of representatives of the public and private sectors of society, as described in detail in the preceding paragraphs of this chapter.

Second, the Nigerian Law Reform Commission (NLRC) needs to be fundamentally reorganized and its authority and power expanded. In doing so, the duties of the NLRC will be reassessed and re-operationalized to emphasize fundamental changes through law and justice reconstruction, rather than cosmetic changes to laws rooted in foreign cultures. Like the Citizens for Law and Justice representatives, the membership of the new NLRC will be broad-based to embody the appropriate government agencies as well as private citizens, groups, and organizations.

Third, it is necessary to separate the office of the Attorney-General (A-G) from that of the Justice Minister (or Commissioner), at the federal and state levels of government. This will entail merging the present A-G's functions with those of the present Solicitor-General (S-G). The combined functions will thereafter be performed by the new Solicitor and Advocate-General (SA-G). The new SA-G will be the chief legal adviser and advocate for the government. On the other hand, the Justice Minister (at the federal level) and the Justice Commissioner (at the state level) will be responsible for (re)building the law and justice system and infrastructures in the federation or state, as the case may be. The Minister's (or Commissioner's) duties will encompass substantive and procedural issues of justice. Specifically, although the Minister (or Commissioner) will be a political appointee, he/she will formulate and pursue policies and programs to advance the rights of all the citizens, not just the interests of the government in power. Overall, it will be the Minister's (or Commissioner's) duty to coordinate all stakeholders' activities towards a more effective and efficient justice system.

Fourth, the need for interdisciplinary approach to legal education cannot be overstated. Expanding law departments' and the law school's curricula by requiring other social science classes, research, and other activities will better inform the law students about the challenges facing lawyers in society and how best to respond to those challenges later in practice.

Fifth, in order to stem the ongoing premature losses of quality professionals from the universities, it is imperative for the mandatory retirement age for professors and lecturers to be raised to 75 years. For the legal profession, raising the retirement age will ensure that skilled and experienced law teachers are able to continue to groom prospective law practitioners, researchers, and future teachers beyond the present mandatory retirement age of 65 years.

References

Okereafọezeke [a.k.a. Okafọ], N. (1996) *The Relationship Between Informal and Formal Strategies of Social Control: An Analysis of the Contemporary Methods of Dispute Processing Among the Igbos of Nigeria.* UMI Number 9638581. Ann Arbor, Michigan, USA: University Microfilms.

Okereafọezeke [a.k.a. Okafọ], N. (2000) "Repugnancy Test (Policy) and the Impact of Colonially Imposed Laws on the Growth of Nigeria's Native Justice Systems" in *The Journal of African Policy Studies*, Volume 6, Number 1, 2000, pp. 55-74.

Okereafọezeke [a.k.a. Okafọ], N. (2002) *Law and Justice in Post-British Nigeria: Conflicts and Interactions Between Native and Foreign Systems of Social Control in Igbo.* Westport, Connecticut, USA: Greenwood Press.

Saanu, S. (2009, February 25) "Lecturers Retirement at 70" in *The Guardian*, http://www.ngrguardiannews.com/editorial_opinion/article03//indexn2_html?pdate=25020...; Internet.

Shaidi, L. P. (1992) "Traditional, Colonial and Present-Day Administration of Criminal Justice" in *Criminology in Africa*, Publication No. 47, Rome, Italy: United Nations Interregional Crime and Justice Research Institute (UNICRI).

Snyder, F. G. (1982) "Colonialism and Legal Form: The Creation of Customary Law in Senegal" in C. Sumter, ed. *Crime, Justice and Underdevelopment*, London, England: Heinemann.

Summary and Conclusion:
Checking the Excesses of Official Criminalization in a Postcolony: Towards Increased Role for Civil Response in a Reconstructed Justice System

Summary

It remains to emphasize the essence of this book for the reader. This book challenges the postcolonial society to appreciate, question, creatively synthesize, and use the good qualities of its indigenous and foreign law and justice systems. The postcolony is urged to make room for and encourage discourses and resolutions to determine the best law, justice, and social control for the society. Citizens and leaders of the postcolony should approach this effort with a decolonized, open mind and with a willingness to challenge those institutions and processes that have been officially presumed to be good for the postcolony for so long. The opportunity for discourses and resolutions will ensure Blagg's (1998) *liminal spaces*,

> where dialogue can be generated, where hybridity and cultural difference can be accepted. It is a place where we accept that what is often taken for granted as normal and unproblematic is a landscape at present imbued with the institutions of the colonizer – a landscape where the cultural artefacts of the colonizers are held to be universal. In this context, decolonization is not only about changing institutions, it also requires a decolonization of the mind and of our imagination; a rethinking of possibilities. What is demanded here is the creation of new spaces where indigenous or minority communities can formulate and activate processes that derive from their own particular traditions and conditions (Cunneen, 2002, p. 42).

Thus, postcolonial law and justice reconstruction involves a challenge of entrenched imperialist ideas and interests. Such ideas and interests are supported by vast State financial, personnel, and other resources, even though the ideas and interests do not enjoy nearly the same amount of support or loyalty among the citizens.

To appreciate, question, creatively synthesize, and use the good qualities of its indigenous and foreign law and justice systems, a postcolonial society has to first understand and take necessary steps to address the historical and contemporary crushing burden of European ideas of law and justice over ex-colonies. In the colonial and postcolonial eras, African societies have typified *The Wretched of the Earth* who have consistently been at the receiving end of European ideas that were designed for Europe's maximum interests at the expense of African societies (Fanon, 1963). The idea of reconstructing law and justice for a postcolony urges all parties in the society (policy makers, policy implementers, leaders, followers, etc.) to transform the society's systemic, substantive, and procedural law and justice elements for improved social control. To do so, however, each postcolony must overcome the following challenge. "The challenge of the post-colonial is to indicate the limits of Western ethnocentricity, to decentre and displace the norms of western knowledge, and to question the assumptions of justice ..." (Cunneen, 2002, p. 47). It is justifiable then to assert that "decolonising the mind" and "moving the centre" [Thiong'o, wa, 1986; 1993; 1997; see also Fanon (1963)] are two critical prerequisites for reconstructing law and justice in a postcolony.

The two concepts, ably explained by Thiong'o, wa (1986; 1993; 1997), exhort the postcolonial leader, follower, policy maker, as well as policy implementer to disabuse their thoughts, reasonings, and rationalizations for continuing and even expanding the legacy of the colonial impositions on the postcolonial society. Rather, the postcolonial leader and the other stakeholders should redirect their focus, energy, and resources to rebuilding their indigenous institutions and ways of life. Yes, with necessary accommodations to account for changes in modern society and to take advantage of the positive attributes of the foreign ideas and institutions. However, the focus of the rebuilding effort should be primarily on strengthening indigenous ideas and institutions. Otherwise, the postcolonial society will remain perpetually without focus or meaningful purpose. Unless the leaders and citizens of a postcolony raise their thought and reasoning processes, rationalizations, self-values, and confidence levels to reassess and reasonably and strategically reposition their indigenous systems and processes in the scheme of social control, the necessary restructuring of the country's law and justice system will not materialize.

As noted in many portions of this book, Nigerian indigenous law and justice differ substantially from their English counterparts in many respects. The differences lead to the logical recommendation to reconstruct the Nigerian law and justice system to reflect the country's peoples and environment. Thus, "we need a change of heart and attitude in our social control [and] legal system in order to have a true and justiciable society," observed a Survey Reaction Participant, a practicing attorney, in response to Question 22 E of Appendix A. Another Participant, a final year law student, accurately observes as follows in answer to the same question: "We should take what is good in the English legal system and what is good in our Nigerian justice system and blend them. We should not allow our legal thinking to be constrained by reference to English precedents and technicalities. We no longer need the clothes of foreign legal order."

Checking the Excesses of Official Criminalization in a Postcolony

Colonization breeds criminalization. This is because a colonizer needs coercive rules and regulations, usually with excessive penalties attached, to obtain compliance with the colonizer's policies, which invariably are out-of-sync and thus unpopular among the colonized. As a consequence of the harsh, strict, suppressive, and tight control actions of colonization, a postcolonial society inevitably emerges from the experience with an expanded number and scope of criminal laws than it had before colonization. However, on emerging from the colonial experience, every society has an opportunity to revisit its laws to determine their suitability for continued, sensible social control. A reassessment of the criminal laws of a postcolony should involve such issues as the number of laws and scope of the laws (including, whether civil rather than criminal law is better suited to address specific issues in society). Considering that criminalization is an essential aspect of colonization, it seems inevitable that a sensible postcolonial re-evaluation of the laws of a society will demonstrate the need to decriminalize certain behaviors. In Nigeria, for example, there is a great and urgent need to lessen criminalization along the lines recommended in this book. Rather than do so, the tendencies of successive postcolonial Nigerian governments have been to sustain and in some respects expand the criminalizing policies of erstwhile colonial regimes.

A more reasoned approach is to formulate policies and take active steps to reduce the number and scope of postcolonial criminal laws generally. Accordingly, alternative civil and semi-civil responses should be incorporated to deal with some criminal violations. One of the areas of key distinction between indigenous Nigerian and foreign (English) law and justice in Nigeria is in the manner of responding to criminal violations. "Criminal violations" are defined generally as norm breaches that negatively and substantially affect the victim's and/or the offender's society, not just the victim and the offender. Usually, pre-colonial Nigerian responses to crimes consisted more of corrective measures and less of punitive sanctions. The imported English responses to crimes contradict the pre-colonial Nigerian philosophy and practice. Pre-colonial law and justice in Nigeria, as in much of Africa, were founded on restoration and peacemaking as means of promoting harmonious coexistence and prosperity in the community.

Regrettably, successive Nigerian postcolonial governments have sustained and expanded the foreign philosophies, principles, and practices of offender management brought through colonial rule. In many respects, the foreign ideas strongly diverge from the indigenous history, knowledge, experiences, practices, and aspirations. The situation is such that the official laws frequently require the average citizen of the postcolony to submit to criminal sanctions that are unknown to the indigenous communities. In view of the profound disconnect between the indigenous Nigerian justice ideas and their English counterparts, official government leadership is required to rediscover less severe and non-criminal sanctions for some criminal violations. In advocating this rediscovery, it should be emphasized that many previously used sanctions will no longer be suitable for the modern era. Thus, as much as is reasonably possible and necessary in view of the enormously mixed postcolonial society in the modern State, relevant indigenous sanctions should be used in a reconstructed law and justice system.

Therefore, a new regime of well considered, less severe criminal sanctions and non-criminal measures should be pursued as responses to nonviolent offenders, minimally violent offenders, first-time offenders, and other offenders with reasonable chances of being corrected or reformed through less punitive sanctions. Over the decades in Nigeria, similar to colonial Britain, successive military and civilian governments have exponentially widened the sphere of criminal laws and sanctions, mostly as a means of controlling the population through intimidation. This trend should be reversed, especially in the era of professed constitutionalism, rule of law, and participatory democracy. It is time for the governments at the federal and state levels to show that they believe in the capacity of the average citizen to control his/her affairs within generally accepted guidelines provided by the State. Entrusting the citizens of each community to contribute to social control in the country by supervising and helping to reform convicts who would rejoin their communities would go a long way towards eliminating or reducing needlessly punitive criminal sanctions. After all, these unduly punitive sanctions likely create more, rather than less, "criminals" by labeling so many citizens so harshly.

Labeling theorists, such as Tannenbaum (1938) and Becker (1963), posit that crime in society mostly results from the capacity of the individuals and groups in the society to identify and define behavior as criminal. Labeling theory contends that crime is best understood as constituting three phases: a citizen's primary behavior, society's reaction to the behavior, and the citizen's secondary behavior (reaction to society's reaction). Thus, "crime" is mainly a consequence of qualitative assessment by groups in society. Conducts are not inherently criminal. Rather, they depend on each society's definition as espoused by the members and the society's application of the definition and label to a person's behavior. It is reasonable to suggest that, at least in some circumstances, a society's members will use their definitional privilege to advance sectional, rather than general society's, causes. This view is sustainable even in an alleged constitutional democracy, such as Nigeria. Thereon rests the fundamental unfairness of some criminal laws. This situation strengthens the argument to limit, rather than expand, criminal law. An effective way to limit criminal law is to redefine some of the present criminal law proscriptions as civil wrongs, manageable between disputing private persons, in civil court. Additionally, criminal law can be further limited by eliminating and replacing some overly punitive sanctions while reducing the punishments in other cases.

Towards Increased Role for Civil Response in a Reconstructed Law and Justice System

It is noteworthy that relative to civil law, criminal law is a later-day development in society. The history of human societal development demonstrates that private individuals and groups do not always have the capacity and/or desire to manage all disagreements, particularly the more serious or contentious variety. Thus, the larger society intervenes due to the wide reach and broad implications of some disputed issues for the society. In such a situation, the disputed issues would affect far more people than the individuals directly involved in the dispute. As a result, the modern State rightly assumes the responsibility to manage the disputed issues. This is consistent with the State's primary duty to ensure the safety and security of its citizens. But, the coercive nature of criminal law, which strips disputants and other participants of voluntariness and choices, means that criminal law must be limited in scope and operation. Citizens of a free society must retain their freedom of choice within the reasonable confines of constitutionalism. This freedom is substantially protected through the civil law process.

Therefore, criminal law is, and must remain, limited. Criminal law was devised to augment, not displace, civil law. Viewing or applying criminal law so widely that it ousts civil law is erroneous. What is needed in a postcolonial State is a restoration of civil law. There should be a presumption that an informed average citizen is capable of working privately (unofficially) in concert with other citizens to manage grievances, conflicts, and disputes among them. Based on this, official government interference will be kept to a minimum. Such interference by way of State criminal law will occur only where it is absolutely necessary to preserve a critical general interest of the citizens. Otherwise, a reconstructed law and justice system will trust individual citizens, communities, and other stakeholder groups to regulate their affairs within the general boundaries of constitutional, participatory democracy.

Trusting the individual in a reconstructed law and justice system to contribute more to social control will require expanding the uses of civil, rather than criminal, processes and sanctions, to manage norm violations. This means that a two-pronged approach is needed.

One, many criminal law violations should be redefined as civil wrongs. In recognition of the importance of the criminalizing process (norm definition as crime) in criminal law and justice, the legislature of a postcolony has the authority and power to redefine appropriate norm violations as civil, rather than criminal, violations. The decision as to the specific norms to be so redefined will depend on the importance of each norm for society. The less important a norm is, the more fitting that it should be redefined as a civil wrong. Another important factor to be considered is the availability of parties' or community's capacity and/or desire to effectively manage an issue unofficially (without official government involvement). The greater the capacity and/or desire of private parties and/or the community to effectively manage alleged violations of a norm, the more appropriate that it ought to be redefined as a civil wrong. On the other hand, less capacity and/or less desire by private parties and/or communities to effectively manage their disagreements privately should mean that a norm violation should continue to be viewed as a crime.

Two, the federal and state governments should expressly empower parties to grievances, conflicts, and disputes to manage their cases by themselves or with the assistance of their community members, at the most local levels, such as the extended family, village (neighborhood), and town, if possible. With the understanding that peace is a necessary ingredient of societal progress, every community has a vested interest in ensuring peaceful co-existence among its members. Therefore, each community will likely assist its members to pursue peace and stability through negotiated and restorative justice model. It should be pointed out that the capacity of postcolonial Nigerian communities to manage many of their affairs, including many "crimes," remains strong even in the modern era. With meaningful, properly targeted support and assistance from the State and its agencies, research shows that local communities have agencies, organizations, and procedures capable of managing most, if not all, of the civil and criminal infractions that occur in the societies (see as examples Okereafoezeke, 1996; 2002; Elechi, 2006).

Conclusion

Postcolonial societies, such as Nigeria, are typically over-criminalized. This is a common and enduring colonial legacy. Over-criminalization means that some behaviors that ought not to be labeled "criminal" are so identified, while some other crimes are punished more severely than necessary. In either situation, the State's policy alienates the citizens by promoting and applying a foreign offender management model to the people. In essence, reconstructing law and justice in a postcolony, such as is advocated in this book, necessarily includes limiting the sphere of criminal law. Strategies for reducing criminal law should include redefining some crimes as civil wrongs, and lessening the penalties for some other transgressions.

The argument to control the role of criminal law in the social control of a society is predicated on the identified benefits of shrinking, rather than growing, the field of criminal law. More active participation of average citizens in the justice system is a major benefit of controlling official criminal law. Such participation is expected to produce more relevant and more acceptable justice that is rooted in the standards of the society, rather than the standards bequeathed by a former colonizer. Moreover, State officials cannot efficiently devise and implement credible and effective social control policies and practices without the citizens' participation. Therefore, within reasonable constitutional boundaries, the citizens' contribution should be secured by empowering them as stakeholders in the society's social control efforts.

In the final analysis, over-criminalization signifies that the State has stolen many citizens' private disputes from the owners (Christie, 1977; Walgrave, 2002). The State should give the disputes back to further the purpose of law as a means of effective social control. The time has come for the State to return ownership of the disputes to their rightful owners by minimizing the role of official criminal law and maximizing the roles of civil law as well as the community (unofficial) criminal law process. As has been shown in this book, these can be successfully devised and implemented within the rules of constitutional democracy. A reduction of the present official criminal law wide net in society will heighten and expand the critical role of community processes for more effective and efficient social control.

References

Becker, H. S. (1963) *Outsiders: Studies in the Sociology of Deviance*. New York, USA: Free Press.

Blagg, H. (1998) "Restorative Visions and Restorative Justice Practices: Conferencing, Ceremony and Reconciliation in Australia" in *Current Issues in Criminal Justice*, 10 (1).

Christie, N. (1977) "Conflicts as Properties" in *British Journal of Criminology*, 1: 1-14.

Cunneen, C. (2002) "Restorative Justice and the Politics of Decolonization" in E. G. M. Weitekamp and H.-J. Kerner, eds. *Restorative Justice: Theoretical Foundations*, , Portland, Oregon, USA: Willan Publishing.

Elechi, O. Oko (2006) *Doing Justice Without the State: The Afikpo (Ehugbo) Nigeria Model*. New York, USA: Routledge.

Fanon, F. (1963) *The Wretched of the Earth*. New York, USA: Grove Press.

Okereafoezeke [a.k.a. Okafo], N. (1996) *The Relationship Between Informal and Formal Strategies of Social Control: An Analysis of the Contemporary Methods of Dispute Processing Among the Igbos of Nigeria*. UMI Number 9638581. Ann Arbor, Michigan, USA: University Microfilms.

Okereafoezeke [a.k.a. Okafo], N. (2002) *Law and Justice in Post-British Nigeria: Conflicts and Interactions Between Native and Foreign Systems of Social Control in Igbo*. Westport, Connecticut, USA: Greenwood Press.

Tannenbaum, F. (1938) *Crime and the Community*. Boston, Massachusetts, USA: Ginn.

Thiong'o, wa, N. (1986) *Decolonising the Mind: The Politics of Language in African Literature*. London, England: James Currey.

Thiong'o, wa, N. (1993) *Moving the Centre: The Struggle for Cultural Freedoms*. London, England: James Currey.

Thiong'o, wa, N. (1997) *Writers in Politics: A Re-Engagement With Issues of Literature and Society*. Oxford, England: James Currey.

Walgrave, L. (2002) "From Community to Dominion: In Search of Social Values for Restorative Justice" in E. G. M. Weitekamp and H.-J. Kerner, eds. *Restorative Justice: Theoretical Foundations*, Portland, Oregon, USA: Willan Publishing, pp. 71-89.

Appendix A

(QUESTIONNAIRE ITEMS USED TO COLLECT SOME DATA)
Reconstructing Law and Justice in a Postcolony

I need you to respond fully to the following questions and items. Your responses will help in successfully carrying out this research project. Your responses will be anonymous and confidential. Thus, do not identify yourself on this instrument or by any other means. However, you may identify yourself by writing your name and title/position on this questionnaire IF you would like your response to be attributed to you specifically, such as by quote in the book that is expected to result from this exercise. Please be detailed in each of your responses. Your candid, clear, complete responses will be greatly appreciated. Thanks.

Nọnso Okafọ, LL.B (Hons.), Ph.D.

---

1. Do you believe that Nigeria's official legal and justice system places too much emphasis on the English system?

2. If Nigeria's official governments promote and encourage the country's native justice and legal systems, are these systems capable of effective social control in the respective parts of the country where they apply?

3. Do traditions, customs, and native laws become ineffective when faced with modernity?

4. Why do you think that Nigeria's post-independence governments at the local, state, and federal levels have 41 years after political independence preferred to maintain the English-type legal and justice system brought to Nigeria by colonial Britain?

5. Do you believe that Nigeria's justice and legal system should be fundamentally changed to reposition the native systems in the country as the *grundnorm(s)* [fundamental, basic system(s)] for the country?

6. Do you believe that Nigeria's native justice systems can be developed into legal systems that are capable of social control in modern Nigeria?

7. Who is responsible for developing Nigeria's native justice and legal systems: the official local, state, and federal governments, including the Legislature and the Executive branches; universities, colleges, institutes, etc; professional groups such as the Nigerian Bar Association, the Nigeria Police Force; private individuals; communities such as towns, villages, groups of towns; or other?

8. Are Nigeria's native laws, customs, and traditions capable of effective social control in modern Nigeria?

9. Which system of laws do you prefer: the customary law of your ethnic group or English law, and why?

10. Should Nigerian laws and those of its constituent parts be based on the relevant Native Laws, Customs, and Traditions, or English law?

11. In which areas of justice and law, if any, do you see strong disagreements between native customary law and English law in Nigeria?

12. In which law enforcement model are you more confident for effective social control: Native-based law enforcement such as the Bakasi Boys, the Odu'a People's Congress (OPC), etc. or the English-based law enforcement such as the Nigeria Police Force, why?

13. What, if any, principles of civil and criminal offender disposal (such as corrections, prison, reprimand, *igba ekpe*, *iri iwu*, etc.) in your native customary law system do you believe should be continued in modern society, why?

14. Should the official governments (Local, State, and Federal) formulate and pursue policies and programs to indigenize law and justice in Nigeria, why or why not?

15. Do you believe that the Nigerian Law Reform Commission has satisfactorily carried out its responsibility of reforming the country's laws to make them relevant to the average Nigerian and consistent with average Nigerian's lifestyle? Please explain your position.

16. What factors, if any, do you consider to be responsible for the official governments' neglect of Nigeria's native justice and legal systems?

17. Do you believe that local communities (or those to whom each community delegates the function) should be responsible for order and law maintenance in their part of the country?

18. How much of your native customary laws and traditions do you understand? Circle the letter of the response option that most closely matches your answer:
    A. Not at all
    B. Very Little
    C. Much
    D. Very Much
    E. Every Aspect of My Native Laws and Customs.

19. Do the official governments (Local, State, and Federal) have a responsibility to educate you on your native laws and customs, why or why not?

20. Do you know of any official government (Local, State, and Federal) program or policy aimed at educating you on your native laws and customs? If you know of any, please identify and briefly explain the program or policy.

21. Which is more acceptable to you: the English Justice System as practiced in Nigeria or Your Native Justice System, why?

22. What other suggestions do you have for more effective and efficient social control in Nigeria? Your suggestions may be either native-based or official government-based, or a combination. Please address your suggestions under the following headings:
    A. Law Making-
    B. Law Enforcement/Policing-
    C. Law Application/Case Adjudication-
    D. Offender/Responsible Party Disposal, Corrections, Prisons, etc.-
    E. Other Suggestions-

23. To re-design the judicial process in Nigeria and emphasize the native (indigenous) judicial process over other (foreign) judicial processes (including the common law and English statute-based processes), Figure 1.1 is a Hierarchical Representation of the Avenues Recommended for Case Management in Igbo and other parts of Nigeria. Do you agree with the recommended avenues? Do you agree with their hierarchical relationships? What changes, if any, would you make to Figure 1.1 to positively re-engineer justice and law in Nigeria so as to create a justice and legal system that is based fundamentally on the native systems across the country?

Figure 1.1

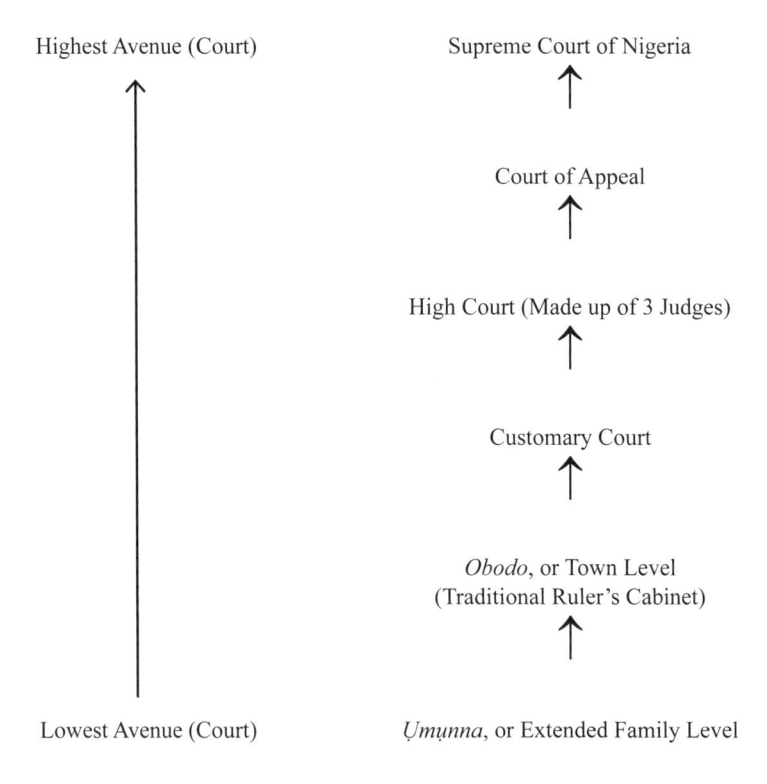

Highest Avenue (Court) ↑   Supreme Court of Nigeria ↑

Court of Appeal ↑

High Court (Made up of 3 Judges) ↑

Customary Court ↑

Obodo, or Town Level
(Traditional Ruler's Cabinet) ↑

Lowest Avenue (Court)   *Ụmụnna*, or Extended Family Level

Please write your suggested changes and opinions on Figure 1.1:

Thanks immensely for taking part in this scientific research.

Index

A-G *see* Attorney-General
Abati, R. 144
Aborigines in Australia 73, 74-5, 85
Abubakar, Abdulsalami 134
Abudu v. Eguakan case 138
accountability in Nigeria 110-11
Achebe, Chinua 225
adjudication in Nigeria 167-93
Afghanistan 39-42, 49-50
    constitution 40-2, 91
    history 39-40
    Islam 92
    United States 40
Al Saud 48
Alemika, E.E.O. 202
American Society of Criminology
    Conference 2003 116
anomic leadership in Nigeria 112
apartheid in South Africa 65-6, 68
appointment of judges in Nigeria 173-4, 178-80
"armed robbery" (Nigeria) 206
"Assimilation" principle 35
ATDs *see* "awaiting trial detainees"
Attorney-General (A-G) in Nigeria 192, 223-4, 227
Austin W.T. 33
Australia 73-5, 85-8
    Aborigines 73, 74-5, 85
        history 73-4
        indigenous rights 87-8
        population 73-4
"awaiting trial detainees" (ATDs) 194

Babangida, Ibrahim 128, 192, 218
Babylonians and Code of Hammurabi 27
Bakassi Boys (Nigeria) 146-7, 154, 156-7, 202
Becker, H.S. 232
Belgore, Alfa 176
Benson, Bruce 13-14

"Bill of Rights" (United States) 84
Black Administration Act, South Africa 67
Blagg, H. 229
Blair, Tony 45
book summary 1-3, 229-34, 234-5
Brazil 53-5,
    constitution 53-5, 69
    history 53-4
    race 53-4
    religion 36, 54
Britain and Iraq 44-5
Brown, M.F. 25
Bush, George W. 45

California and prisoner release 20
Canada 75-7, 86
    constitution 76-7, 86
    France 76
    history 75-6
    indigenous rights 87-8
    population 75
    Quebec 76
capital punishment
    Nigeria 202-7
    United States 204-5
case processing in Nigeria 167-93
character/ethics of law enforcement personnel (Nigeria) 153-4
China and life options 93
Christie, N. 235
citizen education in Nigeria 218-21
Citizen Mass Mobilization Committee on Law and Justice Awareness (CMMCLJA) 219-20, 227
citizen-centered obstacles (Nigeria) 116-17, 118
"citizen-friendly" courts (Nigeria) 171
citizens' acquiescence in Nigeria 116
civil justice in Nigeria 99
civil response role in reconstructed law/justice system 233-4

CMMCLJA *see* Citizen Mass Mobilization Committee on Law and Justice Awareness Code of Hammurabi 27
colonization and criminalization 231-2
common law, English 25-6
Commonwealth of Australia 73
communal character of Nigeria 140
community justice processing (Nigeria) 177
community management in Nigeria 234
"community service" (Nigeria) 197-8, 201
constitution
    Afghanistan 40-2, 91
    Brazil 53-5, 69
    Canada 76-7, 86
    India 42
    Iraq 46-7, 91
    Kenya 56, 57, 69
    Nigeria 61-2, 69
    Saudi Arabia 91
    South Africa 66-7, 69
    United States 84-5, 86-7
Constitution Acts (Canada) 76
Constitution of Brazil, 1988 53-5
Constitution of the Commonwealth of Australia, 1901 74
Constitution of the Empire of Japan 78-9
Constitution of the Federal Republic of Nigeria, 1999 59, 92, 132-3, 138-9, 183
Constitution of India 42
Constitution of Iraq, 2005 46
Constitution of the Islamic Republic of Afghanistan 40
Constitution of the Republic of Kenya 56, 92
Constitution of the Republic of South Africa 1996 (CRSA) 66-7
Constitution of the United States of America 82, 83
constitutional (non-religious) framework for courts (Nigeria) 182-6
consultation with stakeholder groups in law making (Nigeria) 125-6
contemporary, cosmopolitan society (Nigeria) 129-30
"conventional order" of individuals (Nigeria) 148-9
Cook, James 73

"Corrections System" (Nigeria) 199, 200, 202
corrections in trials (Nigeria) 193-207
countries surveyed 1, 35-7, 91-4
Court of Appeal (Nigeria) 174
court structure (Nigeria) 169-71, 181, 197
credible constitution for Nigeria 133-5
crime in society 232
criminal justice, Nigeria 99
criminal justice system, United States 17-19
criminal law control 234-5
criminal Shari'ah law (Nigeria) 180, 183-6
"criminal violations" and Nigerian/English law comparisons 231
criminalization and colonization 231-2
CRSA *see Constitution of the Republic of South Africa 1996*
Cuneen C. 8-9
customary law
    Bruce Benson 13-15
    India 42
    introduction 7
    Nigeria 60-5, 99
    research funding in Nigeria 183
"customary law knowledge test" (Nigeria) 173-4, 179-80
customs 7-27, 27-8
    modern justice 22-7
    rural/industrial societies 10-15

death penalty
    Nigeria 142
    United Nations 142
developed/undeveloped countries 34-5
Dolan, Ronald E. 80
dress code for lawyers/judges in Nigeria 115

Economic and Financial Crimes Commission (EFCC) 189
"education" in Nigeria 116-17
EFCC *see* Economic and Financial Crimes Commission
effectiveness and justice/social control system 9-10
efficiency and justice/social control system 9-10

Eghagha, H. 189
Eisenhower, Dwight 19
enacted authoritarian laws 13-14
England
    Canada 76
    common law 25-6
    justice systems 23-4
English language and Nigeria 57, 186-8
English law and Nigeria 61, 108-10, 115, 123, 137
ethnicity in India 42

family and social control in Nigeria 141-2
Fawehinmi, Gani 192-3
federal court system (Nigeria) 173
Ferreira, A. 159-60
France and Canada 76

Gandhi, Mohandas 42
Giwa, Dele 192-3
government-centered obstacles in Nigeria 106-14, 117-18
governments in Nigeria 112-14
"grounded" law 8
grundnorm (fundamental law) 40, 49
Guantanamo Bay, Cuba and United States 83

History
    Afghanistan 39-40
    Australia 73-4
    Brazil 53-4
    Canada 75-6
    India 42-3
    Iraq 44-5
    Japan 77-8
    Kenya 55
    Nigeria 57-9
    South Africa 65-6
    United States 81-2
Hussein, President 45

Igba ekpe (public shaming) 147-8
Igbo (Nigeria) tribe 215
    crimes 58-9
    indigenous control 130, 190
    justice systems 23-4
    native society 8

"Ignorance of the Law is No excuse", (Nigeria) 129
IGP *see* Inspector-General of Police
independence and Nigeria 101
India 42-4, 49-50
    customary laws 42
    ethnicity 42
    history 42-3
    Mohandas Gandhi, 42
    population 42
    "the world's largest democracy" 43
indigenous control for Igbo tribe (Nigeria) 130, 190
indigenous and fundamental human rights (Nigeria) 139-40
indigenous language and constitution (Nigeria) 135-6
indigenous languages for case processing (Nigeria) 186-8
"indigenous law" 7
indigenous law/justice in Nigeria
    enforcement 154-8
    land matters 137
    obstacles 105-17
    profile 101-5
    repositioning 122-5
    summary 117-18
    systems 111
indigenous rights 87-8
indigenous standards in succession/ inheritance (Nigeria) 138-9
indigenous systems (Nigeria) 218
indigenous traditions, customs and laws (Nigeria) 126
indigenous-based and progressive court model (Nigeria) 169-81
"Indirect Rule" principle 35
industrial societies 10-15, 16-22
Inspector-General of Police (IGP) in Nigeria 144
Iraq 44-7, 49-50
    Britain 44-5
    constitution 46, 91
    history 44-5
    Islam 92
    population 44
    United States 45-6, 82
Islam 36, 92

Iwu Igbo (Igbo Law) 3

Japan 77-81, 86
   history 77-8
   population 78
   social control 93
   World War II 78-80, 86
Jewish religious courts (Beth Din) 185
judges (Nigeria),
   appointment 173-4, 178-80
   inadequacies 114-15
   principles 188-9
judicial activism (Nigeria) 190-2
judicial officers on customary law (Nigeria) 181
judicial recording system (Nigeria) 188
justice system
   effectiveness/efficiency 9-10
   English 23-4
   Igbo (Nigeria) 23-4
   industrial societies 16-22
   modern 22-7
   rural societies 16-22
   United States 21, 27, 28

KANU *see* Kenya African National Union
Karzai, Hamid 39-40
Kenya 55-7
   constitution 56, 57, 69
   history 55
   Kiswahili language 57
   Orange Democratic Movement 156
   population 55
   postcolonial 92-3
Kenya African National Union (KANU) 55
Kibaki, Mwai 55, 156
Kiswahili language in Kenya 57

land inheritance/transfer in Nigeria 137
land matters in Nigeria 137
Lartey, O. 186-8
law/justice
   indigenization in Nigeria 121-2
   international comparison 33-4
laws
   evidence in Nigeria 130-2
   institutions in Nigeria 126
   modern society 25

Nigeria 121-43
   people's statement of their history (Nigeria) 167-9
   publicity (Nigeria) 127-8
   reform in Nigeria 221-3
lawyers in Nigeria 114-15
leadership (Nigeria) 102-3, 112
legal education in Nigeria 224-5, 227
legislation/enforcement for Nigeria 121-65

McCold, P. 22-3
Machel, Graca 68
Mackay, R.E. 22
Madanugu, E. 135
MAMSER *see* Mass mobilization for Self Reliance, Social Justice and Economic Recovery
Mandela, Nelson 68
Marbury v. Madison case 82
marriage laws in Nigeria 136-7
Marshall, John 192
Mass mobilization for Self Reliance, Social Justice and Economic Recovery (MAMSER) 28, 218-19
Minister (Commissioner) of Justice (Nigeria) 223-4
Minton T.D. 200
model law/justice
   adjudication and corrections (Nigeria) 167-207, 207-8
   Nigeria 121-65
"modern" English common law and Nigeria 99-100
modern justice systems 22-7
modern society and laws 25
Moi, Daniel arap 55
Moon, Ban Ki 110-11

Nader, L. 18, 21-2, 27, 28, 34
nation-building vision (Nigeria) 106-7
National Judicial Council (NJC) in Nigeria 178
Native Administration Act, South Africa 67
Native Americans 83-4
"native customs/traditions" in Nigeria 116-17
native laws 7-27, 27-8
   modern justice 22-7

rural/industrial societies 10-15
NBA *see* Nigerian Bar Association
neocolonist craving for foreign ideas/ideals (Nigeria) 112
New Zealand and indigenous rights 87-8
Newswatch magazine 192
Ngige, Chris 192
Niger Deltans 94
Nigeria 57-65
   accountability 110-11
   adjudication 167-93
   appointment of judges 173-4, 178-80
   "armed robbery" 206
   Attorney-General 192, 223-4, 227
   Bakassi Boys 202
   capital punishment 202-7
   case processing 167-93
   case study 1-2, 99
   character/ethics of law enforcement personnel 153-4
   citizen education 218-21
   "citizen-friendly" courts 171
   civil justice 99
   CMMCLJA programme 219, 227
   communal character 140
   community management 234
   "community service" 197-8, 201
   constitution, 61-2, 69
   constitutional (non-religious) framework for courts 182-6
   consultation with stakeholder groups in law making 125-6
   contemporary, cosmopolitan society 129-30
   "conventional order" of individuals 148-9
   corrections 193-207
   "Corrections System" 199, 200, 202
   Court of Appeal 174
   court structure 169-70, 181, 197
   credible constitution 133-5
   criminal justice 99
   criminal Shari'ah law 180, 183-6
   customary law 60-5, 99, 183
   "customary law knowledge test" 173-4, 179-80
   death penalty 142
   Deltans 94

dress code for lawyers/judges 115
English language 57, 186-8
English law 61, 115, 123, 137
family and social control 141-2
federal court system 173
history 57-9
Igbo tribe 58-9
"Ignorance of the Law is No excuse" 129
independence 101
indigenous and fundamental human rights 139-40
indigenous languages
   case processing 186-8
   constitution 135-6
indigenous law enforcement 154-8
indigenous law/justice
   citizen-centered obstacles 116-17
   description 121-2
   expansion 124-5
   government-centered obstacles 106-14, 117-18
   land matters 137
   profession-centered obstacles 114-15, 117
   profile 101-5
   repositioning 122-4
   summary 117-18
indigenous standards in succession/ inheritance 138-9
indigenous systems 218
indigenous traditions, customs and laws 126
indigenous-based and progressive court model 169-81
Inspector-General of Police 144
judges' principles 188-9
judiciary
   activism 190-2
   officers on customary law 181
   recording system 188
land inheritance/transfer 137
land matters 137
law reform 221-3
laws 121-43
   evidence 130-2
   institutions 126

people's statement of their history 167-9
leaders 102-3
legal education 224-5, 227
legislation/enforcement 121-43, 143-60, 160-1
MAMSER programme 218-19
marriage laws 136-7
Minister (Commissioner) of justice 223-4
model law/justice 121-65
    adjudication and corrections 167-211
    "modern" English common law 99-100
National Judicial Council 178
Niger Delta region 94
"no state religion" policy 133
oath/affirmation 189-90
offender management 195-200
"official language" 135
oil 94, 108
OPEC 94
Osun State 113
parole 201
Police Act 147
police training 159-60
police/citizen ratio 158-9
police–citizen partnership 149-50
political control over police 150-1
post colonial attitudes 215
post-trial actions 193-207
postcolonial 63-4, 102, 104-5
pre-colonial 57-9
prisons
    decentralization 198
    living conditions 194-5
    monitoring 195-6
    "Prisons System" term 199, 202
private prosecution 192-3
private sector/equipment for law enforcement 152-3
professors/lecturers 225-6
profile 101-5
proposed laws publicity 127-8
punitive laws 142-3
reconstruction of law/justice 93
rehabilitation 194-5

religion 91-2, 132-3
"repugnancy test" 121
responses to crime 199-202
"responsible adult supervision" 197-8, 201
retirement age 225-6, 227
roots 93
rule making 121-43
rules/law enforcement 143-60, 161-2
sanctions application 202
shaming 140-1, 147-8
shared responsibility for justice 217-26
"*Shari'ah* Court" 171, 174-5
Shari'ah law 92, 183-5
simple statements of the laws 128-9
Solicitor and Advocate-General 224, 227
speed of law enforcement 146-7
State Court System 172, 174
suo moto issue 64
Supreme Court *see* Supreme Court of Nigeria
"The Police are Your Friends" slogan 149
three-tier police 144-6
Town Courts 174, 177, 179
traditions, customs and native laws in school curricula 181-2
unofficial sanctions 207
vigilante law enforcement 150-2
Western individualism 140
Nigeria Police Force (NPF) 2, 143-6, 149-50, 153-5, 159-60, 219-20
Nigeria Security and Civil Defence Corps (NSCDC) 146
Nigerian Bar Association (NBA) 102, 195, 217, 219-20
Nigerian Law Reform Commission (NLRC) 221-3, 227
Nigerian Law School 224-5
NJC *see* National Judicial Council
NLRC *see* Nigerian Law Reform Commission
"no state religion" policy in Nigeria 133
NPF *see* Nigeria Police Force
NSCDC *see* Nigeria Security and Civil Defence Corps
Nzimiro, I. 143

oath/affirmation (Nigeria) 189-90
Obasanjo, Olusegun 106-7, 110-11, 123, 155
ODM *see* Orange Democratic Movement
Odu'a People's Congress (OPC) 154
offender management in Nigeria 195-200
"official language" (Nigeria) 135
Ogwugwu Isiula Shrine 131
Oil
    Nigeria 94, 108
    Saudi Arabia 48
Okereafoezeke, N. (Okafo)
    community law enforcement 149
    community management 234
    customary law development 221, 223
    development 35
    Igbo tribe
        morality based crimes 58
        systems 103
        traditional justice system 24
    law/justice comparison 33
    Nigeria
        British domination 102
        case types 104
        family control 142
        personal beliefs 132
        public shaming 147
        "repugnancy test" 63
        Western ideas 111
        Western/indigenous rights 139
    offender management 207
    sentences and colonial Britain 196
    "Substitutive interaction" 83-4
    US/Iraq war 45, 82
Okonkwo v. Okagbue case 63
Oli, S.I. 104, 108-9, 190
Onagoruwa, O. 60
Onyechi, N.M. 114-15
OPC *see* Odu'a People's Congress
OPEC *see* Organization of Petroleum Exporting Countries
"operation enduring freedom" 45
Oputa, Chukwudifu 191
Orange Democratic Movement (ODM) in Kenya 156
Organization of Petroleum Exporting Countries (OPEC) 94
"oru oyibo" (white man's job) 215

Osun State, Nigeria 113

Panama Canal zone and United States 83
parole in Nigeria 201
PIC *see* "prison-industrial complex"
PMCs *see* Prison Monitoring Committees
Police Act, Nigeria 147
"Police Brutality in Afahakpo Enwang" 153
police training in Nigeria 159-60
police/citizen ratio (Nigeria) 158-9
police–citizen partnership (Nigeria) 149-50
political control over police (Nigeria) 150-1
political will and Nigeria 107-8
population
    Afghanistan 39
    Australia 73-4
    Canada 75
    India 42
    Iraq 44
    Japan 78
    Kenya 55
    Saudi Arabia 47
    United Sates 17
post colonial attitudes (Nigeria) 215
post-trial actions (Nigeria) 193-207
postcolonies
    characteristics 35
    Nigeria 63-4, 102, 104-5
pre-colonial Nigeria 57-9
Prison Monitoring Committees (PMCs) 195-6, 208
"prison-industrial complex" (PIC) 19-20
prisoner release in California 20
prisons in Nigeria
    decentralization 198
    living conditions 194-5
    monitoring 195-6
"Prisons System" term (Nigeria) 199, 202
private prosecution (Nigeria) 192-3
private sector and equipment for law enforcement (Nigeria) 152-3
probation in United States 200-1
Proclamation No 6 of 1900 (Nigerian Law) 63
profession-centered obstacles in Nigeria 114-15, 117

professors and retirement 225-6, 227
professors/lecturers (Nigeria) 225-6
programs for Nigeria 112-14
proposed laws publicity in Nigeria 127-8
public policies (Nigeria) 112-14
public shaming in Nigeria 147
punitive laws (Nigeria) 142-3

Quebec (Canada) 76
quic quid plantatur solo cedit maxim 137

race in Brazil 53-4
rehabilitation in Nigeria 194-5
religion
    Brazil 36, 54
    Islam 92
    Nigeria 91-2, 132-3
Republic of South Africa *see* South Africa
"repugnancy test" for Nigerian law 62, 121
"reservations" in United States 84, 86-7
responses to crime (Nigeria) 199-202
"responsible adult supervision" (Nigeria) 197-8, 201
restorative justice principles 9, 22-4
retirement of professors 225-6, 227
Rudd, Kevin 74
"rule of four", United States 175-7
rule making in Nigeria 121-43
rural societies 10-15, 16-22

Saddam Hussein 82
sanctions application in Nigeria 202
Saudi Arabia 47-9, 49-50
    constitution 48-9, 91
    Islam 92
    oil 48
    population 47
    United states 48
Saudi Arabia Constitution of 1992 48-9
Schlosser E. 19
SCN *see* Supreme Court of Nigeria
September 11 2001 45
shaming in Nigeria 140-1, 147-8
shared responsibility for justice (Nigeria) 217-26
"Shari'ah Court" (Nigeria) 171, 174-5
Shari'ah law
    Nigeria 92, 183-5

Saudi Arabia 48
social control system 9-10
society and crime 232
Solicitor and Advocate-General (S-AG) (Nigeria) 224, 227
South Africa 65-8, 68-9
    apartheid 21, 65-6, 68
    Black Administration Act 67
    constitution 66-7, 69
    history 65-6
    Native Administration Act 67
    Nelson Mandela 68
Soyinka, Wole 225
speed of law enforcement (Nigeria) 146-7
State Court System (Nigeria) 172, 174
statements of the laws (Nigeria) 128-9
statutory law 26
substantial sanctions 12
suo moto issue in Nigeria 64
Supreme Court of Nigeria (SCN)
    community justice processing 177
    court structure 173-5
    judges 178-9, 189
    repugnancy 63-4
    retirement age for justices 225
    "rule of four" 175-7
Supreme Court, United States 175, 192
survey questionnaire 230, 237-40

taliban 40-1
Tannenbaum, F. 204, 232
The Guardian 153, 204
"The Police are Your Friends" slogan (Nigeria) 149
Thiong'o, wa N. 230
three-tier police (Nigeria) 144-6
Todd, H.F. 18, 21-2, 27, 28, 34
Tokugawa Shogunate (military dictatorship in Japan) 78
Town Courts in Nigeria 174, 177, 179
"traditional law" 7
traditions 7-27, 27-8
 modern justice 22-7
 rural/industrial societies 10-15
traditions, customs and native laws in school curricula (Nigeria) 181-2
Treaty of Paris, 1783 81

Index

UN *see* United Nations
Union of South Africa *see* South Africa
"United Nations Declaration on the Rights of Indigenous Peoples, 2007" 87, 93
United Nations (UN)
    death penalty 142
    United States 82
United States (US) 81-5, 86
    Afghanistan 40
    "Bill of Rights" 84, 86
    capital punishment 204-5
    constitution 84-5, 86-7
    criminal justice system 17-19
    federal republicanism 81-2
    Guantanamo Bay, Cuba 83
    history 81-2
    indigenous rights 87-8
    industrial society 8
    Iraq 45-6, 82
    justice system 2, 21, 87
    law/justice system 34
    Marbury v. Madison case 82
    National Criminal Justice Commission, 1996 20
    native American reservations 84
    Panama Canal zone 83
    population 17
    probation 200-1
    "reservations" 86-7
    retirement of professors 225-6
    "rule of four" 175-7
    Saudi Arabia 48
    Supreme Court 175, 192
    Treaty of Paris, 1783 81
    United Nations 82
unofficial sanctions (Nigeria) 207
unpatriotic political leadership (Nigeria) 106-7
US *see* United States

Van Ness, D. 24, 142-3
vigilante law enforcement (Nigeria) 150-2

Walgrave, L. 235
Western individualism and Nigeria 140
Williams, Rowan 185
Worden, Robert, L. 80
World War II and Japan 78-9, 80

Yar'adua, Umaru 107, 132, 154-5
Younkins, E.W. 13, 22, 26-7